FINDING

BOMB

BOOGIE

A Daughter's Search to
Rediscover Her Father—
*the World War II Bomber Boy,
Prisoner of War & American Veteran*

FINDING
BOMB
BOOGIE

Maureen Buick

WEST PORTAL PRESS

Paperback ISBN: 9798987024102
Hardcover ISBN: 9798987024119
ebook ISBN: 9798987024126

Library of Congress Control Number: 2022920115

Library of Congress Cataloging-in-Publication Data
Name: Buick, Maureen, author.
Title: Finding Bomb Boogie: A Daughter's Search to Rediscover Her Father—the World War II Bomber Boy, Prisoner of War, and American Veteran / Maureen Buick

Cover design and interior design by Rachel Valliere of Printed Page Studios

Published by West Portal Press
Website: maureenbuick.com

To Jimmy, my everyday hero.

To my neighbor and others like him—private, anonymous heroes quietly helping others.

✦ ✦ ✦

Contents

PART IV: *The Training Years*

PART V: *The European Theater*

PART VI: *Prisoner of War*

PART VII: *Homeward Bound*

PART VIII: *Looking Forward*

PART ONE

LOOKING BACK

—1—

A True Veteran

Our flag does not fly because the wind moves it . . . it flies with the last breath of each soldier who died protecting it.

—AUTHOR UNKNOWN

My father belonged to the Greatest Generation, a phrase used to describe the group of men and women who grew up in America during the Great Depression and actively served or made distinct contributions to their country during World War II. These remarkable men and women collectively displayed a powerful commitment to a common cause and a mutual determination to make the world a better place. In his book, *The Greatest Generation,* Tom Brokaw claimed these selfless attributes were "the legacy of this generation as much as the sacrifices made and victories gained during World War II."

When my father, who served in World War II, passed away, an American flag was draped over his coffin, visibly validating his status as a veteran. He was buried at the local Catholic cemetery under a bronze gravestone provided by the US Department of Veterans Affairs. At the center of the headstone, a silver ring encircles a metal cross, prominently signaling his past military service. Below the emblem, an inscription reads Donald L. Hayes, US Army Air Corps, World War II, 1921–1986.

My father passed away on March 12, 1986, and I rarely thought about him for the next thirty-two years. Then in September 2018, the dam around my heart broke, and I let him reenter my world. Now, barely a day goes by when I do not reflect on his life and wish he were still around to tell his stories and answer all my questions. But more than anything, I just miss him and wish I knew him back then like I know him now.

For the past several years, I've been on a journey of sorts, rediscovering the truth about my father's past, particularly his role during World War II, and it has given me a better understanding of who he was as a person. It's been a therapeutic and healing process, and I'm grateful I took the time to do it. As I continue to unravel his story and learn more about his life, I've also learned more about myself and the power of forgiveness. I never dreamed that learning my father's narrative would set me on a path toward freedom and genuinely accepting who I am, specifically concerning the circumstances of my childhood and growing-up years.

It is unimaginable to me right now, at this stage of my life, to admit that I did not always view my father as a true veteran. In fact, at his funeral service, when they draped the American flag over his coffin, I felt embarrassed and uncomfortable thinking that my father wasn't truly a veteran like the Vietnam vets I encountered in my young adult years. I thought to myself that World War II was so long ago. Can he still claim veteran status? It almost seemed fraudulent to me, like we, as a family, were trying to cheat the system and get recognition for something that wasn't warranted, including free hospital care, an American flag, and a military plaque on my father's headstone. I'm genuinely ashamed to admit I felt that way and was uninformed and absent for so long because my father *was* a veteran in the most fundamental sense of the word; it just took me most of my life to recognize it.

The following is my father's story—as much as it is mine.

—2—

Veterans Day

We remember those who were called upon to give all a person can give . . . all of them ennobled their nation as they became champions of a noble cause.

—RONALD REAGAN,
40th US President

Lately, I have been thinking a lot about Veterans Day and how we remember our veterans. I now look forward to this day, mainly because I have immersed myself in World War II veterans' stories and finally understand the significance of this holiday.

Before I knew my father was a true veteran, I subconsciously thought Veterans Day belonged to the group of men and women who were actively serving in the military or had served at some point in the past. It was them, and it was me. I did not belong to that group nor believed I could be an active participant in anything related to veterans. I would walk right past the elderly soldier outside the grocery store who was displaying the American flag and selling his poppy pins or other knick-knacks decorated in red, white, and blue.

Occasionally, I would stop and buy something but never engage in meaningful conversation other than a brief hello, and a thank-you for the item I had purchased. If only I had known all along I was a part of this veterans' circle, not simply because my father was a veteran, but because I am an American citizen. I have also discovered that a person rarely has a family member or someone close to them who has not served our country and has a powerful story to tell—providing we take the time to sit and listen.

Recently, I had an opportunity to attend a Veterans Day celebration, including a parade, activities celebrating veterans, and a down-home potluck barbecue. I had never participated in a Veterans Day parade or celebrated the day in this full-blown fashion until a veteran involved in the Veterans Association in Fresno, California, invited me to attend. His name was Vern, and in a telephone conversation, he revealed that he landed in Normandy after the Battle of the Bulge and served in the 90th Infantry Division under General Patton. They were known as the Tough Ombres. He told me he fought from the Siegfried Line in Belgium all the way to Czechoslovakia until the Allies declared victory over Nazi Germany almost a year later. He was nineteen years old at the time.

He proudly reported that the Veterans Day celebration in Fresno hosts one of the country's most prominent Veterans Day parades. I was thrilled to receive his invitation and inspired to meet Vern and hear about his World War II experiences. Vern knew my father's good wartime friend, Toby, through the veterans' organization in Fresno, and I especially looked forward to hearing more about those stories.

When I first contacted Vern to ask him about Toby's experiences in World War II, ultimately hoping to learn more about my father, I hinted that I would be traveling near Fresno. Could we meet over a cup of coffee? Vern sounded delightful and quite welcoming during our phone conversation but said he first had to check his calendar. Luckily, it was open.

At ninety-five years old, Vern remained actively involved in World War II–related activities, which sometimes took him to conferences and speaking engagements across the country. Unfortunately, I had to cancel my Fresno plans last minute due to a family emergency. Regardless, I was awed by the privilege it was that Vern and others like him could still share their time with people like me interested in learning more about our veterans' history. I made plans to attend the parade and celebration on a future Veterans Day. I prayed that Vern's calendar would still be open.

The reality is that time is running out for our World War II veterans. There is a paragraph on the website of the National World War II Museum in New Orleans entitled "The Passing of the WWII Generation," which poignantly describes the urgency of the situation. It states, "Every day, memories of World War II—its sights and sounds, its terrors and triumphs—disappear. Yielding to the inalterable process of aging, the men and women who fought and won the great conflict are now in their late 80s and 90s. They are dying quickly."

The US Department of Veterans Affairs (VA) statistics demonstrate that of the 16 million veterans who served in World War II, fewer than 200,000 will still be alive in 2022. These veterans are in their late nineties, and the data forecast that approximately 300 expire daily. The entire World War II generation will ultimately pass by the end of the next decade. Tragically, they take their stories with them, some of which will never have the chance to be heard.

World War II veterans' sons and daughters are also hitting their golden years and beginning to pass away. They are the ones who listened to their fathers' stories firsthand and learned of the roles their mothers and other family members played in the war effort. Some children heard more than others and may have passed this information on to their children. Importantly, these stories conveyed to the next generation contribute to World War II's general body of knowledge and portray what it was like for parents and family members to serve their country in the most devastating war in recorded history.

Now that I know my father was a true veteran, I permit myself to officially participate in Veterans Day and other military holidays to honor our veterans. I finally feel I belong. This Veterans Day, like all past, I put my flag on the flag pole outside the upstairs window. This year I am proud to be an American and the daughter of a World War II veteran. Other years, before I knew I belonged to this day, I raised my flag because I thought it was the right thing to do, and it made my house look beautiful, like the photos captured in decorating magazines. I am embarrassed to admit that fact. When I hang my flag outside the upstairs window this year, I remember my father and all veterans. This year, I also think of 9/11.

We were in Dublin, Ireland, at the time of 9/11, and the next day after this tragic and shocking event, Dublin closed all the pubs for the afternoon in a sign of solidarity and remembrance. Everyone quietly milled around in the streets in a state of disbelief. A palpable sadness was in the air, and American flags were everywhere. A few days later, when we traveled to London, we saw American flags displayed on buildings and hundreds of bouquets strewn across the lawns and sidewalks in front of the American Embassy. The immense support of the Brits for their cousins across the pond was moving and, at the same time, quite comforting.

A week later, when we returned to the US, I was equally overwhelmed by the dozens of American flags flying in our neighborhood and throughout the city. For some reason, I was surprised by this dazzling display, and I remember thinking what an incredible show of support and remembrance for all those who suffered in this terrible disaster. To an American just arriving from overseas, it seemed to signify we were all in this together and would rise through this tragedy as one nation united.

Never Forget. I am writing these words on Veterans Day and again realizing how unenlightened I have been about veterans and World War II—the war in which my father fought and received his veteran status. This Veterans Day, the phrase Never Forget made the news on *Saturday Night Live (SNL)* and then on the national news stations. The *SNL* incident is what it took for those two words, Never Forget, to reach my world and the world of many people I know.

Dan Crenshaw, the Congressman-elect for Texas's 2nd Congressional District, appeared on *SNL* to accept an apology from cast member Pete Davidson live on the air. During the midterm elections for the House race the week prior, Pete Davidson had mocked Dan Crenshaw's appearance, specifically making fun of the black patch he wears over his right eye. Dan Crenshaw, a former Navy SEAL, lost his eye while serving in Afghanistan. Pete Davidson and the *SNL* late-night show producers had received overwhelming criticism from Democrats and Republicans for this mockery. Hence, one of the reasons for the public apology on Veterans Day.

After a handshake accepting a sincere apology from Davidson, Crenshaw delivered a speech that suggested recognizing veterans by thanking them for their service and saying, Never Forget. He said, "Tell a veteran, 'Never Forget.' When you say 'Never Forget' to a veteran, you are implying that as an American, you are in it with them, not separated by some imaginary barrier between civilians and veterans but connected together as grateful fellow Americans who will never forget the sacrifices made by veterans past and present. And never forget those we lost on 9/11, heroes like Pete's father."

Never Forget—two powerful words that summon multiple meanings and memories. These two words can remind us of 9/11 and the destruction of the twin towers or stir up images of past wars, including the horrors of the Jewish Holocaust under the Nazis' evil regime. Additionally, this phrase can serve as a vow never to forget the past, so we don't repeat the same mistake of allowing a dictator, a psychopath, or an egomaniac to rise to power with empty promises to make life better for their followers—usually at the cost of others. I heard a story from someone whose Dutch parents were liberated during World War II who makes it a point to thank veterans for their service, "not only for our freedom but for the freedom of people you didn't even know."

My father would always say, "Nothing in life is free." Now, I wonder if he was thinking about our freedom and others around the globe when he said this. Did his thoughts travel back to his fellow veterans who, regardless of their role, rank, political preferences, or under which branch they served, made the ultimate sacrifice of giving up their youth and lives so that we and others could remain free?

So Never Forget on this Veterans Day is a day that I begin to remember, begin to discover, and begin to acknowledge my father and his story—the quiet World War II veteran and humble hero, the tail gunner on a B-17 named "Bomb Boogie" flying bombing missions over Germany and Nazi-occupied Europe, the young boy of twenty-one years, scared of heights, parachuting twice out of a plane to his eventual capture by the Germans, the resilient soldier held captive in a prisoner of war (POW) camp for twenty-two months who spent his twenty-fourth birthday on a forced march in one of the coldest winters in over fifty years, the daredevil who rolled down a hill during the forced march to escape detention in another prison camp, and the tired, emaciated young man who finally made it home to get married and have five children, including me, his oldest daughter.

—— 3 ——

VA Benefits

*The farther backward you can look, the farther
forward you are likely to see.*

—WINSTON CHURCHILL,
Prime Minister of the United Kingdom
during World War II, 1940–1945

I am trying to remember when I first started thinking about my father again, and I believe it happened in 2017 when we transferred our ninety-year-old mother to an assisted living facility. At this point, our family became aware that she was eligible for VA assistance. We learned that the cause of death written on our father's death certificate and his years as a POW made his spouse eligible for VA death benefits. Notably, we discovered she had qualified some thirty-one years earlier, the year my father died.

In retrospect, my mother missed out on almost thirty-one years of government services because we were unaware of her eligibility. I do not hold the VA accountable for our not knowing. Perhaps they notified our mother, but we did not take advantage in any case. However, when we truly needed the help, the Department of Veterans Affairs was there for us as our mother's health care costs began to escalate. They provided our mother with a sum of money that helped cover about one-fourth of her monthly costs. She received these VA benefits for two years while in an assisted living facility until she passed away in 2019.

During the process of applying for VA assistance, my father reentered my consciousness. One of the first documents the VA requested was his Discharge Record. Our mother's health was steadily deteriorating, including her mental capabilities, having recently been diagnosed with dementia. She was not able to provide information to the VA about our father's World War II history or able to locate any of the requested forms.

Luckily, after searching around her apartment, we found a manila folder with her handwriting reading "Don Hayes World War II." Inside the folder was our father's original Discharge Record, a photo of his airplane in flight, a picture of his crewmates in front of a white wooden building, and another of his crew with their B-17 aircraft in the background. He kept these photos his entire life, but I don't ever remember seeing any of these pictures. A typed document he had written of the bombing missions he flew from England to Nazi-occupied Europe was also inside the folder. He had highlighted one mission in detail, and it was entitled "Synopsis of the Schweinfurt-Regensburg Mission."

Locating a copy of my father's Discharge Record proved invaluable. This one-page document served as a jumping-off point to uncover other elements of his military history. It revealed his serial number, enlistment date, discharge date, military specialty, training, medals, and service dates, including service outside the US and each return date. According to the Discharge Record, my father enlisted in the Army Air Corps when he was nineteen years old and received an Honorable Discharge five years later at the age of twenty-four.

Familiarizing myself with the Discharge Record and other documents required by the VA, I discovered crucial facts about my father's World War II service. For example, I knew he had been a POW, but I did not know for how long. The VA informed me he was held in captivity for twenty-two months, almost twice as long as the average soldier. However, as I attempted to answer additional questions requested by the VA during the benefits application process, I became painfully aware of how much I did not know about my father's war history.

Recognizing these informational gaps, the VA representative recommended I contact the National Archives and Records Administration (NARA) to request my father's complete Military Personnel File. Promptly, I sent in the paperwork and was informed that it would take approximately three months to honor my request. In the meantime, the VA spokesperson suggested I visit the NARA website and research their World War II Prisoner of War Data Files. These files promised to inform me which POW camp the Germans detained my father in, as his Discharge Record did not contain these facts. And, regrettably, no one in our family could remember those details.

The POW file on the NARA website was reasonably easy to locate, utilizing my father's military serial number on his Discharge Record. In this file, I found the Detaining Power information and the camp information. The Detaining Power listed was "Germany," and the camp was "Stalag Luft 3 in Sagan-Silesia Bavaria," with additional information in parentheses stating, "Moved to Nuremberg-Langwasser." According to the information listed in this online government document, I now knew about the POW camps where my father was held prisoner for almost two years.

The application process for VA benefits initially piqued my interest in finding out more about my father's World War II history, particularly the whereabouts of his POW camp. Shortly after, an opportunity arose that catapulted me on this new path of discovery and reconnection.

This was when my sister Naomi, who had also been involved in the VA benefits process, asked, "Do you want to go to Europe and search out Dad's POW camps?"

I instantly replied, "Yes, it's time. Let's go."

PART TWO

SETTING SAIL

— 4 —

Preparation

*To reach a port we must set sail—Sail, not
tie at anchor—Sail, not drift.*

—FRANKLIN D. ROOSEVELT,
32nd US President

I mmediately, my sister and I made plans to retrace our father's footsteps during World War II. As noted on the NARA website, we specifically targeted the POW camps where he was held prisoner for twenty-two months. I learned that one of these camps, Stalag Luft III, was now in Zagan, Poland, and the other camp, Stalag XIII-D (Stalag 13D hereon), was in Nuremberg, Germany. I also discovered that his POW file listed "moved to Nuremberg-Langwasser" because the Germans forced the POWs detained on their eastern borders to march west, moving them to different prison camps during the war's final months.

Our planned itinerary was to fly into Berlin, rent a car, and drive to Poland, Stalag Luft III's location. From there, we would travel to Nuremberg, Germany, following the path the POWs took on their forced march in the winter of 1945. Last, we made arrangements to drop the car off in Nuremberg and take the train to Amsterdam for our flight back to the US.

Before leaving on our trip, I began doing some homework and quickly realized I needed a crash course on World War II. There was so much to learn. On one of my shelves sat a book called *The Rise and Fall of the Third Reich* by William L. Shirer, published in 1960. I had purchased it sometime in the 1980s when my Book of the Month Club included it in their monthly selection. I never read the book, and as I dusted it off and glanced through the 1,143 pages, I realized it was a publication that required revisiting at a later date.

Right now, time was of the essence as we would be leaving on our trip in a few weeks, and my knowledge of World War II was less than complete. I needed something quick and comprehensive, like the condensed *Reader's Digest* books my father would read each month.

In the history section at our local bookstore, I spotted a book with large red letters on the cover that caught my attention. It was entitled *Nazi Germany History Examined* by Robert Smith Thompson and Alan Axelrod. I skimmed the first few pages and discovered a publishing date of February 2018. Also noted on the cover page was the statement "Reprinted from *The Complete Idiot's Guide to Nazi Germany*." Perfect, that would fit the bill—for now.

This work became an excellent source of information with incredible insights for someone needing the *CliffsNotes* on World War II. Most valuable were the bullet points at the end of each chapter called "The Least You Need to Know." Also helpful was the Chronology Appendix, which defined the critical dates of the rise and fall of Nazi Germany.

With facts at my fingertips, I began to feel somewhat prepared, fully realizing this was the tip of the iceberg as far as my knowledge of this historical period in time. I put William L. Shirer's massive literary work back on the bookshelf, vowing to return to it when I had more opportunity and could fully appreciate the author's enormous undertaking in attempting to explain the rise and fall of the Third Reich.

Because our trip focused on visiting our father's POW camps, I quickly searched the two POW camps listed in his files: Stalag Luft III and Stalag 13D. Additionally, I researched the march the Germans forced the POWs to undertake when they transferred them from one camp to the next in the final months of the war.

Reading about Stalag Luft III, I found it was established in 1942 and was situated in the German province of Lower Silesia, 100 miles from Berlin, in Sagan, Germany (now Zagan, Poland). The Luftwaffe—the name of the German Air Force—was in charge of administering the site, which primarily held Allied Air Force officers, initially pilots from the Royal Air Force (RAF). Later, when the United States entered the war, American Air Force officers joined their British Allies, some of whom were already long-established at this camp.

Notably, Stalag Luft III was the camp where the Great Escape took place in 1944. Over 600 prisoners were involved in an escape attempt by digging three tunnels named Tom, Dick, and Harry. Two hundred of these 600 prisoners participated in the actual escape commencing on the evening of March 24, 1944. Only seventy-six prisoners fled through the tunnel named Harry, as the German guards discovered the attempt midway on the morning of March 25. The Nazis captured seventy-three of the seventy-six men attempting to flee. Only three of the prisoners eventually made it to freedom.

The story goes that Hitler became furious when he heard about the escape and ordered all the recaptured prisoners executed. His officers persuaded him to spare half of them, arguing that a full-out massacre would jeopardize the lives of their own officers held as POWs if the Allies retaliated. Fifty men, more than half, were executed within a short period following recapture. The war would end approximately one year later. So close to being free again, but how were they to know?

I remember when our parents piled us in the family car and we went to the drive-in theater to watch *The Great Escape* when Hollywood first released the movie in 1963. My father eagerly anticipated seeing the film. However, he probably could not fully concentrate until all five of us fell asleep in the back of the station wagon. Already dressed in our pajamas with our blankets and pillows, we eventually drifted off to slumberland with the sounds of that famous theme song floating through our heads.

Although we were too young at the time to fully grasp the significance of this event, my father was thrilled with the film. He seemed so proud of all the brave POWs who participated in this ingenious and daring escape right under the noses of the Nazis, despite the final outcome.

My father's second prisoner of war camp listed in his file was Nuremberg-Langwasser or Stalag 13D. This prison camp was built on what had been the Nazi Party Rally Grounds in Nuremberg, in northern Bavaria, and had initially housed civilian enemies of the state. In 1939, the camp began to hold prisoners of war from all the Nazi-occupied countries, and, at one time, it had over 150,000 detainees.

In late 1944 and 1945, as the Russian Red Army began advancing west, the Germans transferred thousands of POWs to this site from prison camps on their eastern borders. In the winter and spring of 1945, most British and American POWs arrived in Nuremberg after their forced marches away from the advancing Russians—POWs from camps like Stalag Luft III.

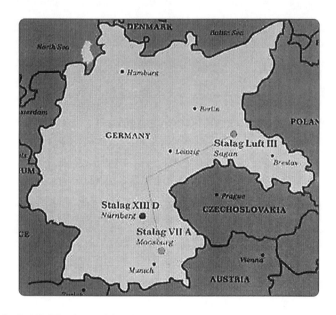

Stalag Luft III: The Long March. Highlighted are the evacuation routes the American POWs at Stalag Luft III were forced to travel in January 1945. From Sagan, Germany, the POWs marched approximately fifty-two miles to the train station in Spremberg, Germany. From Spremberg, the POWs from the South and Center Compound were loaded into boxcars and transported to Stalag VII-A (7A) in Moosburg. The West and North Compounds were transported to Stalag 13D in Nuremberg-Langwasser and eventually to Moosburg, arriving at that site on April 20, 1945.

The routes the POWs traveled on their forced marches, long marches, or death marches, as the Allies termed them, were unique as far as the roads they traveled, depending on the camp's location. Furthermore, within each march from each POW camp that was evacuated, the POWs had varied experiences, such as where they were sheltered, their treatment by the guards, what they witnessed along the routes, and even different end camps. However, they all had similar aspects, such as the harsh weather conditions and the lack of food, clothing, and shelter.

Stalag Luft III's march to Stalag 13D in Nuremberg occurred in January 1945 in one of the coldest winters in fifty years. In the Sagan area, most prisoners in Stalag Luft III marched approximately fifty-two miles to Spremberg, Germany, which took anywhere from four to five days or longer. After arriving in Spremberg, the Germans packed the POWs into boxcars without food or water in filthy and overcrowded conditions. From there, they were transported to their final destinations, either Moosburg or Nuremberg, over 250 miles away. This segment of the journey took another two days and two nights. My father would have been twenty-three years old and just short of celebrating his twenty-fourth birthday.

Everyone Has a Story

I keep my ideals, because in spite of everything
I still believe that people are really good at heart.

—ANNE FRANK

As I made preparations to leave on my trip, I told family and friends about my plans to visit my father's POW camps. These final weeks of preparation were super emotional, something I did not anticipate. I found myself crying throughout the day, and when I talked to people about my plans, my voice would break, and I could barely fight back the tears. I was embarrassed and surprised by my reactions. I had transitioned from hardly thinking of my father for the last thirty-plus years to now when rarely a moment went by when he was not on my mind.

Everything was now framed with him as a reference, and my whole perspective of life changed. For example, when I cleared the dinner plates and threw away the leftovers, I thought about how he faced starvation in the POW camp for almost two years. I envisioned the diseases, lice, battle wounds, and severe cold he and his buddies suffered while imprisoned. Simultaneously, I contemplated my siblings' perspectives about our father's World War II history, realizing we all heard different narratives and even remembered disparate versions of the same story. It began to dawn on me that we never spent much time collectively discussing our father's World War II stories—until now.

Each time I met up with friends and acquaintances, I informed them about my intent to retrace my father's footsteps. More often than not, it seemed to be the first moment in quite some time that they had thought of their fathers and family members who participated in the war. All the stories I heard were unique, but there were many similarities. For example, most said their fathers did not talk much about the war. Many seemed confused and embarrassed that they did not know their father's war history.

At a garden party in the wine country of Sonoma County, California, one friend told me her father was in World War II. I asked her where he served and his role, and she became teary-eyed because she could not remember. She did not know if he was deployed in the Pacific or the European Theater and was visibly embarrassed and filled with emotion. I felt her pain of not knowing the answers to these inquiries; seemingly, at one time, I had all the opportunity in the world to ask my father every conceivable question and then carefully listen and remember his answers.

One good friend reminded me that her father was also a POW. I asked her what camp he was in, and she did not have the answer. She told me she would find out the information before I left on my trip and asked her son to help her undertake the research. Her son was the one who eventually informed me of his grandfather's history. He fought in the Battle of the Bulge, was captured, and spent the remainder of the war in Stalag III-A, just thirty-two miles southwest of Berlin.

Another acquaintance informed me that her father was stationed in the Solomon Islands, fighting in the Pacific Theater. She said he never talked about the war. She added that to the day he died, he never went barefoot. He would take his shoes off just before he got into bed, and every morning before stepping into his shoes, he would thoroughly check them for signs of insects. As demonstrated by his daily rituals, the war stayed with him psychologically to the end of his days.

While walking in my neighborhood, I passed an older neighbor named Margaret, and we exchanged pleasantries. She asked me how my summer was going and had I done much traveling. I told her about my upcoming trip to Europe. Margaret was originally from New Zealand. Her father was sent off to war when England declared war on Germany.

She said, "You know, we were part of the Commonwealth, so when Great Britain made the call, all her nations responded."

Her father left for the European Theater, fighting in Egypt and Italy and then in Germany when she was just two years old. He did not come back until she was eight years old, six years later. She said the most challenging part was when her father returned. She remembers her brother, mother, and relatives going to the train station to meet him when he arrived from overseas. She recalled thinking, Who is that man? I do not know him. Is this man my father? She said it was unfortunate because she and her brother could never feel close to their dad as he was absent during their growing-up years.

Margaret said she and her brother struggled with that fact for the rest of their lives and speculated it might have turned out differently had he been home during their formative years. She also believed her mother experienced similar difficulties when her father returned as she had become entirely independent while he was away. The closeness she felt to him was lost to some degree.

Margaret told me of a Jewish family friend from Denmark who ended up in a Nazi POW camp. Because of his close ties to a wealthy banking family in Denmark who performed some favors for the Germans, he was allowed to stay detained in Germany rather than suffer deportation to an extermination camp in Poland. Margaret quietly stated, "He survived the war."

Finally, another friend, who idolized her father and always spoke about him with the utmost admiration, told me he was a pilot and completed over thirty missions during the war. When asked, she did not remember where he was stationed or what type of plane he flew and had little information about his military history other than those few facts. Her dearth of details surprised me.

But currently, who am I to judge? The more I talked to people, the more similarities there were regarding the limited knowledge we all had of how our fathers participated in World War II.

So just over a few weeks, I realized that almost everyone I knew had a story to tell, even if it only came in bits and pieces. When I visited my mother at her assisted living facility, there were many stories. I no longer viewed the elderly population in the same way. I looked at them with renewed interest knowing that each of them had a tale, and with that somewhat self-centered reason in place, I found myself engaging in many more conversations than I would have previous to my World War II interest. However, it soon became evident that I was the one who was reaping the benefits of these engagements. These seniors gave me more than I imagined when I intentionally carved out time to show interest and listen.

One day at my mother's assisted living facility, I introduced myself to an elderly lady sitting across from us in the main dining room during lunch and engaged her in conversation. Her name was Millie, and she grew up in San Diego. I asked her if she had ever worked, and she told me that one of her first jobs was during World War II working on planes. She mentioned a type of bomber plane that I did not recognize at this stage in my learning. She told me this plane flew in the Pacific during the war.

Millie then recounted a story when the only man at the plane factory, her boss, would make her go back into the plane's tail area to fix the electrical wiring, even though she was not an electrician and had no training in that sort of thing. She said it was because she was smaller and could fit more easily into the tail section.

Millie casually told me that she found a finger back in the tail area one day at work. She said it was probably the poor tail gunner's, and it was most likely frozen or severed during combat. At this point, she looked up at me from her meal, knowing that this segment of her story, which she probably had told many times, always sparked interest—among other emotions—in her audience. I thought of my father as a tail gunner on a B-17 bomber and how lucky he was to return from the war with all his fingers.

These were just a few of the stories I collected in several weeks leading up to my trip, and the more I talked to people, the more information there was to be garnered. The accounts were distinct and engaging and were remarkable windows into a war that shook the entire world.

One day in my book club, someone suggested a story about World War II as we chose our next book to read. One of the members said, "I think I've read about everything there is to know about World War II." I remained quiet. An entire world was at war, nations called millions of their citizens to duty, and countless people died. It is my impression that we will never run out of stories. I often wonder why we read fiction? The real stories, all unique and powerful, are hard to trump.

As I continued talking to friends and family about my upcoming trip, one interesting observation was that many of these people, who seemingly had no interest in World War II, were starting to perform their own private research. It was like a chain reaction. Together, we recognized that our veterans' stories would never be passed on to future generations unless we communicated them now to our children, grandchildren, family members, and friends. The significance of my journey was starting to sink in for many reasons. I was finally ready to stop drifting and set sail.

— 6 —

On His Heels

Greatness is a road leading towards the unknown.

—Charles de Gaulle,
Leader of Free France against
Nazi Germany in World War II

Landing in Berlin, my sister and I allowed two nights and one full day to tour the city. After a deep sleep, the type you get after an exhausting airplane trip, we set out to explore Berlin. Without prior planning, we serendipitously came across the Topography of Terror Museum, situated next to a portion of the existing Berlin Wall. The museum sat directly on top of the former Nazi SS and Gestapo headquarters—all destroyed during the bombing of Berlin. We learned that the persecution and extermination of Nazi political opponents transpired on this site, including plans for the genocide of Jews and other groups marked for ethnic cleansing.

At the time of our visit, an outdoor exhibit entitled "Berlin 1933—The Path to Dictatorship" was on display. Poster boards encased with glass ran along the entire section of this remnant of the Berlin Wall and outlined Hitler's rise to power from 1933 to his demise in 1945. Preserved underground structures were underfoot, and somewhere nearby was the bunker where Hitler and Eva Braun committed suicide. We did not have time to visit every site and exhibit the museum offered, but I made a mental note to return and take it all in at a future date.

The following day we drove from Berlin to Stalag Luft III in Zagan, Poland, where we believed our father was a prisoner from 1943 to 1945. Traveling southeast from Berlin, we decided to reverse the route he would have taken on his forced march from Stalag Luft III to Nuremberg. We made plans to begin at the train station in Spremberg, Germany, and end at the POW camp in Poland. Following the route of the march in this reverse order would allow us to drive from Zagan, Poland, after spending two nights, directly to Nuremberg, approximately a five-hour drive southwest on the Autobahn.

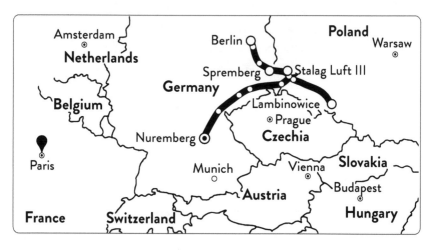

Our Route through Germany and Poland. Outlined on the map is the route my sister and I traveled searching for our father's POW camp. Starting in Berlin, we drove to the train station in Spremberg, Germany. From there, we traveled by car to Stalag Luft III, following the path of the long march (but in the reverse direction). After visiting Stalag Luft III, we drove to Stalag 8B in Lambinowice, Poland. Determining that our father was not at 8B, we went to our destination in Nuremberg, Germany, the location of Stalag 13D.

It took us two hours to drive to Spremberg from Berlin. Arriving at our destination, we traveled through the village down cobblestone streets and parked our car in the town square. Within sight were several quaint shops and a restaurant or two with people sitting outside having a late lunch. The town was so quiet that I swear I heard the village cat purring a few blocks away. Everyone present in the square, which could not have been more than ten total, briefly looked up from their lunches, seemingly out of curiosity or perhaps boredom. I don't recall the sound of any conversations, just the muffled noise of utensils clinking down on plates and drinking glasses landing on tables. Deciding to stay in the car, we punched *Bahnhof* (the German word for train station) Spremberg into our phones and found out it was only five minutes away.

Arriving at the train station was a bit surreal. The Bahnhof in Spremberg was the first place on our trip with any real connection to where we believed our father might have been during the war. I remember parking the car and staring at the old brick building with its large, arched paned windows, fighting back the tears. The station was eerily silent. Several cars were in the small parking lot, but no other visitors were around except for my sister and me. Walking to the main entrance of the Bahnhof, we jiggled the door handle but discovered it was locked. We peered into one of the dusty windows and realized the building was abandoned.

Walking to the back of the Bahnhof, where the tracks were situated, we encountered a forest of pine trees stretching out in all directions as far as the eye could see. There were no buildings in view, and the setting was peaceful, calming, and serene. On the cement walkway near the tracks, a new blue sign displayed the words *Spremberg/Groak*, validating that the train continued to stop at this station.

We took a few pictures of the tracks, and the old brick Bahnhof we learned later looked like every other Bahnhof in Germany—all built with similar architecture. Images ran through my head of the young, sick, malnourished soldiers arriving at this lonely spot after their long march in the bitter cold, only to be crammed into cattle cars and transported to yet another camp days away. I remembered how grateful I was that the train station was still there, even though it stood vacant and neglected. It was such a beautiful building situated in a picturesque and tranquil village in Eastern Germany, and I was grateful to experience this moment. A connection to the past, even if no one in the vicinity seemed to know it.

That thought slowly began to set in, and it bothered me. Did the people living here understand the significance of this train station? Why were there no memorials to be found pointing out the history of this spot and the role that this town played during World War II? I found myself getting upset but ambivalent about where to direct my anger. I never anticipated I would experience these emotions regarding the lack of visible World War II remembrances.

We decided to return to town and visit City Hall to determine if we missed some critical memorial spots or plaques. Back at the town square, we knocked on the City Hall door, but it was already two in the afternoon, and the office was closed for the day. It was getting late, and we intended to visit all the small villages on the long march route on our way to Zagan. We also needed to travel to our final hotel destination in a town a few additional miles away.

Our road trip mimicked the trail the POWs traveled on their forced march in January 1945, near the end of the war. From Spremberg, we headed to Graustein, one of the small hamlets along the route. After driving several miles down a narrow, one-lane road, we ended up on a dirt path in the forest, noticeably absent of any signage of nearby towns. According to Google Maps, we had arrived at the first town on our journey. We stopped the car, got out in the middle of nowhere, and took a picture of the forest with its endless acres of shrubbery and trees.

Google informed us that Graustein was a municipality in the northeastern German state of Brandenburg and was associated with Spremberg, similar to what we would think of as a suburb. I paused and tried to imagine what the scene must have been like, with over 10,000 soldiers and their German guards trudging through the snow through these desolate woods to destinations and fates unknown. The forests were unusual, populated with tall pines with branches that did not sprout until they reached about thirty feet high on their deep rust-colored trunks.

While the POWs most likely marched on trails or small village roads, this type of tree probably offered the guards the advantage of always keeping their prisoners within sight. There was no hiding in forests with this type of vegetation. I learned that this variety of pine was called Scotts Pine. Later on our trip, we discovered that large parts of Eastern Germany and Poland were populated with forests made up of this species—evergreen, coniferous trees sometimes growing up to 100 feet tall, with trunks about fifty inches in diameter. Tall skinny trees with skinny trunks, ubiquitous in this part of Europe.

We decided to continue the remainder of the route we had mapped out, crossing the German border and driving through several Polish villages in the direction of Zagan—stopping only to take pictures of the town signs to remember all these places where our father may have walked so long ago. We did not locate any memorials to honor the POWs, but, in all fairness, we did not linger and investigate each spot along the way.

The roads were one lane, winding through a countryside dotted with farms and occasional villages. Some portions of the road were made up of old cobblestones, and I remembered reading that the POWs had marched through forests and cobblestone roads. I wondered if we were driving down the same cobblestone paths that the POWs traversed decades earlier.

During the drive, I became painfully aware that I had so many unanswered questions I wanted to ask my father about this march and his war history. I longed to know if his feet were warm enough. What shoes was he wearing while he walked all those miles, now that he had been a POW for almost two years? Were his fingers cold? Did he feel weak and ever wonder if he would be able to finish the march? Where did he sleep? Was he scared? And why did it take me so long to take this journey myself?

As we finished the long march route, my sister played a song from her iPhone entitled "Long March to Freedom" written by Lesley Loughlin to remember her father-in-law who took this same journey. Greensand Ridge performed the music; the words were powerful, the tone woeful, and I was driving and trying to hold back tears.

It began to dawn on me that little remained to signify the presence of Allied POWs in Germany. It took us approximately five hours by car to cover the fifty-two to sixty miles the POWs took from Zagan to Spremberg, stopping at every conceivable town and village, searching for proof of the long march. In the end, we could not uncover one shred of evidence that something so significant and historical had ever occurred.

We arrived in Zagan, Poland, at around 6 p.m. The light was beginning to change, and it would be dark soon. We were staying thirty miles outside the town of Zagan in a Polish castle called Zamek Kliczkow in the tiny village of Osiecznica, Poland. Our thoughts were to quickly drive through Zagan, where Stalag Luft III was located.

As we approached the town, we saw the POW camp off to the right of the road. It was impossible to miss it with its tall, foreboding watchtower, surrounded by a barbed-wire fence. We were tempted to stop, but it was late, and the museum on site had already closed for the day. We made plans to wake early and spend the next day visiting the camp museum, exploring the grounds—especially the tunnels—and speaking to any person who could provide us with more information about our father.

+ + +

The next morning, we woke up early, full of anticipation and excitement about what lay ahead. Flinging open the shutters in our castle bedroom, we were greeted with the most beautiful bluebird day Poland had to offer. The camp museum opened at 10 a.m., and we arrived at around 10:30. Luckily, Stalag Luft III was a POW camp that had been preserved, primarily in part to *The Great Escape* that occurred there and the famous movie by the same name starring Steve McQueen.

As we drove through the prison gates, the primary feature that jumped out was the intact barbed-wire fence and the tall wooden watchtower looming over the entrance. We parked the car and went directly into the museum. A Polish lady at the ticket counter asked us in her limited English if we were family members. We told her our father was a POW at this camp, and she let us know there was no charge. My eyes, once again, immediately welled up with tears. This first small act of kindness on the museum granting access to all POW families felt overwhelming. It seemed like the kind, smiling Polish lady was all but taking my hand and saying, "It's all right, honey. We understand how difficult this was for your father and your family. We appreciate all the sacrifices these young boys made so our country could eventually regain its freedom and end all the suffering."

We then asked her if we could speak to the museum director or someone who could give us more information on our father's stay at the prison camp. The kind Polish lady told us that the person who could help us was named Mirek. He was currently leading a group of Polish soldiers on tour but would be with us soon. She then instructed us to visit the museum on our own until he returned.

As we strolled through the building, we ran into Mirek, still touring the group of Polish soldiers. He briefly stopped, introduced himself, and informed us he would return shortly after showing the soldiers the outside grounds. He bowed toward us, looked directly into our eyes, shook our hands, and said how sorry he was that our father was a prisoner of war. My sister and I fought to hold back our tears, to no avail. It was our first contact with someone who could validate our father's POW story, and he came across as genuinely kind and understanding, similar to the Polish lady at the front desk.

On our self-guided tour, we learned that Stalag Luft III was a POW camp for Air Force pilots and other aircrew officers. Our father was not an officer, but this was the first camp listed on his veteran papers. We eagerly anticipated learning how long he was at Stalag Luft III and obtaining more information about the forced march to Nuremberg. We patiently waited for Mirek to return to answer all those questions.

The museum was one large room sectioned into three areas. The first section held information and memorabilia about British prisoners. There were photos of officers and pilots, uniforms on display, eating utensils, and other paraphernalia. They even had a copy of a Christmas menu decorated with green and red holly that the prisoners had put together, with fantasized food items such as turkey and gravy. This menu emphasized the POWs' attempts to stay calm and carry on and create distractions to escape the day-to-day prison life.

The second section in the museum had a replica of the men's sleeping quarters, complete with a bunk bed and table. There were personal items the POWs managed to keep, including pictures of family or poster girls pinned up on the walls around their bed space. This display provided a snapshot of how the POWs made efforts to create a safe and homey area, despite their little personal space and freedom to move about as they would like.

The last room had a small number of American POW items that included uniforms, boots, US aircraft pictures, and World War II propaganda signs enticing young men to enlist. Also displayed were artifacts from Poland, the Low Countries (Belgium, Netherlands, and Luxembourg), Canada, and other nations that contributed to the war effort.

I noticed how the items in the British section far outnumbered the items in the American display. Later, Mirek reinforced that few Americans were at this camp early in the war compared to the British soldiers. The small numbers made sense since the British entered the war in 1939, right after Hitler invaded Poland. That was almost two and a half years ahead of the Americans, providing them with more time to be casualties of war.

After our self-guided tour, we watched a short fifteen-minute film on the camp's history. While I waited for Mirek to conclude with the Polish soldiers, I grabbed a pamphlet about the museum and found out that Stalag Luft III was built in the spring of 1942 and was explicitly for officers of the Allied air forces. By 1945, the camp held more than 10,000 captured Air Force officers, with Americans now outnumbering the British.

As previously mentioned, Stalag Luft III became famous worldwide with the Great Escape in March of 1944. The museum had partially reconstructed the escape tunnel and replicated POW "Hut No. 104"— the barrack where the British officers built the famous tunnel, Harry. Information about the other tunnels, Tom and Dick, all constructed simultaneously, was also displayed. Pictures on the hut walls indicated one tunnel started under the wood-burning stove, one under a large wooden exercise horse, and one under a heavy piece of furniture. Harry was cleverly hidden under the wooden exercise horse.

The tunnel-making was ingenious and poignant at the same time, knowing the fated outcome of all their plans. Even though I had heard this story many times, it seemed more palpable and tragic at the site where it occurred. Sadly, I envisioned family members overcome with emotion as they received notices that their loved ones while trying to escape had been executed by their Nazi captors.

In Stalag Luft III, the Americans were housed primarily in the South, Center, and West Compounds, while the British were predominantly in the North Compound. The Germans aimed to keep POWs separated by their country of origin for the most part. Apart from one another, most American prisoners remained unaware of the British plans to escape. I don't remember my father talking about the Great Escape as a POW, but at this point in my search, I was uncertain if he was in the camp during the actual escape attempt.

After about one hour, Mirek said goodbye to the Polish soldiers and met us outside the museum carrying a handful of thick spiral notebooks. Each notebook contained the names of all the prisoners at Stalag Luft III. Mirek inquired about our father's name and POW number. We did not have his POW number, and we discovered that this was an essential piece of information when searching for a POW. All we had was his Army serial number. Since we had planned this trip at the last minute, our research and knowledge were limited.

We carefully scoured the files that Mirek provided us but could not find our father's record. I refused to believe it at first. It was such a disappointment not seeing his name in print. A wave of doubt descended over me for a brief moment, and I questioned if he was actually in the war and a POW in Germany. Now, here in the middle of Poland, his story resembled a ghost story—fleeting, intangible, and impossible to pin down. It was incredibly frustrating, but I made an effort to hide my feelings and the bitter disappointment of not finding tangible evidence of our father's whereabouts. I remembered saying that he had to be recorded in the book.

I said, "Look at his POW file. Don't you see Stalag Luft III listed as his first camp?" Mirek was a gentle soul. He told us not to worry, that we would eventually find our father.

Mirek asked that we follow him to his office where he could review other records and obtain additional information by asking us a few more questions. We followed him into a small room crowded with piles of papers and books. He explained that while Stalag Luft III was listed in our father's file, primarily only officers and pilots in the Air Force were interned at this camp.

He said, "Your father was a technical sergeant, and he would not have been interned at this camp." He informed us that after capture, the Germans would often bring a few of the airmen here to be interrogated and then reassign them to other centers according to their rank. He could have been transferred to many other camps from this location if he had made it here in the first place.

It began to sink in that we were missing valuable information about where our father spent almost two years as a POW. My sister said she remembered a conversation she recently had with the son of our father's close friend, Toby, his bunkmate, in the POW camp. She shared that Toby's son remembered his father talking about a prison camp he called 8B. Mirek informed us that Stalag 8B (Stalag VIII-B according to the German designation system) was one of the prison camps where the Germans transferred enlisted men like our father. He said our father might have been moved to that camp.

I asked, "Why was Stalag Luft III listed on my father's Army Air Corps papers and not Stalag 8B?" Mirek informed us that the Germans organized their camps into districts and assigned airmen to prison camps under the jurisdiction of the Luftwaffe. Stalag Luft III was the main camp out of ten camps that fell under the Luftwaffe's parachute. All mail first went to the district's main camp to be sorted and delivered to the sub-camps. So Mirek said that while most POWs, like our father, had Stalag Luft III listed on his war records for mail purposes, they did not reside in that camp but were assigned to others.

Now I was even more confused and frustrated. I was also disappointed for not being adequately informed, both in doing my homework and not asking my father more questions, including listening carefully to his stories when he was around to tell them.

Mirek informed us that Stalag 8B was about two and a half hours away in Lambinowice, Poland (formerly known as Lamsdorf, Germany). It was now 1 p.m. If we wanted to visit this camp, which we did, we needed to do it today. Tomorrow we would leave for Nuremberg, and we did not have the flexibility to veer from our itinerary. If we hurried, we could make it to the camp by 4 p.m. before the museum closed at 5 p.m. We asked Mirek if he could call the museum to let them know we were coming and if they could locate any records that authenticated that our father was a POW at that camp.

Mirek called the museum and had a Polish conversation with the person on duty who said we needed to visit in person to obtain additional information. Mirek reassured us that Stalag 8B had an excellent museum and extensive, well-preserved grounds to explore. He copied our father's records for safekeeping, gave us his business card, and asked us to stay in touch with any new information we could find out. We thanked Mirek for his time and headed out in a hurry without exploring Stalag Luft III's grounds. We also did not have time to explore the town of Zagan to see for ourselves if any memorials commemorated the young soldiers that spent time in this part of the world—the many who made countless sacrifices not so long ago.

It took us almost three hours driving at high speeds on the Autobahn to reach Lambinowice, Poland. Driving on the Autobahn was an adventure unto itself. There was no such thing as letting your mind wander or relax in deep thought because, before you knew it, a car going over 100 miles per hour would be on your tail until they forced you to move over to the slower lane behind a row of trucks. The trucks were traveling over seventy miles per hour, and after a while, I found myself driving as fast as everyone else.

Finally, we veered off the Autobahn into the bucolic and beautiful Polish countryside, where I could take a deep breath and decompress. It was peaceful to experience all the lush farms and expansive fields sown with crops, broken up by the picturesque villages every so many miles—their cottages and window boxes overflowing with flowers. After driving through the narrow one-lane country roads, we finally arrived in the town of Lambinowice. It was 4 p.m., and we had one hour to tour the museum and talk to someone in charge before it closed at 5 p.m.

Peter, the manager, had been waiting for us. He immediately let us know that there were few Americans at this camp, fewer than 100. Peter also informed us that they did not have records with lists of the American POWs' names. He told us that a research project was underway to gather information from POW families and requested that we contact him again if we found that our father spent time at this prison camp. Why hadn't Peter told us all of this before we started our journey? Perhaps he was hoping we would have information for him, not the other way around.

Since we had made the long drive, we toured the small museum, which primarily had information on the Polish POWs, most of whom were forced to work in Upper Silesia's mines and industries in this part of Poland. There was also an entire section in the museum dedicated to the Katyn Massacre. Peter asked us if we knew about the Katyn Massacre, and we replied no. He told us that after Russia invaded Poland, the

Russian Army, in 1940, executed approximately 22,000 Polish military personnel upon Stalin's direct orders and buried them in mass graves in and around the Katyn forest.

I was embarrassed that I had never heard of this massacre. I remembered wondering what was going through Peter's mind when we admitted we were oblivious about this horrific war crime. We had traveled to this museum and POW camp to find out about our father and American POWs. In the process, we were becoming educated on other nations' plights, such as the Polish prisoners who suffered even harsher conditions than POWs of different nationalities. As I studied more about World War II, I learned how much the Polish people endured from the Russians and the Germans. Their country was sandwiched in between two warring nations, and they tolerated immeasurable hardships from both sides.

After we quickly toured the museum, we said goodbye to Peter with promises to send him any information we could gather about our father's whereabouts as a POW, hoping to contribute to their ongoing research project. It was getting late, and we wanted to explore the areas where the actual POW camp existed. A billboard outside the museum displayed a map with additional points of interest, including the Polish cemetery and other POW cemeteries of different nationalities.

An area on the map, designated as Stalag VIII-B (8B), was situated on the same route we took to the museum. We drove back out the way we came, and on the left side of the road, we noticed a large yellow billboard displaying the words *Lamsdorf-Stalag VIII-B*. I swerved into the dirt path under the sign and parked the car. Walking over to the billboard, we studied the detailed map highlighting all the structures that were in the POW camp. There were no actual structures from this vantage point, but a narrow cobblestone path bordered with trees on each side reached far into the woods. We could not view what lay at the end of the trail, but it seemed to be beckoning us forward. We decided to head out on foot, nervous about driving the rental car down the path, not knowing what lay ahead.

As we walked down the path into the woods, a car slowly drove up beside us. The driver, a young male, rolled down his window and, in broken English, asked us if we needed help. I peered inside the car and saw a young woman seated beside him and two young blond-haired children quietly sitting in the back of the car strapped into their car seats. The entire family had red-stained hands as if they were just on an outing picking berries.

We informed him that we were looking for a POW camp, and did he know what was up ahead? The young man told us that acres spread out in all directions once housed POWs. He went on to say that sprinkled throughout the land were remnants of old structures and buildings, but nothing remained in its entirety. He also let us know that, currently, the Polish Army has its headquarters on this land. That made us nervous, thinking we were not on a guided tour of any sort and may have been trespassing into areas that could be dangerous.

We decided we did not have permission to explore independently, especially in a deserted place with no souls around. We thanked the young family for their knowledge and decided to head back toward the museum and follow the cobblestone road in the opposite direction.

This new road led us to the Polish POW cemetery. It was a beautiful, secluded, stunning area that, at first sight, took our breath away. The graveyard was isolated, with no visitors except my sister and me. There were deep green freshly mowed lawns, and on the far backside of the cemetery was a semicircle of massive, manicured fir trees. The actual cemetery was surrounded by a low wrought-iron fence, allowing the gravesites, marked by enormous rocks, to be easily viewed. Engraved plaques on the ground outside the fence were also present, but the stones inside the fence were spellbinding, and each caught our attention.

It was a peaceful but sad place, and I imagined all the suffering that must have taken place at this site so many years ago. Something about those large jagged stones haphazardly placed over graves was both haunting and beautiful. The Polish prisoners would be remembered, even if it was only with a rock. It was the first memorial to POWs that we had witnessed on our trip, and it would be a place I would never forget.

We did not want to leave; there was so much we did not get to explore, but it was now almost dusk, and we needed to get back to the Polish castle where we were staying overnight, a few hours away. I was not looking forward to driving on the Autobahn in the dark. As we left, I had a premonition or was it a deep yearning that I may be returning one day. If that were to happen, I would certainly allow more time to take this all in leisurely. There was so much to see and learn in this historical, beautiful area in western Poland.

The next day, we made the five-hour drive to Nuremberg. Our hotel was in the town center where no cars were allowed. We were able to drive up to the entrance, drop off our luggage, and return the rental car. I was now ready to relax and enjoy this picturesque city in southern Bavaria, complete with its hilltop castle, especially after driving five hours on the crazy Autobahn. An outdoor restaurant was located next to our hotel with umbrellas and blue-checkered tablecloths, with the waitresses wearing typical Bavarian dirndls and white peasant blouses.

My sister immediately decided to explore the Old Town on foot. However, I was happy to plop myself down at a table and order a large beer and grilled Nuremberg sausages complete with sauerkraut, mustard, and horseradish. It was heaven—people-watching and relaxing after the long drive and emotional visits to the POW camps. The next day we planned to visit the museum on the Nazi Party Rally Grounds and the area where the Nuremberg-Langwasser POW camp existed, but right now, I was perfectly content and wanted this moment never to end.

— 7 —

Nuremberg, Amsterdam, and Back to Base

The story is not about heroes and villains, but about
ordinary people who, in a time of scarcity and oppression,
were faced with dilemmas and had to make choices.

—Verzets
(Dutch) Resistance Museum

After a delicious Bavarian breakfast, we took the trolley bus to the Documentation Center—the museum built on the Nazi Party Rally Grounds. The current exhibition was titled Fascination and Terror and provided a comprehensive view of Nuremberg's role as one of the Nazi Party headquarters.

In 1934, Albert Speer, Hitler's favorite architect, was commissioned to design these grounds on approximately 2,700 acres in the southeast part of Nuremberg. Between 1933 through 1938, up to one million people came each year to Nuremberg in the late summer for the Nazi Party rallies. The buildings were constructed around two lakes and included a stadium, Congress Hall (unfinished), large fields to host sporting events and parades, and a Great Street.

The Great Street was 200 feet wide and one-half mile long and was the central marching avenue for Hitler and the Nazi soldiers. At the south of the grounds were the training barracks used to house SS soldiers and the Hitler Youth during their special events. With the start of World War II in 1939, all construction came to a halt, and they turned the barracks into POW camps. The district was called Nuremberg-Langwasser, and this was the name listed on my father's POW file.

When we arrived at the Documentation Center, we immediately went to the information area and asked for a map of the grounds. After glancing at the map, we asked the young woman at the desk to point out the POW camp because we could not identify its location. She pointed to a large area on the map labeled Langwasser situated in the southernmost section of the Nazi Party Rally Grounds. However, she informed us there were no remnants left of the POW camp; it was now an extensive housing development.

Despite this disappointing news, I remained determined to tour the area. I was also hopeful that I would finally find evidence of old structures or memorials commemorating the POWs detained on these sites during World War II.

We gathered our maps and rented a headset and tape recorder and proceeded to tour the museum, which took about two hours. The exhibit provided a powerful and comprehensive history of the rise and fall of the Nazi regime and was accurately named; it was fascinating and terrifying and left us spellbound.

When you first entered the museum, there was a natural light-filled, modern theater where you could sit or stand and watch a short ten-minute film. The documentary alternated between current times and the days of Nazi rule. In the film, two teenagers, a young boy and a young girl, arrive at the Documentation Center on skateboards. They got off their boards and entered the doors to the museum. On the other side of the doors, the teenagers were transported back in time, where thousands of frenzied Nazi soldiers in the stadium were shouting and saluting Hitler. After watching this short film, we felt transported back to that brutal era. The deafening cries of "Heil Hitler" resonated from the sound speakers and followed us into the main exhibit hall, creating a frightening effect.

After two hours, we were emotionally exhausted. We located the museum café and bought a warm pretzel with mustard. The pretzel would be our lunch, along with fruit and cookies left over from breakfast. We planned to picnic in the Langwasser area, where the POW camps once stood. I hoped to sit quietly and capture my father's spirit and times past, regardless of whether we discovered evidence of World War II structures or memorials. So far, as I could comprehend, the focus at the Documentation Center Museum had been on the rise and fall of Nazi Germany and not so much on the POW camps. We would have to discover that information on our own.

It took us about forty-five minutes on foot to reach the area where the POW camps once stood, now the Langwasser housing development. To get there, we walked along the Great Street, which stretched from the north around the unfinished Congress Hall to the south, along a large lake called Dutzendteich Lake. During our visit, the area was quiet, with only a few people walking and enjoying the beautiful weather. The lake setting was tranquil, with flocks of birds and ducks on the water and others flying in the skies above the lake's thick woods. The Eurasian aspen leaves were beginning to turn their golden hues, and now and then, a gentle breeze would catch them, causing them to shimmer and flutter in the warm afternoon sun.

While I was walking, I imagined the thousands of SS troopers and Nazi soldiers marching in goose-step fashion with the throngs of German citizens loudly cheering them on during their large parades and Nazi Party rallies. Countless human beings paid with their lives, I thought, for me to enjoy this lovely, leisurely walk down Great Street.

When we arrived at the Langwasser area, we realized it was much larger than expected. There was a south, mid, and north section. We arrived in the north section. There were bus and train routes through the development, and we proceeded to walk toward the midsection in the direction of the train station. The Langwasser area was wooded, peaceful, and beautifully designed. The development consisted of small homes, townhouses, and condominiums, surrounded by lawns and forested areas. Numerous paved and dirt paths to walk on or ride bikes were scattered throughout, making it possible to hike for miles and not see cars or hear traffic.

We eventually found a park-like area with a bench and settled down to have our picnic. At this point, I did not have a clue where the POW camps and barracks once stood. They could have been miles further north, south, east, or west, or we could have been sitting smack dab on the site.

Absent was any information or memorials indicating that Langwasser could be anything more than what it was now—a suburban housing development filled with young people, families with children, and senior citizens going about their daily lives in a suburb in southern Nuremberg.

We sat on the park bench, quiet with our thoughts. I breathed in the air, closed my eyes, and tried to connect with my father's spirit and a tumultuous period of years past. Something was unsettling about not knowing precisely where the camp stood or if he was at this camp—despite Nuremberg-Langwasser listed on his POW papers. Regardless, this site had significance. After more time with my thoughts, I realized what I felt was emptiness and frustration. Zero traces were left behind to indicate the human tragedy that transpired on these grounds before becoming what it was now—a peaceful suburban development. What was missing were the reminders—the memorials. Just one would have made me feel at peace.

The next day, we took the train from Nuremberg to Amsterdam. I was not eager to leave Germany. There was so much I hadn't discovered related to my father's time here between September 1943 and May 1945. It was disturbing that we had come all this way only to leave empty-handed—knowing less now than when we started. I felt I was leaving my father behind as we boarded the train to Amsterdam. Despite all the horrors of the Nazi regime, I loved being in this country and experiencing all it had to offer, even though the focus of my visit was to relive World War II history and retrace my father's footsteps.

We arrived in Amsterdam early evening and settled into our hotel room. This visit was my first time in Amsterdam. I had heard so many wonderful, exciting stories about this city, which was why we made it our final stop before heading home. We have close friends who, whenever they travel to Europe, make a point to stop there. Sometimes you either like places or do not like places, depending on where they land on your itinerary. That is how it is for me. Amsterdam was at the end of what proved to be an emotionally exhausting trip. No offense to Amsterdam, but I was not as excited to be there as anticipated.

On the following morning, we went for a canal tour, which was lovely. While on the boat, the guide pointed out the neighborhood where the Dutch Resistance Museum was located. I was not aware there was a

Dutch Resistance Museum in Amsterdam. The guide also pointed out the house where Anne Frank and her family hid from the Germans. We had plans to visit the Van Gogh Museum and Rijksmuseum that afternoon, but I vowed to see the Dutch Resistance Museum the following day. Suddenly, I was extremely interested in Amsterdam.

The Dutch Resistance Museum was fascinating, mainly because it was a completely different angle for me to absorb. The entire exhibit was framed from the perspective of situational ethics. What would you do if you were in the same situation? How would you react? For example, if your country was occupied by the Nazis (or any other terrorist regime), would you (1) collaborate, (2) do nothing, or (3) resist the occupation? Resisting the occupation could take many forms, from helping others who were being persecuted, aiding Allied evaders, or being an active participant in the organized Resistance.

No matter one's role in resisting the occupation—a courier or someone offering a safe house—the consequences were harsh, including torture, forced labor camps, or execution for yourself and possibly your entire family. The Dutch Resistance Museum housed a powerful exhibit that portrayed life under Nazi occupation and the choices the Dutch people had to make every day. There were tales of utmost bravery and extreme hardships, and accounts of cowardice.

Some of the most compelling stories were about the thousands of Dutchmen between the ages of eighteen and forty-five who were forced to leave their families and work in German factories. Those who refused to go were forced into hiding, and many of those who returned suffered permanent physical and psychological disabilities. Based on Red Cross estimates, of the over 500,000 Dutch citizens transported to Germany in the labor deployment programs during World War II, 30,000 perished.

Other tragic stories were the Jewish citizens' narratives of how they were forced to register as Jews, and how they were eventually rounded up and transported to the concentration camps. Of the 140,000 Jews living in the Netherlands in 1941, only 38,000 survived the war. Roughly, 75 percent of Dutch Jews perished under the Nazi regime.

One section of the museum effectively highlighted the Jewish and Dutch people's plight through an exhibit with a bright red front door with various doorbells on the left side of the entry. Each doorbell had a sign above it, posting a different language. When you pressed the door-bell in your language, you could hear a Jewish family knocking on the door, pleading with the family inside to give them refuge. The responses varied from "Go away; we can't help you" to "We would like to help, but my wife is scared, and we have our children to worry about" to saying nothing and closing the door.

This interactive display was one of many exhibits in the museum that portrayed the choices people had to make at that time in history. So many tragic scenarios played out in the exhibition, and I thought that no one knows how they would react to these extreme situations until they happened to them. Honestly, I am not sure if I would have been brave enough to hide a family, but I don't know. I could almost say with certainty that I would not collaborate, but I don't know, especially if it came down to my family's lives being at stake. What these people in the occupied countries had to experience—the unimaginable heartbreak and suffering they witnessed—is almost inconceivable.

We ended our trip and headed home. It was a life-changing expe-rience. I learned so much, but most of all, I realized how much I didn't know. I looked forward to devoting time to researching my father's war history and educating myself about the war in general. I anticipated receiving his complete set of service records with details of his mili-tary history. I expected to speak with World War II veterans' families, including friends of my father's, especially the family of his bunkmate in the POW camp. After reviewing my father's records, I hoped to reconnect with the people in Germany and Poland, specifically at the Documentation Center in Nuremberg and the Stalag Luft III Museum in Poland.

I know I'm not the only one trying to piece together my veteran's war history. I am also painfully aware that time is of the essence, as the Greatest Generation is passing away, and their children are not far behind them. It would have been so much easier to gather this information when my father was alive. But truthfully, I didn't know what to ask, and I wasn't present when he wanted to have a conversation. Now I long to talk, but he's not here to answer my questions. If I don't uncover his story soon, it will most likely quietly disappear. For someone like me, a baby boomer, there's no time to lose.

— 8 —

My Generation

I didn't get old on purpose, it just happened. If
you're lucky, it could happen to you.

—ANDY ROONEY,
American Journalist and Broadcaster, World
War II News Correspondent

A baby boomer is a name that identifies a generation of children—now older adults—born in the United States between 1946 and 1964. This booming explosion in the US birth rate happened when millions of young men who served in the Armed Forces during World War II returned home *en masse*, got married, and started families. Their children became known as baby boomers. I'm proud to report that I'm a baby boomer, born just six years after the war ended.

Most baby boomers' parents lived through the Great Depression and suffered severe hardships due to a lack of jobs and extreme poverty. People were hungry and destitute. Families were large, life was tough, and it wasn't easy to make ends meet. Then World War II happened, and after years of isolationist policies, the parents of baby boomers—mostly the fathers—were unexpectedly called to fight overseas in what was known as the greatest war of modern history.

When they returned home from the war, they became eligible for veterans' benefits—thanks to a Congress that worked together to pass the GI Bill of Rights in June 1944. Veterans could now apply for loans that helped them purchase homes and farms at low-interest rates. Veterans were also offered the chance to pursue higher education. My father took advantage of both of these opportunities, first graduating from college on the GI Bill and later buying his first house with the help of a VA loan. He, and others like him, began living the American Dream regarding financial stability. Jobs were plentiful, and life was relatively cheap and straightforward. Americans generally enjoyed a brief period of postwar peace and Norman Rockwell–type innocence a few years after the Korean War and before the Vietnam War.

Compared to World War II's more recent hardships and atrocities, these were relatively carefree years—the mid-1950s and early 1960s. Baby boomers learned to walk, talk, ride bikes, play baseball, swim and have picnics, take Sunday drives, and engage in other baby boomer–type activities during their early childhoods. They watched TV shows like *Lassie, Leave It to Beaver, My Three Sons*, and *Father Knows Best*. Some mothers worked, but most stayed at home in those early years, raising their families and preparing home-cooked meals. Our mother was one of the exceptions. She worked full-time as a registered nurse and was not fond of cooking.

In our house, our father did all the cooking. I still remember him peeling potatoes for dinner almost every evening, just like in the Army when he was on KP duty. Our father may have been the only young man in the Army Air Corps who enjoyed military rations, including the food in his Red Cross parcels. His simple taste was evidenced by the fact that he continued to cook up plain, boiled potatoes and fried SPAM® for us kids, just like he ate in the Armed Forces, until the day he died.

Eating was an adventure in our house, and not because of the gourmet cuisine. Our father habitually shared many POW anecdotes at the dinner table. Our parents did not require us to stay at the table as a family until we ate all our peas. Whatever food item we did not finish, our father used to say, "Great! More for me!" He would go on to share that was how it was in the POW camp—you ate what was put in front of you, or you starved.

One of his favorite stories was about a fellow prisoner who could not eat anything if there was a hair in it. All his buddies would point at this prisoner's food portion and say they saw a hair floating around in the soup. The guy would get nauseous, refuse to eat anything further, and then the meager meal was theirs to engulf. I had visions of this poor prison mate being extremely hungry and the skinniest of them all.

Another story was about worm soup. He explained that the soup was supposed to be broth with potatoes, but worms were in all the potatoes. Again, you ate what was in front of you or starved. He would end his POW stories with a big laugh, and we never quite knew how true they were or if they were tall tales embellished with fragments of truth.

Those early halcyon baby boomer days during the innocent '50s soon turned into the turbulent '60s. Baby boomers experienced war protests and civil rights marches, witnessed the Kennedy and MLK assassinations, and watched an astronaut's first steps on the moon. We were finishing our grammar school years, beginning to graduate from high school, and many of us were heading off to college. Others were dropping out of college or starting their first career jobs. And still others were being drafted and heading off to Vietnam. For some of us, this was also when we began experimenting with "sex, drugs, and rock and roll."

In my life, it was a time when I began to experience what was known as the generation gap. Unlike our parents, we questioned our involvement in wars, religion, consensual relationships outside marriage, birth control, civil rights, women's rights, and other hot topics. Our music, clothes, hair, and values seemed miles apart from the Greatest Generation's values.

While living at home, I limited most of my conversations to pleasantries in those teenage years, and when I moved away, I would go days and weeks, even months, without picking up the phone to say, "Hi, just checking in." Not like today, when I witness family and friends, including myself, texting or emailing or calling our kids, and vice versa, at least once a day. If a few days go by and there is no text from the kids, I think something is wrong, and I rush to my iPhone to fill in the gap. We are deep in our kids' business, unlike our parents, who gave us space, maybe because we rebelliously demanded that space.

I did not spend much time in deep conversations with my parents and did not seriously take the time to listen to their stories. I half-heard their words and did not ask all the questions I now desperately want to know, especially about my father's war stories. I was busy growing up and was self-centered, focusing on my issues, like so many children naturally do. We were in school, going away to school, meeting friends and future partners, getting married, and raising children of our own. Only now do I finally have the time and awareness to ask my parents those crucial questions I never asked before. But now, the truth is elusive as there is no one around to give me answers. It is heartbreaking knowing that something so close and available has slipped away forever.

We baby boomers are aging, just like our parents before us, and all too soon, we will slip away. With our passing, the veterans' stories we know will disappear if they are not written down or told to others. For those who are inspired, I believe now is the time to uncover those stories and share them with our families by retelling them or writing them down so they can be passed on to future generations. And for baby boomers whose parents served during World War II, all had important stories that deserve to be remembered and passed on to their children and children's children. Each bit of knowledge, each tale told at the dinner table, contributes to World War II's overall body of knowledge.

Time is running out for me and others like me to uncover my veteran's story and pass it along either verbally or in writing, so others can learn about the Greatest Generation and their unselfish contributions to halting a world gone mad. I long for my family to know that my father served in World War II because our country called upon him to do so, and I want them all to know what part he played in that war. I ache for my children and grandchildren to know the valuable lessons we learned from that war and never forget that they have a true veteran's blood running through their veins.

I am determined to uncover my father's narrative and solve all the puzzle pieces. I'm afraid his story will not be passed on correctly or, worse, not passed on at all. When I returned from my first trip to Amsterdam, I was driving in the car with a group of old-time, close friends. I passionately related the story about the Dutch Resistance Museum I had just visited a week before. It was fresh in my mind, and I had tears in my eyes as I shared some of the poignant and horrific stories of ordinary people making extraordinary sacrifices.

As we were driving, one of the friends in the car said, "Excuse me, not to interrupt, but what is our next exit? Are we going the right way?"

After a brief discussion among the passengers about our correct whereabouts, I waited for the person who interrupted me, or any person in the car for that matter, to say, "Go on, continue with your story," but no one did. They started a conversation about an entirely different subject as if what I was saying had never happened. I was quietly saddened.

At that moment, I thought, something like this needs to be heard, and maybe I need to write these stories down. At least seeing the words in print would assure me that the story is real, not just words falling on distracted ears. Sometimes people are better readers than they are listeners.

Maybe this is how all our fathers felt. A story so worthy needed our full attention; otherwise, it would not be worth wasting the strength to tell it. How often has it been said repeatedly, "My father was in World War II, but he never wanted to talk about it?" How could so many fathers not want to talk about it? At first, it seemed reasonable to conclude they just wanted to get on with life and forget all the unspeakable atrocities they had witnessed and the pain and suffering they had endured. But now I am not so sure.

Did fathers not talk about the war because they wanted to move on and spare their children these negative experiences, or did they just not have receptive audiences? Perhaps a combination of both? And maybe the children did not listen as attentively as their fathers needed them to because they were young and preoccupied with just being children— incapable of fully understanding something so incomprehensible and removed from their current reality. When a human has such a compelling story, they can feel sad and vulnerable when the person on the other end cannot provide the level of attention their words deserve. It can be emotionally draining. Is a heartfelt and powerful story worth sharing with someone who can only give it half an ear?

I have heard accounts of World War II veterans joining groups, such as the American Ex-Prisoners of War Organization, Bomb Group Memorial Associations, and Veterans Service Organizations. Here they were together with their military buddies with similar backgrounds. It was in these settings that the floodgates often opened. In their comfort zone, surrounded by other veterans, they shared their experiences and listened to each other's stories. Usually, this happened many years after the war was over.

Currently, baby boomers, we young children who were not entirely capable of listening and understanding these powerful events, seemingly having all the time in the world, are retired, and more often than not, many of us have plenty of leisure time, including the liberty to reflect. Like me, some realize that if they do not pass on their fathers' stories, then who will? If our veterans were still alive, it would be easy to ask them our burning questions about their service. But now we need to do the rigorous work to unravel their pasts, and in many instances, it is not that straightforward.

Nonetheless, discovering their unique histories is comforting and well worth the effort. I believe my father would be honored that I took the time to learn about his role in World War II, passing this on to his future generations. He would be proud that I now fully understand the high price he paid for freedom in his youthful years. It was not all for naught. He knew that. And now I will too. Forever.

PART THREE

UNRAVELING THE TRUTH

— 9 —

Starting from Scratch

*The first and absolute requirement of strategic air power
in this war was control of the air in order to carry out
sustained operations without prohibitive losses.*

—CARL A. SPAATZ,
Commanding General, US Strategic Air
Forces in Europe, 1944–1945

Back in the US, I patiently waited for the arrival of my father's military file back from the National Personnel Records Center (NPRC) in St.Louis. I anticipated these files would hold comprehensive information regarding his World War II history, primarily the POW camp where he was for almost two years. In the meantime, eager to start my research, I visited the National Archives website on my own, hoping to find facts that would help unravel my father's story.

I was shocked to uncover that on July 12, 1973, there was a disastrous fire at the NPRC in St. Louis, the repository for all US personnel military records. Firefighters arrived on the scene only four minutes after the first alarm sounded, but the fire was so intense that they had difficulty containing the flames. The fire crews poured millions of gallons of water on the building, but the blaze continued to actively burn for another twenty-two hours. After almost five days, they completely extinguished the fire. Due to the extensive damage, investigators never figured out the primary cause.

When all was said and done, the blaze destroyed 16 to 18 million

Official Military Personnel Files. The estimated loss of Army files was 80 percent. The Air Force files' estimated loss was 75 percent, specifically for files listed alphabetically after Hubbard, James E. According to information on the National Archives site, the government agency did not maintain duplicate records.

After firefighters completely contained the fire, there were immediate efforts to recover the millions of burned and water-damaged records. Also, there were efforts to reconstruct partially damaged or destroyed files by obtaining information from alternate sources outside of the NPRC. That process is still going on to this day. A quote from the National Archives website summed up the impact the damage had on our country: "In terms of loss to the cultural heritage of our nation, the 1973 NPRC Fire was an unparalleled disaster."

As I finished reading all this information, my initial thought was how could something like this have happened? How flabbergasted (a baby boomer expression that goes back to Old English and before) and embarrassing was it that I was only finding out about this significant national catastrophe now? But more importantly, it was heartbreaking to think about the devastation it caused all the veterans and their families to have their histories erased. My second, somewhat selfish thought was that my father's records, listed as Hayes, Donald L., preceded Hubbard, James E.; his records may still be intact, I hoped.

A month after we returned from Europe, we finally received an envelope in the mail from the NPRC. Before I tore it open, my first impression was that the package was relatively thin. I realized my worst expectations. A letter from the NPRC in St. Louis informed us, "The complete Official Military Personnel File for the veteran requested is not in our files. If the record was here on July 12, 1973, it would have been in the area that suffered the most damage in the fire on that date and may have been destroyed. Fortunately, there were alternate records sources that contained information that was used to reconstruct some service record data lost in the fire. However, complete records could not be reconstructed." End of story.

So it appeared we received a partially reconstructed file. I looked through the enclosed paperwork and discovered no new information. The file consisted of my father's World War II Prisoner of War Data File, which we already had accessed online before leaving for Germany. (This file gave us misleading information by listing his POW camps as Stalag Luft III and Nuremberg/Langwasser.)

The only additional information in the file was my father's last paycheck upon separation from the Army in September of 1945—a total sum of $10,708.82. I surmised that being a POW for twenty-two months was like having a savings account with regular deposits that he could not touch. And while this seemed like a large sum of money for the time, I wondered what went through my father's mind when he received this lump check and if he thought the military paid him handsomely enough for all he had endured.

I now started my exploration with increased earnestness, trying to locate other sources of official government records documenting my father's World War II history, specifically his POW camp. As it stood now, I had four documents in my possession to initiate my research: the NARA POW War File, the Honorable Discharge Record, my father's notes of flight missions from England to Nazi Germany, and a copy of his Personal Military File from the NPRC, which was limited to his last paycheck information.

Of all these documents, his Discharge Record provided the most valuable data, especially regarding dates of service, dates of entry in and out of the US, and names of US cities and countries he was stationed in during his military service. I was grateful that my father kept the original copy of his Discharge Record his entire life, as it was absent in the St. Louis file.

Knowing what was available and missing, I was ready to examine everything related to World War II. I became fixated. Looking at one detail of an event brought me to others, and before I knew it, I was spiraling out of control in disparate directions. For example, one could read forever how the young men parachuted out of their planes and the myriad obstacles they encountered, from jumping out of the aircraft to landing on the ground and then trying to stay alive.

Sometimes, the airmen were fortunate enough to be greeted by friendly French, Dutch, or Belgian farmers (depending on their navigation routes) and, eventually, the Resistance, who helped them evade capture. Other times, German soldiers captured them, or German civilians assailed them if they were unlucky enough to land in Germany.

Frequently, the American soldiers experienced more deadly threats from angry German citizens than the German soldiers. Sometimes, the German civilians killed the young airmen before they had the chance to be captured and imprisoned.

I read one remarkable story of how a young American soldier parachuted safely to the ground only to be greeted by an even younger sixteen-year-old German boy with a gun. The young boy took the American to his farmhouse where he introduced him to his entire family. After feeding and sheltering him, the family later handed him over to the authorities, as failure could result in the whole family's execution. Many years later, when the American soldier returned to Germany to retrace his steps, he found the family and learned that three of the boy's sisters had used the silk from his parachute to sew their wedding dresses.

Incredible stories like this are numerous, and it was challenging to stay on track researching my father's history alone. I slowly realized it would take me much longer than I thought to unravel the truth, but it was proving well worth the time and effort.

What I Heard

Loose Lips Sink Ships

—WORLD WAR II PROPAGANDA POSTER

My father's stories were a jumble to me at this stage. As I began my research, I tried to sort out what I heard from him while he was still alive. In summary, I heard stories of his training in Panama before the war and how he wanted to be a pilot. While in Panama diving in a river with his buddies, he said he scooped up a handful of muddy dirt from the river's bottom, some of which got into his ear, which resulted in a severe ear infection and a significant loss of hearing in that ear. I heard him say that this incident ended his dream of being a pilot.

He completed training as a tail gunner and flew eleven missions from England to Nazi-occupied Europe and Germany. He said he parachuted out of an airplane twice. After his first parachute jump, he said, "They sent me right back."

He continued to fly missions until enemy fighters shot down his plane, and he parachuted out a second time. I distinctly remember him saying a group of young German soldiers surrounded him as soon as he hit the ground, all pointing their rifles at him. Later, I discovered he had landed on a German fighter base in Reims, France. The date was September 6, 1943. He remained a prisoner of war until the war ended in May 1945.

I heard his story about being marched to another German prison camp, but I was unsure of the exact timing. Was it after the Germans first captured him? Or was he marched to another POW camp during the war? Or was the march later at the end of the war?

During this march, I remember he told me that another American POW in front of him turned around and said, "I'm rolling down this hill. Do you wanna join me?" The two rolled down a hill to escape into what my father thought was the Black Forest. He said they met up with Russians who shared their food with them for two weeks. He repeatedly said he loved the Russian people, most likely because this group of men safeguarded him and his buddy from harm and from dying of starvation.

Initially, I was not sure at what point in the war my father rolled down that hill and met the group of friendly Russians. Nor was I clear if these Russians were POWs like himself or escaped forced laborers or soldiers. At first, I thought he met the Russians after he parachuted out of his plane, was captured, and then transported to his designated POW camp. Maybe he escaped on the way to the first POW camp. Later, I concluded that his escape had to be when the Germans forced the POWs to evacuate their camps and begin their long marches toward the end of the war—as the Russian Red Army advanced into Germany and Nazi-occupied Europe from the east.

Most memorable was hearing my father tell stories about his bunk-mate in the POW camp. His name was Toby. When I listened to my father talking about Toby, I remember thinking how comforting it was to have a best friend at camp. It seemed they helped each other combat loneliness through their friendship, surviving the tough times they faced daily for almost two years as prisoners of war.

Ultimately, I heard my father talk about being transported back to the States on a ship. Once back in the US, he had to spend three months in a hospital where the medical staff slowly reintroduced him to food. Working with these bits and pieces of his story, I was ready to discover the proper sequence of these events, endeavor to fill in most of the blanks, and eventually unravel the truth about his service during World War II.

— 11 —

Where to Start?

The hate of men will pass, and dictators die, and the power
they took from the people will return to the people.

—CHARLIE CHAPLIN,
Actor and Director, *The Great Dictator*

Where does one begin to find the absolute truth behind all the war stories? As I painstakingly familiarized myself with information on the internet, I discovered a bounty of resources readily available in specific locations. Some materials were on government sites, and some were on private websites organized by family members and World War II–related historical groups. Locating and becoming familiar with these online sources, including the abundance of published literature about World War II, became an ongoing enterprise.

During this process, I also discovered several excellent museums devoted to preserving World War II history—notably the National WWII Museum in New Orleans and the American Air Museum in Britain. The information on these sites was phenomenal. Still, considerable gaps existed in what was available from the government, private sources, museum sites, and published literature related to my father's personal story. I gradually realized these gaps would only be filled by interviewing relatives, other veterans, and their families or locating personal family letters and documents.

And I was coming to a painful awareness that I would never discover the entire truth. That was the most disturbing part—knowing I would never know. At one time, it could have been just a simple question to my father and an eager answer back.

— 12 —

What Camp?

*Only when sharing your experiences with another
former POW can you be sure that he knows what
you are feeling. You can see it in his eyes.*

—John Nichol and Tony Rennell,
Authors, *The Last Escape*

Before deciphering my father's discharge papers and additional documents in my possession, I needed to learn more about German POW camps. It was challenging to focus on other segments of his World War II history until I discovered where the Nazis detained him. I became obsessed with that detail of his story.

After all my father's conversations about his life as a POW, it was disheartening that our family could not remember the name of his camp. There were hazy memories of him mentioning 8B, Stalag 13, and Stalag 17. There were also vague recollections about *The Great Escape* film and the *Hogan's Heroes* TV series. I remember him saying that the TV tales were entertaining but did not accurately portray life in the POW camps. Ultimately, when I compared narratives with my other siblings, none of us could collectively shed additional light on our father's POW whereabouts.

As I searched for information about Nazi POW camps, I found out the Germans established over 1,000 POW camps in Nazi Germany and Nazi-occupied countries. About 100 centers held American POWs, with populations that rose to over 100,000 by the war's end. The German word for POW was *Kriegsgefangener*, shortened to *Kriegie*, as the POWs came to call themselves. When we visited one of the prison camps in Poland, the museum director mistakenly called me a Kriegie. I corrected him and said I was the daughter of a Kriegie. He smiled, and to this day, I am not sure what that exchange entailed.

The number of POW camps for captured soldiers was not to be confused with the thousands of concentration and extermination camps in Nazi Germany and Nazi-occupied Europe to detain Jews, forced laborers, and other perceived enemies of the state. On the United States Holocaust Memorial Museum website, a reference states the following: "Between 1933 and 1945, Nazi Germany and its allies established more than 42,000 camps and other incarceration sites (including ghettos). The perpetrators used these sites for a range of purposes, including forced labor, detention of people thought to be enemies of the state, and mass murder."

I read that number a few times and checked different literature sources because it seemed incredible. The estimate was based on continuing research of German war records, and still today, it has been challenging to pinpoint how many of these concentration camps existed. I am now aware it is more than I ever imagined or had initially been reported. The number is staggering.

As I tried to recapture all my father's stories, I recalled him repeatedly saying that while he and fellow POWs lived in deplorable conditions and suffered starvation, their plights could not compare to the suffering of the Jewish prisoners. I remembered the tone of his voice and how sad he was when he said these words. He described accounts of Jewish people who looked like walking skeletons at the end of the war. They wandered the countryside, slaughtering cows and then trying to eat them only to throw up because their stomachs could not handle the richness of any foods, especially freshly killed livestock.

After the war ended, my father told us he was admitted to a hospital in the States for three months to be slowly introduced to food. These reintroduction diets started with bland mashed potatoes, maybe some rice, and a banana if you were lucky. Juicy hamburgers with onions and pickles (probably something he dreamed about while in the POW camp) would have to wait. At this point, out of curiosity, I researched "Reintroducing Food after Starvation." I came up with articles on

"Refeeding Syndrome," which confirmed my father's narrative that food needed to be slowly introduced if you suffered from starvation and were severely malnourished.

I now made a determined effort to get back on track and focus specifically on POW camps and not on all the other horrors of concentration and extermination camps, although POW camps were horrific enough. There were essentially four types of Allied POW camps created by the Nazis in World War II: Stalags, Oflags, Stalag Lufts, and Dulags. Stalags, short for *Stammlager*, were camps for drafted and enlisted Army personnel, and Oflags were POW camps for Army officers. The German Army, known as the Wehrmacht, administered these camps. A Stalag Luft was for Allied Air Force crew, including officers, and the Luftwaffe, the German Air Force, had jurisdiction over those camps. Dulags, short for *Durchgangslager*, were transit camps.

After learning the definitions of these four types of camps, I concluded that my father would have been a prisoner at a Stalag Luft POW camp because he was in the US Army Air Force. Camps for Allied airmen run by the Luftwaffe were separate from POW camps run by the Wehrmacht. Under the Luftwaffe administration, there were ten primary camps, including Dulag Luft, the interrogation and transit camp for aircrew members. The following are the names of the ten primary Luftwaffe-run POW camps: 1) Stalag Luft I in Barth, Germany; 2) Stalag Luft II in Litzmannstadt, Poland; 3) Stalag Luft III in Sagan, Germany; 4) Stalag Luft IV in Gross Tychow, Poland; 5) Stalag Luft V in Halle, Germany; 6) Stalag Luft VI in Heydekrug, Lithuania; 7) Stalag Luft VII in Bankau, Poland; 8) Stalag Luft VIII-B in Lamsdorf, Poland; 9) Stalag Luft XI-B in Fallingbostel, Germany; and 10) Dulag Luft in Oberursel-Frankfurt, Germany.

Dulag Luft's primary purpose was to act as a collection and interrogation center for newly captured aircrew before they were transferred in groups to their permanent camps. When Allied Air Force men parachuted out of their planes and were captured, the protocol was that the Germans would transport them to Dulag Luft. It is highly likely that my father, after his capture, was sent to Dulag Luft, where he was first interrogated and then, in time, transported to his designated POW camp.

Next, I systematically reviewed all the Luftwaffe-run camps to determine the probability that my father was at one of them. I started with Stalag Luft I in Barth, Germany, near the Baltic Sea. After opening in 1940 to hold captured British officers, it closed in April 1942 after the Germans moved all the British officers at this camp to other POW camps. The camp reopened in October 1942 when the Germans moved 200 Royal Air Force (RAF) noncommissioned officers (NCOs) back to this site from Stalag Luft III due to overcrowding.

In 1943, American POWs were transferred here, and by the end of the war, it held approximately 7,700 American and 1,400 British POWs. As indicated in this description of Stalag Luft I, a complicating and frustrating factor about tracking POW camps was that camps were continually changing. These changes related to the types of prisoners they held, their naming conventions, and population numbers—with more prisoners added as the war progressed.

In my search, I found an excellent website dedicated to Stalag Luft I. A World War II veteran's family organized this site in honor of their father who flew in the Eighth Air Force. He was shot down over Nazi Germany, captured, and then spent the rest of the war in Stalag Luft I. Like my father's story as with many other veterans' families, their father did not talk much about the war. He died suddenly, taking all his memories with him. Years later, his family began researching their father's war history and completed this informative and comprehensive memorial website in dedication to his memory.

The site contained extensive materials about Stalag Luft I, including tips for anyone searching for more information about their World War II veteran. Here, I found advice that confirmed my theories about my father's camps being incorrect. Under one of the links, there was a written warning stating: "Please note this information is by no means complete or necessarily accurate—it is the best they could do from trying to reconstruct information from several sources considered official. I have found many POWs that I know were in Stalag Luft I listed in other camps. In some cases, they may have been at the camp listed for a short while and then transferred to Stalag Luft I. Many POWs were moved around a lot, especially as the war progressed and the camp they were held in was in danger of being overrun."

I wish I had discovered this warning before leaving on our trip to

Europe. I may not have been so disillusioned when the camp directors at the three camps we visited could not find our father's name in any of their directories.

The Stalag Luft I site also contained thousands of POW names when the war ended. The administrators stated they strongly relied on veterans and family members of veterans to update their records. My father's name was not in any of these documents. After reviewing this roster of POWs, I was confident my father was not at Stalag Luft I. Like Stalag Luft III, it seemed most of the Allied soldiers held captive at this camp were officers—at least in the early years of the war. My father was not an officer. He was a Technical Sergeant.

One important factor I discovered in searching for my father's camp was that sometimes it was not the government websites that contained the bulk of data about veterans, especially POW veterans. Often, the families of veterans spent years of research putting together information on a website containing the most comprehensive information. Additionally, specific bomb groups, such as the 91st Bomb Group Memorial Association, or groups such as the American Ex-Prisoners of War Organization, also are excellent resources.

Government sites such as the US Air Force website and Maxwell Air Force Base have branches dedicated to World War II historical research. And I found that museum websites, such as the National WWII Museum in New Orleans, the National Museum of the Mighty Eighth Air Force in Pooler, Georgia, the Planes of Fame Air Museum in Chino, California, and the American Air Museum in Britain, have compiled extensive amounts of World War II knowledge—lest we forget.

The second Luft camp I investigated was Stalag Luft II in Litzmannstadt, Poland. I immediately ruled this camp out as it was primarily a labor camp for Russian prisoners. The thought of a labor camp for Russian prisoners sent chills down my spine. From all I had read about the Nazis and their disregard for the Russians and Poles, they clearly subjugated them to inhumane treatment. Labor camps seemed nothing more than death camps, just a slower process. The Nazis conceived these camps to be extermination through labor, and millions died, including children—forced to work to fuel the Nazi war economy. It did not surprise me that the Germans situated this camp in Poland. The

Nazis ultimately located most of their concentration and extermination camps farther away from Germany. Out of sight, out of mind.

The third Luft camp on my checklist was Stalag Luft III in Sagan, Germany, now Zagan, Poland. I had determined that my father was not at this camp as he was not on the roster we reviewed when we visited the site. At first, I had hoped he was at Stalag Luft III, not only due to the notoriety of the famous Great Escape but because accounts confirmed the Germans treated the Allies, primarily officers, better at this camp. That was not the case for other nationalities at this site, particularly the Russians and Poles, whom the Germans starved, outright murdered, or worked to death.

Stalag Luft IV at Gross Tychow in the Reich province of Pomerania, now Poland, was the fourth camp I researched. The site opened to Americans on May 12, 1944, and over 7,000 prisoners were detained there that year with numbers swelling to nearly 10,000 by January 1945. The camp was for sergeants, and guards were especially cruel to prisoners at this site. My father was probably not there since it opened in May of 1944. Additionally, the camp roster I found on a website created by the veterans and families of Stalag Luft IV and Stalag Luft VI did not list his name.

Stalag Luft V in Halle, Germany, was a concentration camp that provided forced labor for the Siebel aircraft manufacturing factory, constructing parts for airplane wings. This camp was listed under the Luftwaffe jurisdiction because it was related to airplane construction. The POW file on the National Personnel Records Center website documented that Americans were, in fact, at this camp, but it appeared they arrived there in 1945, late in the war. It also seemed that the rules changed as the war neared an end, with who was held at individual camps as the situation became more chaotic.

I determined my father was not there, mainly because the Americans arrived later in the war. It was also a working camp, and my father never mentioned participating in forced work as an American POW, thanks to terms outlined in the Geneva Convention that prohibited this practice for staff sergeants and higher ranks. The Army Air Corps had the foresight to promote all aircrew members that were not officers to the rank of sergeant, thus circumventing the possibility of forced labor practices during their imprisonments.

I now researched Stalag Luft VI in Heydekrug, East Prussia (now Lithuania). This camp was built in 1939 and initially held Polish POWs, French and Belgians, and, later, Russians. In June 1943, Stalag Luft VI began to admit British and Canadians who were former prisoners at Stalag Luft I due to the overflowing conditions.

The first Americans arrived in February 1944. In July 1944, as the Russians advanced toward Germany, American and British POWs were transferred from Stalag Luft VI to Stalag Luft IV—from the frying pan into the fire. During this transfer from one camp to another, their treatment is one of the most horrific examples of cruelty Allied POWs received under the Germans' hands. What these prisoners experienced has been termed the "Heydekrug Run."

The Germans first packed the POWs from Stalag Luft VI into cattle cars, transporting them to the Baltic Sea. The guards next herded the POWs into the holds of old freighters in appalling conditions without fresh air, food, or bathroom facilities. After two days at sea, the POWs were loaded into boxcars and handcuffed in pairs for the remainder of the trip until they arrived at their destination the following day.

Once the prisoners were out of the boxcars, the guards forced them to run for two miles as they were hit with rifles and stabbed with bayonets. It was impossible to flee as the German guards would unleash their viciously trained dogs at any signs of escape.

Claude Watkins, an American POW who experienced this event, summed up the experience as follows: "After arrival in the village and while handcuffed in pairs, we participated in what has come to be known as the 'Heydekrug Run,' a morale-jarring incident brought about by the actions of one psychopathic German captain that resulted in bayonet stabs and dog bites to a number of helpless prisoners, and the loss of much of our already meager personal possessions."

I don't remember my father mentioning a town called Heydekrug. Americans did not show up here until 1944, and I would have recalled a story as terrifying as the Heydekrug Run. I determined my father was not at this camp—thank his lucky stars.

Near the Polish border, the next Luftwaffe camp to be checked off was Stalag Luft VII in Bankau, Germany, now Bakow, Poland. The site opened in June 1944 for RAF NCO flying crews, and by January

1945, the camp held approximately 1,500 prisoners. I determined that my father was not at this camp. It opened in 1944, and, according to the reports, it was a camp primarily for RAF prisoners with only a few Americans.

Noteworthy at this camp was the long march these British POWs had to endure at the end of the war. On January 19, 1945, with the Russian advance almost encircling the camp, the Germans urgently forced 1,500 prisoners to march out into the bitter cold (8° F), crossing the Oder River bridge before German special forces could blow it up to slow the Russian advance. The POWs commented that the air was so cold, breathing in was painful, and the pace of the march left them exhausted. At one point during the march, twenty-three men were reported missing, and no one knew if these men had escaped or simply fallen in the snow and died.

Next on the list was Stalag 8B in Lamsdorf, Poland—the camp we visited the same day after visiting Stalag Luft III. By 1943, Stalag Luft III had become so overcrowded that about 1,000, primarily noncommissioned flight personnel, were transferred to 8B in Lamsdorf. The Germans had built barbed-wire fences around a section of the existing camp to house these transferred airmen. Having heard 8B mentioned somewhere in my father's past, we thought he might have been among the group of prisoners transferred there from Stalag Luft III. The camp director had told us few American prisoners were at this camp, but I am unsure if that was actually the case or just not documented in any saved records. Nevertheless, I could not confirm he was ever at 8B.

One thing I didn't know at the time we toured 8B, set in the beautiful, tranquil Polish countryside, was the horrible conditions and treatment that the Poles and Russians suffered at the hands of the Nazis. I was ignorant of the tragic incident when hundreds of Russian POWs were machine-gunned down by German guards while trying to escape, nor did I know of the Katyn Massacre where, in this incident, the Russians were the perpetrators.

There was so much history in this Polish village, and 8B remains one of the few Nazi POW camps with a museum and dedicated grounds to preserve that history.

The last Luftwaffe-run camp to research on my list was Stalag Luft XI-B in northwestern Germany near Fallingbostel. Toward the end of

1940, 40,000 POWs were at this camp and assigned to various forced labor camps nearby, unless they were from countries protected by the Geneva Convention. By mid-1944, the prisoner numbers reached 96,000 POWs, including many American POWs captured after the Battle of the Bulge.

Conditions continued to deteriorate, and disease was prevalent as the prison camp became increasingly overcrowded. It is unlikely my father was in Stalag Luft XI-B. Even though there were many nationalities, it seemed most Americans did not arrive until early 1945, almost two years after his capture.

The town where Stalag Luft XI-B once existed is now called Bad Fallingbostel. "Bad" (pronounced *bod* in German) means bath or spa, so any city with the word *Bad* in front of it piques my interest as a place worth visiting. I paused to reflect on Germany's abundance of natural beauty, including all the spa towns and picturesque villages tucked along the beautiful rivers and rolling green countryside. All that natural beauty our fathers were not able to enjoy. Even now, for people who remember World War II, that beauty remains tainted by the past.

I recalled talking to a friend who enjoys visiting Germany but described the experience as feeling like a filmy substance descends over you when entering the country. You catch yourself continually brushing off your skin, trying to remove the film. The description was striking. It is difficult to erase a tarnished past that seems to forever settle over you like a shroud.

— 13 —

Out of Many, One

E Pluribus Unum

—LATIN FOR "OUT OF MANY, ONE"
was the motto for the new United States in 1776.
E Pluribus Unum is also the reverse inscription on the 1994
United States Prisoner of War Commemorative Silver Dollar, which
features a chained eagle breaking through a ring of barbed wire.

I researched all ten Luftwaffe (Luft) designated camps but did not find a trace of my father. However, while exploring this list of ten camps, I stumbled across a website organized by the 392nd Bomb Group Memorial Association members. Here, I found three additional camps where the Germans held airmen.

The 392nd Bomb Group flew B-24 Liberators (another heavy bomber that the Eighth Air Force flew in addition to the B-17) out of Wendling Air Force Base in Norfolk, England. Their website offered information about the airmen, the aircraft they flew, the air bases they flew out of, the POW Stalag Lufts where the men were prisoners, and the death marches they had to undergo.

I found a link on this site entitled, "World War II POW Stalag Luft Camps in Germany." It stated, "One of the internet's largest and most complete research on the German POW camps for airmen during World War II." On the site were eight POW camps. I had already researched five of these camps—Dulag Luft, Stalag Luft I, Stalag Luft 3, Stalag Luft 4, and Stalag Luft 6. Three were not on my original list—Stalag 7A, Stalag 13D, and Stalag 17B. Eureka! I just located three more Allied prisoner camps where I might get closer to finding my father.

Later, I discovered that these three camps were not on my original list because, while they were camps for Allied airmen under the Luftwaffe jurisdiction, they were inside larger prison camps under the Wehrmacht administration. Camps within camps.

I began with Stalag VII-A (Stalag 7A hereon)—not to be confused with Stalag Luft VII, where I had already determined that my father was not a prisoner. Stalag 7A was twenty-one miles northeast of Munich and less than one mile north of Moosburg. It was a camp for the US Army Air Forces NCOs until October 13, 1943, when the Germans transferred all 1,900 men at this camp to Stalag 17B.

As Germany started to collapse in the spring of 1945, the camp became the final assembly place for POWs moved from other sites closer to the advancing Russian Army. Numbers at this camp were colossal, with more than 70,000 Allied soldiers detained in the main camp and over 40,000 forced laborers *(Arbeitskommandos)* in labor sub-camps. A total of 150,000 POWs passed through Stalag 7A by the war's end.

Possibly, my father was at Stalag 7A for a few weeks and then transferred to Stalag 17B in October 1943, along with the other Air Force POWs forced to move earlier in the war. His plane was shot down on September 6, 1943, and the transfer of Air Force personnel from 7A to 17B was on October 13, 1943. If he was at this camp, it was only for a brief time. All this was speculation, but I was beginning to see glimmers of light at the end of a long tunnel.

Next on this updated list was Stalag 13D, the camp we visited in Nuremberg. It seemed most of the American POWs at this camp were there because of the forced march from Stalag Luft III at the war's end. I don't believe my father was ever at this POW camp, even though his veteran papers stated the opposite.

The last camp listed was Stalag XVII B (Stalag 17B hereon), located four miles northwest of Krems, Austria, in the small village of Gneixendorf. In October 1943, when the Germans transferred NCO Air Force officers from Stalag 7A to Stalag 17B, the camp already contained POWs from France, Italy, Russia, Yugoslavia, and the other Nazi-occupied nations. By the war's end, the American population had reached over 4,000, and the entire camp population contained over 30,000 prisoners.

Reviewing the names of POWs and men listed on the 392nd Bomb Group site under the tab titled "Airmen Roster Search," I could not locate my father's name anywhere. However, the site administrators did not claim to have complete rosters of all the POWs, and the site was genuinely dedicated to the 392nd Bomb Group airmen who flew on B-24 heavy bombers. At this point, I was not sure what bomb group my father was associated with, but I knew he was crew on a B-17 heavy bomber, not a B-24.

I performed my due diligence in reviewing the most likely camps where the Germans would have detained my father, and I still came up empty-handed. It was now time to try another tactic. My father frequently talked about his friend Toby, his bunkmate in the POW camp. I was determined to find out what camp Toby was listed in. Toby's real name was George Dillard, and I entered this name into the NARA site, specifically the World War II POW Data File. Toby's name came up as being a POW at Stalag 17B in Austria. I searched for my father under Stalag 17B, but his name did not appear. At this point, I was confident that my father was at Stalag 17B because this was the camp where Toby, his bunkmate, was listed.

Believing there must be existing directories of POWs for each camp, either on official government sites or on personal, individual sites, I explicitly searched online for POW rosters. When I entered World War II Prisoners of War Rosters in Stalag 17B, three links appeared: 1) the government NARA site categorized with a list of all POWs in Stalag 17B; 2) a PDF of a Stalag 17B roster on a site named "Valerosos"; and 3) the 392 BG website with a specific section dedicated to Stalag 17B in Krems, Austria. The latter was the site I had just reviewed, and my father's name was not there.

This time, I entered Stalag 17B in the search field at the NARA site rather than my father's name as in previous searches. I found 3,220 records for POWs listed as being in Stalag 17B. Everyone listed had the same information next to their names: "Detaining Power—Germany" and "Camp—Stalag 17B Braunau Gneixendorf Near Krems Austria 48-15." The source of this file was as follows: "File unit: World War II Prisoners of War Data File, 12/7/1941–11/19/1946 in the Series: Records of World War II Prisoners of War, created 1942–1947, documenting the period 12/7/1941–11/19/1946."

Further explanations about the source stated that the War Department Adjutant General's Office compiled the list from POW names gathered from 1941 to 1946. "Using copies of reports from the International Committee of the Red Cross, the agency produced records on US military and civilian prisoners of war and internees, as well as for some Allied internees. The agency used these records to generate monthly reports." For whatever reason, my father's information did not make it to these Red Cross–generated reports, at least not to the final report now listed on the NARA POW website.

Next, I visited the Valerosos site that promised a Stalag 17B roster in a PDF document. At first, I was unsure who Valerosos was, and, initially, I believed it to be the last name of a person. Opening up this document, it was evident that someone compiled quite an extensive list of POW names at Stalag 17B. The file had two distinct sections.

The first section was a typewritten document with a large, bold header stating: "Stalag 17B Roster American Prisoners of War." Under the heading read: "Source—National Archives & 1994 Directory of American Former Prisoners of War 1943–1945 Stalag 17B." It further stated, "The following names are missing from the Access to Archival Database (AAD) World War II Prisoners of War Data File for Stalag 17B." A grouping of nearly 1,000 names followed, including their respective bomb groups and date of capture information.

The second section of this PDF document included scanned pages that held additional names of POWs detained at Stalag 17B. The information in this second section was more comprehensive than in the first segment. Each POW name had a service number, grade, date of capture, and date of return listed. This scanned document was hard to read as visible creases were present from the original form. The top of the first page stated the following: "US Military Personnel who were Prisoners of War During World War II In The European Theater And Who Were Returned Alive (Not a Complete List). Listed Numerically By POW

Camp Code And There Under Alphabetically By Prisoner Name." The author indicated that the list was incomplete, but 2,983 entries were in this section.

Reviewing more information on the NARA website, I concluded that the government's complete lists of POWs were an ongoing project. In the 1990s, the government located additional files (including additional information from punch cards) and merged them to create a complete POW list in the National Archive records. I reviewed both sections of this Valerosos document—the original with 2,983 names and the one updated in 1994 with approximately 1,000 names, and I could not locate my father on either list. I again wondered if my father had actually been a POW.

This document compiled by this person or organization called Valerosos piqued my curiosity. The PDF listed its sources—both government sites—but I was unsure if this Valerosos document was legitimate. I discovered that *Valerosos* translated to *courageous* in Spanish. When I typed in www.valerosos.com, it brought me to the following web page statement:

> Welcome to the Borinqueneers Website! The 65th Infantry Regiment, comprised primarily of Puerto Ricans, began as a volunteer regiment in 1899 and participated in WWI and WWII. It was during the Korean War that they made their mark and saw extensive combat. In this website dedicated to their accomplishments, you will find their history, photographs, newspaper articles, listings of their many award recipients, and sadly, a listing of those who sacrificed their lives defending American ideals. As we celebrate over a century of service to the nation and commemorate the 50th Anniversary of the Korean War, we invite you to pay tribute to those Puerto Ricans and fellow Americans who served proudly. Visit these pages and remember and honor them.

It was ironic, I thought, that the first place I located a Stalag 17B roster, other than the NARA website, was from the Valerosos website—ironic for me because my father married my mother, a native of Puerto Rico. Also on the website was a 122-page wartime log about the life of a Puerto Rican POW at Stalag 17B.

A paragraph went on to explain: "This is a copy of my uncle Clem's wartime log at Stalag 17B, Clem did a lot of the drawings in this log from personal experience, and included are some of his writings reflecting his situation and his experience during the war." Clem's wartime log was another beautiful example of family members' preserving their veteran's history for posterity.

For the first time researching my father's POW whereabouts, I realized I needed to switch my attention to his flight history. I thought I would get to that later after finding out where he was a prisoner. Now, I questioned what happened to his crewmates when they bailed out and if that could provide clues about my father's POW camp.

I started with the American Air Museum in Britain website, a phenomenal repository of information on the US Army Air Force soldiers who served their country from the United Kingdom during World War II. All my father's crewmates' names were listed, though there was no mention of what POW camps they were detained in. After German fighter planes and flak hit their aircraft, the site confirmed that all ten crew members parachuted to safety. Four evaded capture, and the other six, including my father, were captured and spent the remainder of the war in POW camps.

Next, I examined the American Ex-Prisoners of War Organization. The home page described the organization as a "not-for-profit, Congressionally-chartered veterans' service organization advocating for former prisoners of war and their families." A special report included the names of 30,000 POWs and their POW camps. Most of the POWs had more than one camp listed. The site also had information on selected POW camps and some members' biographies and obituaries. I searched for my father's name, but apparently he did not join this organization. However, I found his buddy Toby's name (he had five prison camps listed).

Finally, I went back to my old friend, the NARA website, and the World War II POW Data File to research the whereabouts of the five other captured crew members, speculating that my father may have ended up at the same place. Punching in the five crew members' names, I discovered four were at Stalag 17B: the radio operator, the two waist gunners, and the top turret gunner. One crew member, the navigator, evaded capture for a few months. He was ultimately caught and ended up at Stalag Luft I, a camp for officers and higher-ranked airmen. His placement made sense because the navigator was a second lieutenant, and all the rest of the captured crew were sergeants. My father, the tail gunner, was a Staff Sergeant at the time, and it was logical that he went to the same camp as the rest of his aircrew, who were also NCOs—Stalag 17B. I just needed to see this confirmed in writing.

— 14 —

Eureka!

If a man falls freely, he would not feel his weight.

—ALBERT EINSTEIN
(experiencing a eureka moment)

O ut of frustration, I returned to the Stalag 17B website I had already visited, hoping I had missed something significant in my previous searches. Instead of punching in Stalag XVII B like many times before, *I accidentally typed in Stalag 17b.* The following new website appeared: http://web.archive.org/web/sitemap/stalag17b.com.

I had just landed on an excellent online site brimming with information about Stalag 17B. On the introductory home page, the website's author described the reason behind the site's creation:

> I started this website and another one about my father's bomber squadron twenty years ago in memory of his service in WWII, and to help find and share answers to the many unanswered questions I had about what he experienced during the war. Over the years, as I read more books, found other websites, and met and spoke with other POWs and their families from around the world, I now have a better idea of what happened in Stalag XVII B and how it has affected the lives of so many people. In this website, I can only present a small part of the whole story of Stalag XVII B, but I hope it can help us

understand what the prisoners experienced, what so many of them did not want to talk about after they returned home.

Several sections on the website included information on Stalag 17B's history, details of the long march, treatment of prisoners, and daily life and activities. Personal drawings and stories of the POWs existed, along with a copy of the author's father's diary he kept while held captive in Stalag 17B. The author stated, "Like all the other American prisoners, my father received a 'Wartime Log'—a hardbound book with numbered blank pages, donated by the YMCA and distributed through the Red Cross—and a set of colored pencils. Many of these diaries were either confiscated by the Germans or left behind when the prisoners began the long, forced march across Austria in April 1945. My father kept his diary." The diary showed how POWs spent their time—also preserved on this site for posterity.

One section particularly captured my attention. It was entitled "Books, Links and Files." I clicked on the File section, and nine files appeared. The first file was named "My list of American prisoners held at Stalag XVII B." I could hardly contain my excitement as I opened the document. Could this be what I had been searching for all these months?

The file was sixty-nine pages long and held over 4,000 names. Each name had a last name, first name, MI, US serial number, state, bomb group number, plane serial number, MACR number, year, month, date plane crashed, and POW barrack number. I scrolled down to page twenty-six, where the Hs were, and saw my dad's name: Donald L. Hayes. I confirmed that all the information was correct and stared at the page for a few minutes, almost in disbelief. After the initial emotions subsided after finally finding factual information on my father's whereabouts, I telephoned my sister Naomi and quietly said, "I found Dad."

After six months of obsessively searching for some thread of evidence of years past, I felt an incredible sense of accomplishment. At the same time, it was bittersweet. The search had come to an end, but seeing my father's name in print was also hard evidence that he had spent almost two years in captivity in the worst circumstances imaginable.

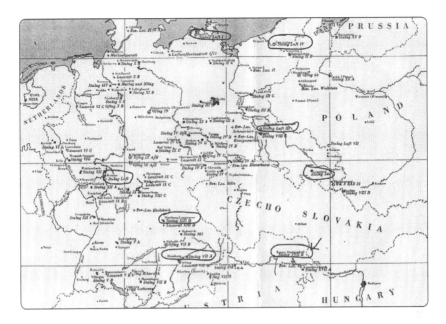

American Red Cross Map of POW Camps. The caption reads: "Location of German Camps and Hospitals Where American Prisoners of War and Civilian Internees are Held. (Based on information received to December 31, 1944)." I circled the main camps where American airmen were held captive—Stalag Luft I, Stalag Luft III, Stalag Luft IV, Dulag Luft, and my father's POW camp—Stalag XVII B (17B), circled with an arrow. I also circled Stalag VIII-B (8B), the POW camp we visited in Poland, later known as Stalag 344. Last, I circled Stalag XIII-D (13D) in Nuremberg and Stalag VII-A (7A) in Moosburg—the final destination camps for many American POWs forced to evacuate their primary camps toward the last months of the war. Stalag Luft VI in East Prussia is missing in this depiction of POW camps, as the Americans—victims of the infamous Heydekrug Run—were already transferred to Stalag Luft IV in July 1944.

I was immensely grateful to the person (William Doubledee) who put together this website and this roster, which must have taken countless hours. Immediately, I located the author's contact information and sent him an email. I thanked him profusely for his devotion to his father and for putting together all these fantastic resources so family members like me could close gaps in our loved ones' stories. I asked him about the source of his information, not doubting, but I was baffled why I could not find these details myself. He had cited the same sources I had researched, but I didn't recognize one reference.

That source was a document that someone in Stalag 17B compiled many decades ago. His name was Luther Victory, and the manuscript was titled *A Chronicle of Stalag XVII B*. The book is extremely rare, and I could not locate a copy to confirm if this was the missing source. But now, I was grateful and satisfied that the information displayed was correct. Even the barrack number of 39A was the same as my dad's friend and bunk-mate, Toby. I also located four of my dad's crewmates on this list, two of whom were in the same barrack, just like old home week.

Enclosed is a copy of the email I sent to William (Bill) Doubledee, the author of the Stalag 17B website:

> Hello, first of all, I would like to thank you for creating your two websites in memory of your father. I have been trying to find out more about my father's POW history in WWII and have not been able to locate his name on any written POW list until today, when I found your website. It has been a long search, and I can't thank you enough for all your research. My father was a tail gunner, shot down over Germany on September 6, 1943. He spent 22 months in a POW camp. His records list Stalag Luft III and Nuremberg/Langwasser—the same as your father's records. I visited both POW camps because those were the camps listed on my father's service papers. I looked through all the documents at Stalag Luft III with the camp directors, and they did not have his name listed. Same for the other camp—no recordings that he was a POW at these camps. Later, when I returned home, I found that four of his captured crew members were sent to Stalag XVII B. My father also had a friend (his bunkmate) whom he talked about often, who I later found out was at Stalag XVII B. I finally located a POW list online of Stalag XVII B. My father's friend was on this list, but my father was not. I assumed he was not at this camp. Not until today did I find your list and see my father's name in print. I have a few questions if you have the time. I am wondering how you got this list of names? I wonder why our fathers had Stalag Luft III listed on their service records (also Nuremberg/Langwasser) and not Stalag XVII B? Thank you for your time and excellent research, especially for sharing it online.

And here was his reply:

Thank you, Maureen, for writing to me, and thank you for visiting my website. I am glad you have found it helpful. I have been researching the American POWs in Stalag XVII B since 1996. I started with a partial list from the Stalag XVII B Ex-POW Association (now disbanded) and then spent the next 20 years filling in the blanks. Along the way, I was extremely lucky to get a copy of Luther Victory's "Chronicle of Stalag XVII B." I scanned it and spent more time comparing it with the National Archive Online database. Then I searched online sites of bomber groups and squadrons for more information. The MACR data from fold3.com helped, too. The result is my list. The reason why the Germans didn't let the Americans know where they kept their POWs was because the Germans didn't want us to know where they kept our boys, period. Most of the men who were sent to Stalag XVII B show up in National Archive records as being held in Stalag Luft III.

Again, many thanks for writing and visiting my site.

Best regards,

Bill

PART FOUR

THE
TRAINING
YEARS

— 15 —

Enlistment

*We will not be driven by fear . . . if we remember
that we are not descended from fearful men.*

—EDWARD R. MURROW,
World War II American Broadcaster and War Correspondent

My father was not driven by fear when he joined the Army Air Corps. He was driven by adventure and the thought of being a pilot someday. As I embarked on the experience of unraveling his story, it gave me strength to recognize that I did not descend from a fearful man but a brave young man fulfilling his patriotic duty.

My father's time in the air was the component of his war history that I remember him being most excited about and the only part he wrote about after the war ended. While he would tell us kids the stories of being a POW, mostly humorous for our young ears, he could go on for hours talking about his B-17 airplane and the missions he flew from England to Germany and Nazi-occupied Europe. I was not as interested in this part of his journey until I solved his imprisonment enigma. However, once my questions were answered, I became fascinated with my father's aviation history and associated stories.

Empowered by knowing his correct POW camp, I investigated the remainder of his World War II years, from enlistment to his return to the US. I began with his Discharge Record, which told the complete story—almost. My goal now shifted to recording my father's World War

II story in chronological order, and his Discharge Record proved to be a valuable guide toward accomplishing this task.

To begin with, I was impressed with the Army for the Discharge Record's thoroughness—formally called the "Enlisted Record and Report of Separation/Honorable Discharge." I reviewed this one piece of paper for over a year, and every time I examined it, I found another number or another term I did not observe before. The Discharge Record outlined my father's entire military history; I just had to fill in the gaps, which was not always easy—seventy-five plus years later.

The record was divided into five sections. The first section was a combination of personal data at the time of enlistment. Individual boxes contained the following information: Permanent Address, Date Of Birth, Place Of Birth, Color Eyes, Color Hair, Height, Weight, Number of Dependents, Civilian Occupation, Army Serial Number, Grade, Arm Of Service, and Date and Place Of Separation. There was one box entitled Organization, which stated his Army Air Force (AAF) Base Unit.

The second section was entitled Military History. This area had information about Date Of Enlistment, Place Of Entry Into Service, Military Occupation Specialty, Battles And Campaigns, Immunization Dates, Decorations And Citations, and Service Outside Continental US, including return dates. There were details about the Reason And Authority For Separation, Service Schools Attended, and Education Years.

The third section provided Pay Data, and the fourth section was related to an Insurance Notice. The fifth and final section was a signature area complete with a thumbprint, Adjusted Service Rating Score (ASR Score) number, and the statement, "Lapel Button Issued." Using his Discharge Record as a guide, I attempted to piece together my father's war story, starting from when he first decided to enlist. After more than two years of research, the following description is what I now know about my father during World War II.

✢   ✢   ✢

Donald L. Hayes was born in Brockton, Massachusetts, on February 27, 1921. He enlisted for the Army Air Corps on August 8, 1940, when he was nineteen. According to his Discharge Record, he had brown eyes and blond hair, was 5 feet 9 inches (always seemed taller), and weighed 138 pounds (seemed exceptionally light). I was unsure if this was his weight at the time of enlistment or the time of his discharge, but later, I discovered a document explaining how to read a World War II Discharge Record.

According to this document, the Army obtained all personal data at induction—or enlistment, as in my father's case. It made me wonder what his weight was at his time of separation from the military. Given his POW history—most likely, frighteningly underweight.

My father grew up in Brockton, Massachusetts, where he attended eight years of grammar school and four years of high school. He graduated from Brockton High, the same high school that Rocky Marciano, the heavyweight boxing champion, attended. He often said he was a pitcher, and Rocky was his catcher. Not long ago, I had the opportunity to visit Brockton High. Sure enough, there is a large bronze statue of Rocky Marciano in a beautiful grassy, fenced-in area designated for his remembrance. I did not find any information about Rocky's baseball catching years and my father being his pitcher, nor did I expect to, but nevertheless, I heard that story recounted repeatedly. It was one of my father's favorite boyhood memories, and I believed it to be true. I still have a photo of my father and Rocky after the war ended, with their arms around each other, smiling for the camera.

At enlistment, the military recorded my father's civilian occupation as a Clerk Typist, a standard occupational title for clerical work defined by the United States Employment Service. His Army Qualification Separation Record stated that Franklin Creamery employed him in Brockton, Massachusetts. He performed office duties such as simple bookkeeping, accepting telephone orders, keeping an account of drivers' deliveries, operating an adding machine, and balancing the books. It also stated he typed sixty-five words per minute.

After reviewing the records of many young men who ended up in World War II, I found it fascinating to read what jobs were listed on their files in the late 1930s and early 1940s before they enlisted or were drafted. Many seemed to hold mundane jobs that paid the rent and put food on the table, but not much more. They could never imagine how extraordinary their lives were to become and how different their training

My Father and Rocky Marciano. Rocky Marciano—the World Heavyweight Boxing Champion from 1952 to 1956—is pictured on the left. Donald L. Hayes is shown on the right. The photo was taken years after World War II ended. My father would often say of his boyhood friend, "I was the pitcher, and Rocky was my catcher."

and jobs would be once they entered the Army and a military preparing to embark on a world war. These new jobs would change their lives forever, and if they survived, they would also provide new opportunities for them once they returned home. I contemplated how many of these young men ended up in the same occupations they had before the war. Or were new horizons and myriad opportunities waiting for them upon their return?

I read about one young soldier who collected bridge tolls for four years before enlisting. Once in the Army Air Corps, he trained to become a navigator on a B-17 plane, flying multiple missions until he was shot down, captured, and became a POW. At the end of the war, he made the military his new career. I wondered if my father ever dreamed of what lay in store for him while he sat at his desk performing his clerical duties, including typing sixty-five words per minute. With thoughts of enlisting, he probably anticipated life would be a bit more exciting.

Although my father enlisted in the United States Army, the Army Air Corps was the Arm of Service highlighted on his Discharge Record—the title used at that time to refer to what we now know as the United States Air Force (USAF). I learned that during World War II, there was no independent Air Force; the United States Army Air Corps (USAAC) and later the United States Army Air Forces (USAAF) served as the aerial warfare components under the United States Army's command.

I also discovered that American aviation could be traced back to 1907 when the US War Department created the Aeronautical Division within the US Army Signal Corps—the first forerunner to the USAF. In 1917, when America entered World War I, the American Expeditionary Force (AEF), a branch of the US Army, was sent to fight on the Western Front. In 1918, one year later, the first major US aviation combat force, known as the Air Service, was created and became part of the AEF.

After World War I ended, the Air Service became less of a force but remained critical to the advancement of aviation technology, with many of its officers becoming key leaders during World War II. In 1920, the Air Service became a branch of the US Army, and in 1926, it was renamed the USAAC.

In mid-1941, as aviation began to play an increasingly important role in modern warfare, the Army renamed the USAAC the United

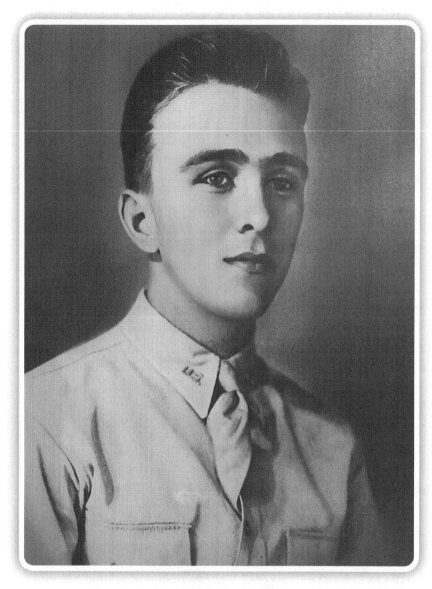

My Father's Photo Shortly after Enlistment. Donald L. Hayes is pictured in his Army Air Corps Enlisted Aviation Student uniform. In this photograph, he is wearing a cotton khaki shirt with his tie tucked between the first and second visible buttons. Regulations specified that the tie must be tucked in when the shirt was worn without the outer coat.

States Army Air Forces (USAAF). The USAAF had greater autonomy but remained within the Army's command structure throughout World War II. The United States Air Force did not become independent from the Army until 1947. It was interesting to observe how quickly aviation technology and the Air Force evolved from a fledgling organization consisting of minimal numbers of men and aircraft during World War I and during the 1920s and 1930s to a full force of men with the most advanced aviation technology in the world by the end of World War II.

An article in *Air Force News* states, "All told, US Army Air Forces strength in World War II would swell from 26,500 men and 2,200 aircraft in 1939 to 2,253,000 men and women and 63,715 aircraft in 1945."

Going back to my father's Discharge Record, his enlistment date was noted as August 8, 1940, but the record did not state the actual place where he enlisted. I was able to locate his Enlistment Record, a public document available through the National Archives. There were two additional pieces of information on the Enlistment Record that were not on the discharge paper. The first detail was that his actual place of enlistment was in Boston, Massachusetts. The second was that the "Term of Enlistment" section stated, "Enlistment for the Panama Canal Department."

Only now did I realize that my father enlisted with the primary intention of going to the Canal Zone, something unknown before. Previously, I thought he enlisted and planned to go wherever the Army told him. It seemed there was intention and he had a choice, especially in the early 1940s—the prewar years.

Several years later, a family member showed me a letter from my father's oldest brother—my uncle Johnny. The letter confirmed that Johnny was stationed in Panama when my father enlisted, working as an airplane mechanic and flight engineer in the Canal Zone, aspiring to become a pilot. When I read this letter, it finally made sense why my father had intentionally requested to serve in Panama—he was following in his brother's footsteps.

After enlisting, my father entered the service at Fort Slocum, New York. It is unclear if he went directly from Boston to Fort Slocum, which would have been about 195 miles and approximately four hours, depending on travel mode. I contemplated if he went back to Brockton from

Boston to gather his belongings and say a final farewell to his family and friends, or had he already said all his goodbyes, knowing he would be off to training camp that same day. One could speculate that he had spoken to a recruitment officer in his hometown of Brockton and already knew what was in store for him before heading off to Boston and ultimately off into the wide blue yonder—not returning home again for a long five years.

— 16 —

Fort Slocum, New York

*They answered the call to help save the world from the two
most powerful and ruthless military machines ever assembled,
instruments of conquest in the hands of fascist maniacs.*

—Tom Brokaw,
Journalist and Author, *The Greatest Generation*

Fort Slocum, New York, was where my father first experienced military life. The base was on an eighty-acre island called Davids Island, located in the Long Island Sound, approximately one-half mile east of the mainland of New Rochelle, New York. During World War II, Fort Slocum was a busy assembly point, a central staging area, and an embarkation camp for recruits bound for positions overseas, including the Panama Canal Zone. Here, the Army provided soldiers housing and hot meals while they completed their final training in preparation for their transport to posts elsewhere. Perhaps the primary reason the Army ordered my father to report to Fort Slocum may have been because of his future assignment in Panama.

On this island, my father received his basic training and introduction to military service. According to the *AAF The Official Guide to the Army Air Forces*, every newly enlisted person learned to be a soldier by completing a five-week basic training course. Training included drills and marches, physical exercise, marksmanship, care of equipment, map and photo interpretation, understanding defense against air attacks, and other essential military procedures. Six weeks later, my father departed for Panama with basic training under his belt.

As an aside, I discovered Fort Slocum was also the training ground for the Army Bakers and Cooks School. Old photos depicted the cooks putting dozens of pies in massive steel ovens with oversized wooden paddles. The Westchester County Archives site states: "In the late 1920s, the Quartermaster Corps established one of its bakers and cooks schools at Fort Slocum (in operation ca.1928–1943). Its students learned to plan, prepare, and serve meals for hundreds of soldiers at a time, essential tasks for keeping the Army functioning. This technical school was the first to be housed at Fort Slocum."

My father loved his pies, especially New England blueberry pies. I pictured he took advantage of some delicious cooking before transferring to other destinations during his World War II years of service—places where the cooking was not as good and settings like the POW camps where it was often inhumanely nonexistent.

— 17 —

The Republic of Panama

There's nothing stronger than the heart of a volunteer.

—JIMMY DOOLITTLE,
Commanding General, Eighth Air Force, 1944–1945

On October 1, 1940, my father arrived in the Republic of Panama, staying there until August 14, 1942—just short of two years. The journey took five days, and it is unknown to me if he traveled by boat, plane, or a combination of modes. Upon arrival, his discharge papers indicated that he attended the Airplane and Engine Mechanic School in Rio Hato. Although my father dreamed of being an airplane pilot, it seemed his career path began with technical training in Panama.

Rio Hato Air Field, also known as Rio Hato Army Air Base, was located on the Gulf of Panama, seventy miles southwest of the Panama Canal. It was one of several US air bases in Panama during World War II. Other air bases included Albrook Field, where my father started his Aviation Cadet training, and France Field on the Atlantic side of the Canal Zone, where my uncle Johnny was first deployed. Howard Air Force Base, nine miles southwest of Albrook Field, was where Uncle Johnny was later stationed after the attack on Pearl Harbor.

Even before the Japanese attacked Pearl Harbor in 1941, the Canal Zone had a significant deployment of American troops overseas. Their primary aim was to protect American interests in the region, which meant defending the Panama Canal so ships could safely cross from the Atlantic to the Pacific and vice versa.

In 1940, when my father reported to Rio Hato Air Field, the Army Air Corps had one fighter group stationed there—the 37th PG—and one heavy bomber group—the 9th BG. Later, in 1941, squadrons from the 32nd PG and the 6th BG group arrived, providing increased reinforcements. With all these fighter planes and bomb groups in Panama, my father began solidifying his dream to be a pilot, starting from the ground up.

As I familiarized myself with the planes stationed at the airfields in Panama from 1940 to 1946, several numbers and letters describing the different groups and squadrons were unrecognizable. When I first glanced at the long list of all the aircraft, it looked cluttered and dull, but it became more interesting as I understood the significance of these characters. I had become accustomed to the letters BG, which signified bomb group, but I had never seen the letters PG. After some research, I realized this stood for pursuit group, and the letter P signified pursuit aircraft adapted from the French phrase, *Avion de Chasse*. This phrase translated to pursuit or hunt airplane and eventually fighter plane as the Americans referred to these aircraft.

The initial fighter planes that occupied the airfields in Panama in the early 1940s were the P-26s and P-36s, and later the P-39s and P-40s. They had nicknames like Peashooter, Hawk, Airacobra, and Warhawk, respectively.

I also discovered that the chief US fighter planes in the European Theater of Operations (ETO) were the P-38s, P-47s, and P-51s—and held nicknames like Lightning, Thunderbolt, and Mustang, respectively. I was now jumping at the throttle to learn more about these fighter planes, or "Little Friends," as the young men flying in the big bombers affectionately called them. And important friends they were as the aircrew in the heavy bombers depended on them to escort them into Nazi-occupied territory, fighting off enemy fire on the way to their missions and back.

Studying the earlier and later versions of pursuit fighter planes was fascinating, but I realized I needed to narrow my scope and put that aside for now. However, when my father said he wanted to be a pilot, was he referring to a fighter pilot? I had always assumed he meant a B-17 pilot, but perhaps that was not the case.

During his time in Panama, my father completed his technical training in Rio Hato and became an Aviation Cadet. He began a pre-aviation eight-week training course at Albrook Field, not far from Rio Hato in the Canal Zone on the Pacific Ocean near Panama City. His Army Qualification Separation Record stated that the institution that accepted him was West Point Prep. As indicated on his Separation Record, he did not graduate from the course. His brother Johnny wrote in his military career notes: "My brother, Donald, was rejected for flight training as a pilot because of an ear infection contracted in Panama."

The only account I remember my father talking about during his time in Panama was his desire to be a pilot. I vividly remember him telling us kids about the day he was swimming in a nearby river with his buddies. Diving to the bottom of the river, he scooped up a handful of muddy dirt, some of which entered his ear. After that, he developed a massive ear infection and lost hearing in that ear. He would say that his chances of being a pilot were over because of that swimming incident. My father repeated this swimming anecdote many times, and, years later, Johnny confirmed the story in his military memoir.

Another excerpt from Uncle Johnny's military notes stated the following: "On December 7, 1941—a most memorable day—I was having dinner with my brother, Donald, who was an Aviation Cadet at the time, in the mess hall at Albrook Field (Pacific side of the Canal). Suddenly, we heard the loud boom of a cannon, followed by many more. An old, deeply tanned Master Sergeant at a nearby table said in a loud voice, 'That means an attack somewhere.' Much to our amazement, we learned that the 'attack' was on Pearl Harbor."

My uncle Johnny's words not only confirmed that my father was following his dream to be a pilot, but they also conjured up powerful images of two brothers far away from home, together, sharing a meal and a decisive moment in history that would soon change their lives.

Uncle Johnny went on to successfully achieve his dream of becoming a pilot. He never saw live action like my father, as the Army Air Forces assigned him to be a flight instructor in the States, training pilots to fight in Europe and the Pacific. After the war, Johnny decided to make a career in the US Air Force, achieving his highest rank of Major.

I know my father was proud of his oldest brother and that he had fulfilled his pilot dreams. I never heard him mention it, but I wonder if he felt he got the short end of the stick—rejected from aviation training and spending almost two years in a POW camp. On the other hand, I know Uncle Johnny had regrets that he never saw live action, like my father. But both lived to tell their tales, regardless of how imperfectly they viewed their scenarios.

— 18 —

Las Vegas, Nevada

*It takes all kinds of guys doing all kinds of jobs to win
this war, and it makes you feel big just to be in it.*

—REAR GUNNER,
1943, American Air Forces Training Film

After staying just short of two years in Panama, my father departed
on August 15, 1942, for his return trip to the US. He arrived on
September 8, 1942, twenty-four days later. Absent are the documents
on how he journeyed back to the States, but one could speculate it was
by boat, given the number of days it took to complete the journey. Upon
returning to the US, his Discharge Record indicated he attended the
Flexible Gunnery School in Las Vegas, Nevada. He did not depart for
the ETO until almost nine months later, on May 31, 1943.

I assume the Army Air Corps transferred my father to Flexible
Gunnery School in Las Vegas because he could no longer pursue his
dream of being a pilot. He may have requested gunnery training with
hopes of being a crew member on a bomber plane, or he may have had
no choice. The war was ramping up after the bombing of Pearl Harbor
almost a year earlier, and aircrews were being deployed to England to fly
bomber and fighter planes in organized attacks against Nazi Germany.
When my father received his assignment to report to Las Vegas, he
probably knew he would soon join a ten-man crew flying on a B-17
heavy bomber.

So, what was flexible gunnery? I learned that it had to do with firing machine guns mounted on a turret that allowed them to swivel—hence the name flexible. There were ten crew members on a B-17 Flying Fortress heavy bomber—the type of plane my father flew on. The crew consisted of the pilot, copilot, navigator, bombardier, top turret gunner/flight engineer, radio operator, ball turret gunner, left waist gunner, right waist gunner, and a tail gunner. Eight of the ten crew members on the B-17 bomber plane operated flexible guns, except the pilot and copilot. As I read more about flexible gunnery, I found several training videos, booklets, and films devoted to the subject. The movies and reading materials were fascinating, especially when I put myself in the shoes of the young men training to become gunners.

The Flexible Gunnery School in Las Vegas, Nevada, was the first flexible gunnery school that the Army opened in the US in 1941. The school provided training and instruction on handling .50-caliber machine guns mounted on the B-17 Flying Fortress, the B-24 Liberator, and, later, the B-29 Superfortress. The students received five weeks of intensive training while assigned to small groups called "flights." Each flight had an instructor who tracked their progress hour by hour and day by day throughout the entire five weeks.

The instruction began with education about .30- and .50-caliber machine guns, taking them apart, and putting them back together. The young men then learned about a bullet's flight path and about sights and sighting moving targets. Next, they studied turret manipulation—becoming familiar with shooting on turrets, putting them together, and installing the guns. Other instruction included learning about the clothes and equipment they would be wearing in their planes, all necessary for flying in high altitudes in freezing conditions. They also learned about the need for oxygen when flying at these high altitudes. In addition, exercise programs were introduced to increase their fitness and strength.

After all this, the young men were ready to shoot at fixed and moving targets. The trainees started with BB machine guns in an indoor range, learning to aim ahead of targets. For some of the men raised with guns, or as several described, "cut their teeth with guns," this must have been very simple. However, I am not sure how easy it was for young men like my father, raised with just a New England hockey stick.

Next, the trainees progressed to the outdoor skeet range using 12-gauge shotguns until tracking and leading the target became instinctive. Their first experience with a real machine gun was on the malfunction range. The instructors intentionally manipulated the guns to malfunction, and they expected the trainees to figure out what was wrong and fix them when they jammed or stopped firing. After that, they cleaned and adjusted the guns as the expectation was that they would "know a machine gun better than its mother does."

After they understood their guns inside and out, they studied how to identify enemy aircraft and then progressed to shooting at fixed and moving targets. The training started on the ground using mounted shotguns and then progressed to shotguns installed on the backs of trucks that the trainers drove through a course. Finally, the young men went up in the bombers, shooting at targets pulled by other aircraft. The instructors assigned the students ammunition dipped in paint throughout their training to track if they were hitting their targets. Their shooting skills and written tests determined if they graduated from their course.

While researching educational materials about flexible gunnery, I came across a training film entitled *Rear Gunner*, created in 1943, directed by Ray Enright, and produced by Warner Brothers. The cast members included names that I quickly recognized—Ronald Reagan, Burgess Meredith, and Frank Coghlan, Jr., to highlight a few. The film started with a version of the "Air Force Song" I was already familiar with, having sung it many times, albeit not precisely using the exact words:

Off we go into the wild sky yonder, Keep the wings level and true;

If you'd live to be a gray-haired wonder, keep the nose out of the blue.

Flying men, guarding the nation's borders,
we'll be there followed by more!

In echelon, we carry on, for nothing can stop the Army Air Corps.

Rear Gunner was about twenty minutes long and depicted a youthful, handsome Ronald Reagan playing the role of Lieutenant Ames. He spotted a young mechanic working outside a plane—Pee Wee Williams, played by Burgess Meredith. Ames asked Pee Wee if he'd like to get inside that plane, saying, "How'd ya like to go to gunnery school?"

Pee Wee replied, "Yes, sir, I'd like that just fine."

The film was slightly hokey and over-the-top rah-rah, but at the same time, it was well done and pulled at your heartstrings. Poor Pee Wee, who turned out to be a crack shooter, having received plenty of practice shooting crows down on the farm, was told by his classmates at school that he would never amount to anything. I reckoned bullying goes way back in time.

Pee Wee successfully graduated from gunnery school, and during a mission, he saved the lives of his crewmates from a fighter pilot shooting at them after they crash-landed. After abandoning the plane and hiding in the brush, a Japanese fighter pilot was determined to finish them off. Pee Wee ran back into the aircraft and operated his guns in the tail section, shooting down the fighter and saving the day.

The film showcased how the Army Air Corps could transform a young boy, full of self-doubt, into a war hero proud of himself and looked upon with admiration by all his comrades. At the end of the film, the Army Air Corps awards Pee Wee the Distinguished Service Medal. A bit corny, but very effective. *Rear Gunner* received a bounty of accolades, citing it as a prime example of how Hollywood helped boost morale and recruit men into military service. The film also offered the public a glimpse into what type of training it took to be a gunner on a big bomber plane—from the ground to the sky.

I also discovered an AAF 1943 training film by the War Department entitled *Flexible Aerial Gunnery: Making a Gunner.* This film had a more serious tone than *Rear Gunner* and focused intensely on gunnery school and what it entailed. At the start, it highlighted the purpose of the training—"to take our bombers to smash the Axis." Clearly, it made the point that every man at gunnery school must want to be a gunner and emphasized how important a gunner's role was, noting "the success of the mission will depend on you." In one part, during the training film, the instructor stated, "This is what you are here for—to fire guns—to kill."

A short training pamphlet called *Get That Fighter* was interesting and entertaining, complete with explanatory drawings. Detailed instructions were in a forty-three-page manual that the military instructors handed out to the young men training to be flexible gunners. The pamphlet's information was specifically about shooting a fighter plane coming directly at you for an attack. I was struck by how the pictures tried to make the images look funny or light-hearted, maybe because, in reality, the subject was mentally difficult, nerve-racking, and, at the core, was about survival.

Life versus death probably was not the first thought of the young guys eager to try their new skills on the German pilots. But at some point, it had to sink in that you shot them, or they shot you. One of the training manual pages explicitly explained "how to get the fighter pilot before he gets you." The first page read, "The success of the mission and the lives of the crew depend on your gunnery." After watching these training films and reading a few training pamphlets, I better understood what flexible gunnery training was all about.

Get That Fighter. This short booklet was distributed to the aerial gunners and illustrated how to get that fighter before he gets you. Shown are pages four and five.

Over 44,000 students eventually graduated from the Flexible Gunnery School in Las Vegas. In the year my father attended, 10,562 enrolled, and 9,117 graduated, so it was not a given that everyone passed. To be a gunner, you had to want to be a gunner, have excellent eye-hand coordination, the ability to lead the target correctly, and, ultimately, the intellectual capability to pass all the tests. You also had to function in a crisis, possess nerves of steel, and have an innate yearning to be part of a crew on a bomber plane. My father was one of the honored graduates, and his discharge papers listed his Military Occupational Specialty as a Flight Maintenance Gunner.

I have a photo of my father taken after graduating from gunnery school that he kept his entire life in a drawer with the rest of his World War II photos and papers. In the photo, he proudly displays his new Air Force wings and updated rank of Staff Sergeant (later promoted to Technical Sergeant). He is smiling but looks slightly apprehensive—as if he knew he was about to embark on an adventure of a lifetime, but during immensely uncertain times with no guarantee of survival.

My Father with Wings. My father, Donald L. Hayes, is smiling for the camera after receiving his Aircrew Badge (Wings). To qualify and receive their wings, each crew member completed advanced training in aircraft in-flight support roles.

US Army Air Forces Aircrew Badge (Wings).

US Army Air Forces Aerial Gunner Badge (badge my father earned after gunnery school).

— 19 —

Crew Training

*Your limits are somewhere up there, waiting
for you to reach beyond infinity.*

—HENRY H. ARNOLD,
Commanding General, US Army Air Forces, 1942–1946

A fter my father completed gunnery school and until deployment overseas, the Army Air Forces, as per protocol, transferred him to another Air Force base to participate in a Bombardment Training Program. During this training, he received his assignment to a ten-man crew. He completed several months of flight training with the same team, as they learned to operate together as a cohesive unit. Finally, with training completed, the crew was notified of their assignment to the Eighth Air Force and deployment to the European Theater of Operations (ETO).

The Army Air Forces carefully laid out requirements for bombardment crew instruction in published training standards. The standards contained measurable outcomes to determine if the trainees passed each directive objectively. "The training standards established requirements to be met at all levels of performance." If the young men did not meet the standards, they were required to complete additional instruction. The ultimate goal of each of these standards was to create "a closely-knit, well-organized team of highly trained specialists of both the air and ground echelons." As they would later find out, operating as a highly functioning

113

team over the skies of Nazi-occupied Europe often became a matter of life or death.

The Second Air Force oversaw most heavy bombardment training and divided the program into three phases. The book entitled *The Army Air Forces in World War II*, under the "Combat Crew and Unit Training" chapter, best described the heavy bombardment training as follows:

> During the first phase, individual crew members received instruction in their specialties, with particular attention given to instrument and night flying exercises for pilots, cross-country tests for navigators, target runs for bombardiers, and air-to-air firing for gunners. During the second phase, the teamwork of the combat crew was stressed: bombing, gunnery, and instrument flight missions were performed by full crews. The third phase aimed at developing effective unit operation—the goal of the entire program. It included extensive exercises in high-altitude formation flying, long-range navigation, target identification, and simulated combat missions.

In 1942, in the early part of the war, when entire bomb groups were being transferred overseas, these three phases of training took place while still in the States. Replacement crews, like my father's crew in 1943, most likely received the third phase of training in formation flying with an entire squadron after arriving in the ETO.

The unwritten training standards of forming a tight-knit, high-functioning crew were equally important. These standards involved learning about each other's personalities and the roles each member was responsible for performing. "The crew was the family circle of an air force; each member knew that long hours of work, play, anxiety, and danger would be shared."

Every crew learned to operate as a unit, with the planes in their squadron and the entire formation. They had to master how to take off, assemble into formation, complete their missions, and then land together at the end of the mission. They had to operate together in the air under radio silence and through the overcast skies of England. Being able to get along and function as a highly skilled crew could determine if the young men returned home to base—or not.

In an interview, Conrad L. Lohoefer, a World War II veteran assigned to the Eighth Air Force, 91st Bomb Group, described his experience after being assigned to a crew and selected to participate in operational overseas training: "That was actually where the crew learned to be together and how to operate as a crew and where the pilot and co-pilot learned to fly together. Then that's when we became a crew."

He went on to say that everyone on the crew was indispensable. "We couldn't have done without a tail gunner. We couldn't have done without a navigator. They were all equally important, and the ground crew especially was because we couldn't have flown that B17 if we hadn't had a decent ground crew."

Lohoefer reported that after several months of crew training complete, the AAF assigned him and his crew to the Eighth Air Force in England. He said some crews were assigned new airplanes and flew directly to Great Britain, but there were not enough airplanes for everyone to fly; therefore, some crews went by ship. Lohoefer said the Army Air Forces appointed him to go by ship, and that ship was named the *Queen Mary*, "if you can believe it," he exclaimed.

My father was a member of one of the replacement crews assigned to fly a new airplane to Europe. According to his Discharge Record, the voyage took three days; he departed the US on May 31, 1943, and arrived in the ETO on June 3, 1943. His plane most likely took one version of the North Atlantic Air Ferry Route, starting in New England and flying to intermediate airfields in either Newfoundland, Labrador, Greenland, or Iceland. From there, the crew would have flown to an airfield in Great Britain—the most common being Prestwick, Scotland.

The three-day time frame suggested that my father stopped at one of these points along the way before reaching the ETO. My father's plane likely took the same North Atlantic Air Ferry Route that his 91st Bomb Group took in 1942—from Bangor, Maine, to Gander, Newfoundland, to Prestwick, Scotland.

Once at Prestwick, the replacement crews often would be transported to Bovingdon Air Force Base in England for familiarization with operations in the ETO and eventual assignments, parting ways with the plane that ferried them across the Atlantic. Often, their aircraft would travel on to Burtonwood Air Force Base in Warrington, England, to have additional equipment and field modifications installed before being assigned to a bomb group and corresponding air base. I am not sure when my father was informed he would be joining the 91st Bomb Group based at Bassingbourn Air Force Base, but most likely it was after landing in the ETO. He did not arrive at Bassingbourn until three weeks later, on June 25, 1943.

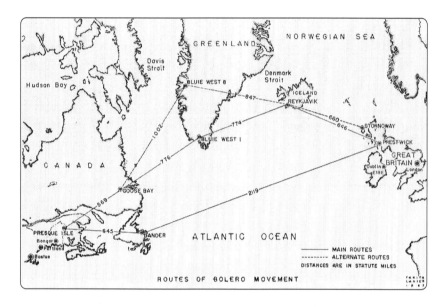

The North Atlantic Air Ferry Routes. The caption reads: "Map No. 30: Routes of the Bolero Movement." Operation Bolero was the code name for the movement of US forces across the Atlantic to the United Kingdom. The southernmost route is most likely the path my father and his crewmates flew to the European Theater on May 31, 1943—from Bangor, Maine, to Gander, Newfoundland, to Prestwick, Scotland.

Later, I discovered a crew photo my father had saved and realized this was the crew he flew with from the US to the European Theater. I am unsure who took the picture and when the ten crew members posed together in front of a white wooden building in the background. Five of the young men in this photo—the pilot, the copilot, the radio operator, the top turret gunner, one of the waist gunners, and my father, the tail gunner—arrived at Bassingbourn on the same day. Comparing this photo with another crew photo in front of their aircraft on the runway, I realized that these five crew members were also together on their last mission when they were shot down over Nazi-occupied Europe on September 6, 1943.

I couldn't help but wonder what these young bomber boys thought of one another. What types of relationships did they have after being together in the most dangerous and exhilarating circumstances? Was there mutual respect? Did they laugh, hang out together, and share jokes during their free time? When the war was over, did they ever wonder how the other guys were doing?

I don't know the answers to these questions because I never asked, and my father never talked about his crew members. Only decades later, out of the blue, did the son of my father's pilot make contact with our family. Come to find out, my father and his pilot did keep in touch many years after the war ended. And their love of baseball finally brought them together, watching their beloved teams and my youngest brother, a professional baseball player, playing on one of those teams. I found this information years after my father and his pilot passed away. Still, the memory of their collegiality was endearing and answered many of my questions about whether theirs was a close-knit crew.

Crew Picture. This is a photo my father kept tucked away in a drawer his entire life. Pictured is the crew he flew with from the US to the European Theater. The image was most likely taken in the United States before their departure overseas. My father is in the back row, the first crew member on the left (with his eyes closed). He obviously did not get the memo, as he is the only one wearing his bomber jacket. Five of the crew members in this photo were also in the official crew photo taken at Bassingbourn, England, in front of "Bomb Boogie." They are as follows: Back row, left to right: S/Sgt. Donald L. Hayes, Tail Gunner; unable to identify; S/Sgt. Dean W. Millward, Waist Gunner; unable to identify; T/Sgt. John B. Wenninghoff, Radio; unable to identify. Front row, left to right: unable to identify; 2nd Lt. Howard Sherman, Copilot; 1st Lt. Elwood D. Arp, Pilot; unable to identify. Although the names of the remaining crew members are not available, their smiling faces are preserved here for posterity.

Everyone Had a Role

Here's looking at you, kid.

—*CASABLANCA,*
a Hollywood film released in January 1943

During World War II and the years building up to America entering the fight, the US government strongly communicated to its citizens that everyone had a role in winning the war. Americans were encouraged to purchase war bonds, plant Victory Gardens, and volunteer wherever needed. It seemed every civilian participated in the war effort, either by joining a branch of the military stationed in the States or fighting abroad. American families assisted by volunteering on the home front or working in jobs that contributed toward victory.

Propaganda posters played an essential role in the war and were produced by the thousands. Who can forget the posters of Uncle Sam pointing his finger, saying, "I want you," or Rosie the Riveter flexing her muscles with the message, "We Can Do It." Like Rosie, during World War II, the women kept the fires burning back home, taking care of children and working in jobs traditionally held by the men who were now off to war on two fronts.

Women worked in factories, on farms, in offices, in hospitals, drove trucks, and did whatever was required to help win the war. They also enlisted in the Women's Army Corps (WAC), Women Airforce Service

Pilots (WASP), and the United States Naval Reserve (Women's Reserve) (WAVES), serving their country domestically and abroad.

Planting Victory Gardens was one of the ways citizens at home performed their patriotic duty and lent a helping hand. The United States rationed most food items and emphasized that the troops abroad were top priorities. Government agencies urged all Americans to plant their own Victory Gardens and provided instructions on growing and preserving their garden produce. Neighbors formed cooperatives and pooled their resources. Over twenty million Victory Gardens were planted throughout the war producing approximately 40 percent of all vegetables consumed in the US.

Early on, the War Department understood Hollywood's vital role in the war effort and in raising American morale. Many years after the war ended, the Palm Springs Air Museum held an exhibit entitled "Hollywood and the Home Front." This presentation detailed the critical role Hollywood played in boosting the war effort:

> During WWII, the War Department realized the importance of not only keeping up the morale of America's fighting forces abroad but the morale of those at home. The result was an unprecedented push by Hollywood to contribute morale-building war dramas, troop entertainment, and training films to influence the war effort. These films told Americans at home that they too could serve in the defense of their country by purchasing war bonds, participating in scrap drives, planting Victory Gardens and volunteering.

When the United States officially entered the war after the bombing of Pearl Harbor in December 1941, so did Hollywood. Although President Roosevelt did not believe in censorship, he had specific guidelines for the film industry. One question Roosevelt and the Office of War Information asked Hollywood to ask itself was, "Will this picture help to win the war?" The Roosevelt Administration encouraged Hollywood to make films depicting people from all walks of life rising to their patriotic duties, such as men from diverse backgrounds joining the war effort or women at home volunteering or working as combat nurses, riveters, and welders. The film industry emphasized that Americans were making small sacrifices and doing it of their own free will, cheerfully, and all in the name of victory and a greater cause.

The Bureau of Motion Pictures, an agency under the Office of War Information, helped produce educational and propaganda-type films similar to *Rear Gunner* that my father and other young men in the military were exposed to during their training years. Actors and actresses volunteered to lead recruitment and bond drives. The movie industry made documentaries and training films explaining the war and why America needed to fight.

Hollywood stars like Bob Hope, Marlene Dietrich, Bing Crosby, and Judy Garland entertained the troops at home and overseas. Some actresses, such as Rita Hayworth and Lana Turner, boosted morale more than they probably ever realized. The young soldiers pinned up pictures of these movie stars next to their sleeping quarters in countries far away from America—places like England, Austria, Germany, and Poland. Still others joined the Armed Forces. Clark Gable and Jimmy Stewart flew in the Eighth Air Force, similar to my father—albeit not on the same plane.

Clark Gable also starred in and narrated the documentary film *Combat America* produced in 1943 and released by the Army Air Forces in 1945. The film was initially intended to serve as a recruitment tool for aerial gunners, but by the time it was finished, the need for gunners had decreased. The film transitioned to become an account of aerial combat over Nazi-occupied Europe and a tribute to the Eighth Air Force. Filming began around June 1943 at Bassingbourn Air Force Base, where my father was stationed. It is not too far-reaching to say my father may have glimpsed Clark Gable on the base in between missions. And, who knows, they may have exchanged a few words in passing—or at least a salute.

Even Walt Disney Studios rose to the challenge of educating the American public and raising morale, fully embracing the question, "Will this picture help win the war?" Cartoons featuring Bugs Bunny encouraged viewers to purchase war bonds and join volunteering efforts. Several Disney animated films and cartoons propagated the war as a just and worthwhile cause while simultaneously demonizing the enemy as an evil force that needed to be crushed. Other movies and cartoons ridiculed and poked fun at the Axis powers and their leaders. Additionally, Walt Disney artists created over a thousand military insignia, which were used as nose art for bombers and as unit logos.

Two highly acclaimed Disney works stood out during the war years. One was a short animated film about Hitler Youth called *Education For Death*. The other was a cartoon starring Donald Duck called *Der Fuehrer's Face*. The animated Disney film entitled *Education For Death* was dark and sinister, with an overlying element of sadness lingering throughout. It told the story of the Hitler Youth, from the beginning when parents registered their child to the end of their training after the child had been indoctrinated and was goose-stepping and yelling, "Heil Hitler," arms raised.

One scene in the film left an everlasting impression. It showed the young children in a classroom looking at a drawing of a fox eating a rabbit on the blackboard. The teacher asked who was stronger, the fox or rabbit? One little boy was crying and said he felt sorry for the rabbit. That was the wrong answer, and the instructor punished him by making him sit in the dunce corner. All his classmates fervently agreed with the instructor, who enforced that there was no room for weakness.

The impressionable part was watching the little boy's face as he looked at his classmates, who stood up and yelled the correct reply, "The world belongs to the strong and to the brutal." "The rabbit is a coward and deserves to die." "I spit on the rabbit." The little boy's face slowly transformed from sympathy to anger toward the rabbit, succumbing to peer pressure and groupthink. Properly brainwashed, the last scene showed all the boys marching off to war and their eventual deaths. In his book, *Mein Kampf*, Hitler said, "Whoever has the youth has the future." Frightening how so many parents went along with his plan.

The animated film starring Donald Duck was nine minutes long and depicted poor Donald having a nightmare as the Nazis forced him to work in a munitions factory in Germany. His alarm clock wakes him up to Heil Hitlers everywhere. Even the bird in the cuckoo clock is Heil Hitlering. The cartoon portrayed the German people as a starving nation, highlighted by a scene where Donald has one coffee bean tied to a string that he dips into a cup of hot water. At the end of a long forty-eight-hour shift, Donald wakes up again to the sounds of his alarm clock, but this time he is in America with the Statue of Liberty on his bedstand. Donald hugs Lady Liberty as never before. He would not, for a moment, take his freedom for granted ever again.

The Donald Duck film featured the popular tune, "Der Fuehrer's Face," written by Oliver Wallace, a songwriter at Disney Studios. Spike Jones and the City Slickers performed the song and released it before the Donald Duck cartoon came out; it was an overnight success. Due to overwhelming requests to play the jingle, radio stations announced they would provide a free copy of the tune to anyone who pledged to purchase a $50 war bond. After listening to the song, I think it should come with a warning that states you may never get it out of your head.

Originally, Disney Studios planned to name the cartoon "Donald Duck in Nutziland," but the name was changed to *Der Fuehrer's Face* after the popular song's lyrics. Walt Disney Studios understood that one way to reduce the tenets of Hitler's Nazism was to poke fun at them while simultaneously prodding Americans to laugh and reduce their anxieties. If there was anything the Nazis hated, it was to be ridiculed. One could say there was not one ounce of self-deprecating humor in that Nutzi-bunch, and no one showcased that better than Disney. And, perhaps, Charlie Chaplin.

In 1940, Charlie Chaplin produced, directed, and starred in his first talking film, *The Great Dictator*. Charlie Chaplin played two roles in this movie—a Jewish barber and a dictator who resembled Hitler down to that infamous mustache. It was rumored that Hitler copied Charlie Chaplin's mustache because Charlie Chaplin was much beloved, and Hitler thought it would be good for his image. The movie was a satirical comedy that ridiculed Hitler and his generals and staff. Some parts of the film were hilarious, like the segment when General Goring accidentally causes Hitler to slip on a banana peel and fall down a flight of stairs.

At the end of the movie, Charlie Chaplin gives one of the most widely acclaimed monologues in film history in his role as Hitler. In this final scene, he denounces fascism and tyranny and delivers an impassioned speech expounding on brotherhood and goodwill. "Soldiers! Don't fight for slavery! Fight for liberty! In the 17th Chapter of St. Luke it is written: 'the Kingdom of God is within man' not one man nor a group of men, but in all men! In you!"

John Steinbeck was also determined to help crush tyranny and fascism during World War II. In his short novel, *The Moon Is Down*, he demonstrated how people subjected against their wishes will always resist their subjugators. When Steinbeck first published his book, it received harsh criticism from folks in America as too subtle—almost humanizing the German people—to be an effective propaganda tool. It was the opposite of the exaggerated nature of previous propaganda efforts. However, throughout Nazi-occupied Europe, the novel was considered highly effective in boosting Resistance efforts.

Hundreds of thousands of copies were clandestinely translated into several languages and distributed throughout the occupied countries at risk of death. Donald V. Coers described the following in his introduction pages of *The Moon Is Down*: "Against the fiercest assault on freedom during this century, John Steinbeck calmly reaffirmed in *The Moon Is Down* the bedrock principles of democracy: the worth of the individual, and the power deriving from free citizens sharing common commitments."

There were also many magnificent books and training manuals geared to educate soldiers and the American public. One that stood out was the *AAF The Official Guide to the Army Air Forces*, published in 1944 by the AAF. The AAF wrote this book with the American public in mind, and their philosophy was that every American was entitled to know the underpinnings of their country's Air Force.

The book included a foreword by General H. H. Arnold, Commanding General of the Army Air Forces. It then provided an introduction and comprehensive overview of the AAF, including who they were, how they trained, what they fought with, how they kept the AAF flying, where they fought, historical highlights, awards, insignia, drawings, maps, and diagrams.

I read this extensively detailed book from cover to cover, and when I finished, I was confident I could repair and fly an airplane. More importantly, I felt that regardless of a person's role—man, woman, ground crew, pilot, or airplane factory worker—the AAF highlighted all equally important in the fight for freedom.

It suddenly dawned on me that in none of my readings and research thus far had I come across the words *Republican* or *Democrat*, except back home as the country grappled whether to support the Allies or remain in isolation. I encountered no documented political conversations between the men in training and those headed off to war. There were no partisan debates on who was right or wrong or more patriotic or religious. It was fastidiously refreshing. Most everyone affiliated with a party, but it did not seem to be front and foremost. There were other more demanding issues to deal with, and our country needed to act as a whole—and we did—as one nation, indivisible, with liberty and justice for all.

And with the help of everyone—including Hollywood.

PART FIVE

THE EUROPEAN THEATER

— 21 —

The Friendly Invasion

They're overpaid, overconfident, and over here.

—THE BRITS

It was a unique time in England after the bombing of Pearl Harbor on December 7, 1941. The whole dynamic of Great Britain changed as Americans arrived by the thousands to fly their big B-17 and B-24 planes, dropping bombs across Nazi Germany. The British nicknamed this massive influx of Americans "The Friendly Invasion."

Between 1942 and 1945, so many Americans were stationed in England that the Brits said the island had started to sink a bit—in that dry British humor sort of way. At first, the English were not thrilled to see all these young airmen taking over their towns and countryside. A local saying went, "They're overpaid, overconfident, and over here." I have also heard versions of this same quote, such as "They're overpaid, oversexed, and over here," but I prefer the first version, especially when thinking my father was one of those stationed over there. When visiting the area, I never noticed anyone strolling about that looked like me, but I must admit the thought did drift through my mind, if only for a few seconds.

With such drastic changes happening to these quaint, quiet villages and countryside, and even in the larger towns and cities, it must have been quite unsettling for the English people. Their lives were disheveled, already fighting a war for several years. And now they had the young bomber boys to contend with using their farmland for airfields and hanging out with their daughters whenever opportunities arose. It was quite a lot to absorb in such a short amount of time.

In preparation for this enormous influx of Americans, the military created pamphlets and training manuals for the US troops with instructions on how to interact with the British. An adage in one of the training manuals entitled *A Short Guide to Great Britain*, produced for the US soldiers, summed it up: "The British don't know how to make a good cup of coffee. You don't know how to make a good cup of tea. It's an even swap."

The publication date was January 1943, so I am sure my father received a copy and read a few other suggestions such as these: "Don't show off or brag or bluster." "Don't make fun of British speech or accents. You sound just as funny to them but they will be too polite to show it." "If you are invited to eat with a family, don't eat too much. Otherwise you may eat up their weekly rations." "NEVER criticize the King or Queen." "It is always impolite to criticize your hosts; it is militarily stupid to criticize your allies."

Over time, there came to be a better understanding and appreciation for each other on both sides. The British appreciated these young boys who were sacrificing their lives day in and day out. The Americans respected the British who had stayed calm and carried on for so many years, enduring relentless bombing by the Nazis until America was ultimately ready and prepared to help out.

— 22 —

East Anglia

We won't do much talking until we've done more fighting.
We hope that when we leave you'll be glad we came.

—IRA C. EAKER,
Commanding General, Eighth Air Force, 1942–1943

In 1941, after the bombing of Pearl Harbor, the US designated Air
Force units worldwide, starting with number one. Each unit had a different mission. The Army assigned the Eighth Air Force to England
with the primary goal of bombing German military targets throughout
Western Europe. Brigadier General Ira Eaker was the first Commander
of the VIII Bomber Command (a.k.a. the Eighth Air Force) and was
charged with starting this newly formed group from scratch.

When General Eaker arrived in England in February 1942, he had
zero airfields, zero planes, and seven men. He was literally starting from
ground zero. By August 1943, when my father was stationed in England,
the Eighth had established thirty-five bases, 864 bombers, 750 fighters,
and 105,000 men. These numbers continued to increase as the war progressed. By mid-1944, the Eighth Air Force reached a total strength of
more than 200,000 men and over fifty airfields that accommodated their
bomber and fighter planes.

The growth of the Eighth Air Force over the war years was quite
remarkable. Their first regular mission was on August 17, 1942, when

the 97th Bombardment Group flew twelve B-17 Flying Fortresses on the first VIII Bomber Command heavy bomber mission of the war. A year later, on August 17, 1943, the Eighth sent out sixteen bomb groups and 376 bombers for the famous Schweinfurt-Regensburg mission. The Eighth lost sixty bombers on that mission. And on December 24, 1944, the largest raid of the war thus far, the Eighth Air Force launched 2,046 bombers to attack a wide range of German airfields and military installations.

So, in just over two years, the Eighth Air Force went from 12 to 376 to 2,046 bombers in a mission. Starting from scratch in 1942, the Eighth Air Force had grown in size and might, from a fledgling group to a formidable force deserving of its nickname, "The Mighty Eighth."

During World War II, the Eighth Air Force was principally located in an area of England called East Anglia. In this district in southeastern England bordered by the North Sea, over 130 British and American military airfields were scattered over the countryside in a geographical area about the size of New Jersey. The location of these newly built air bases in East Anglia was necessary given its distance to Nazi-occupied Europe and Nazi Germany. Most of these bases had sprung up hastily and were not known for their comfortable accommodations except for a few like Bassingbourn—an older, preexisting RAF property.

East Anglia also had an abundance of flat land, necessary for airfields. Often this meant "requisitioning" from its owners some of the best farmland in England. The airfields were built right into the farmlands and occasionally on the country estates. It was prime real estate, especially as fertile soil became increasingly precious as the entire nation struggled with a limited food supply. The British planned for these airfields to be temporary, and the farmers and the country landowners expected their land to be returned to them as soon as the war ended.

Planes would take off right next to cows and farmers tilling their fields. It was said there were so many air bases all next to one another that if you had any trouble, all you had to do was hop over a hedge and land on the closest one you saw. In *One Last Look* by Kaplan and Smith, an Eighth Air Force pilot expressed amazement at the number of airfields to choose from as he came in for his first landing: "The sight of all those airports as you came in made you feel like a beggar who had suddenly come into an inheritance."

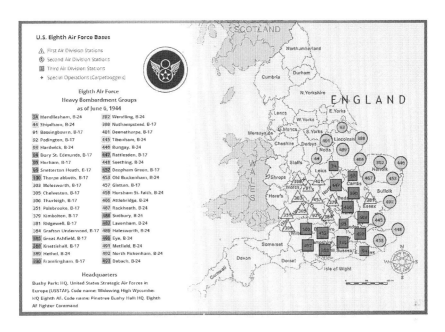

U.S. Eighth Air Force Bases

△ First Air Division Stations
⑥ Second Air Division Stations
▣ Third Air Division Stations
+ Special Operations (Carpetbaggers)

Eighth Air Force
Heavy Bombardment Groups
as of June 6, 1944

34 Mendlesham, B-24	392 Wendling, B-24
44 Shipdham, B-24	398 Nuthampstead, B-17
91 Bassingbourn, B-17	401 Deenethorpe, B-17
92 Podington, B-17	445 Tibenham, B-24
93 Hardwick, B-24	446 Bungay, B-24
94 Bury St. Edmunds, B-17	447 Rattlesden, B-17
95 Horham, B-17	448 Seething, B-24
96 Snetterton Heath, B-17	452 Deopham Green, B-17
100 Thorpe abbotts, B-17	453 Old Buckenham, B-24
303 Molesworth, B-17	457 Glatton, B-17
305 Chelveston, B-17	458 Horsham St. Faith, B-24
306 Thurleigh, B-17	466 Attlebridge, B-24
351 Polebrooke, B-17	467 Rackheath, B-24
379 Kimbolton, B-17	486 Sudbury, B-24
381 Ridgewell, B-17	487 Lavenham, B-24
384 Grafton Underwood, B-17	489 Halesworth, B-24
385 Great Ashfield, B-17	490 Eye, B-24
388 Knettishall, B-17	491 Metfield, B-24
389 Hethel, B-24	492 North Pickenham, B-24
390 Framlingham, B-17	493 Debach, B-24

Headquarters

Bushy Park; HQ, United States Strategic Air Forces in
Europe (USSTAF). Code name: Widewing High Wycombe:
HQ Eighth AF. Code name: Pinetree Bushy Hall: HQ, Eighth
AF Fighter Command

Eighth Air Force Installations: June 1944. This illustration highlights the US Eighth Air Force installations scattered throughout England, primarily in East Anglia. As of June 6, 1944, forty US bases were designated for the heavy bomber groups, with additional bases for fighter groups, training facilities, and reconnaissance. RAF bomber and fighter bases were also strategically positioned throughout England, complementing the newly constructed American air bases. Initially built for the RAF, some bases ended up occupied by the Eighth Air Force—Bassingbourn, a prime example. Over 400 Allied air bases dotted the landscape in the United Kingdom by the war's end, with the USAAF occupying approximately 200 of the airfields.

Before gaining notoriety for its numerous airfields, East Anglia was initially recognized for its beautiful, lush countryside and peaceful, quaint villages. For Americans first arriving in this area, the beauty may have been beyond their expectations. A quote by one of the bomber boys said it all: "And if you flew there, . . . it not only matched but exceeded your imaginary pictures of it. You had expected England to be green, even your childhood storybooks had told you that, but you had not expected it to be this green—actually to be, well . . . storybook green."

Another unique characteristic was that, back home, the Americans had buildings that may have been one hundred years old, but in England, if a building was less than 300 years old, it was considered new. It was a dramatic change of scenery for these young boys, and the stark differences in culture and landscape further emphasized that they had landed in a faraway place. The language was the same, but even that required translation from time to time. By all accounts, they weren't in Kansas anymore.

— 23 —

Bassingbourn

Gentlemen, you are cleared for takeoff, and good luck.

—From the Tower

Bassingbourn Air Force Base, home of the 91st Bomb Group, was located in East Anglia, outside Cambridge and not far from London. My father drew the lucky straw assigned to the 91st because Bassingbourn had a reputation as the "country club" of all the American Air Force bases in England. Its brick-based barracks with solidly built quarters, including amenities such as tennis courts and flower beds sprinkled throughout, were the envy of the other Eighth Air Force bomb groups.

In October 1942, the Army Air Corps first stationed the 91st at an airfield called Kimbolton, originally a RAF base in East Anglia. It soon became evident that Kimbolton was unsuitable for heavy bombers, as the airstrips were not sturdy enough to support the weight of the planes taking off and landing. In addition, its runways were of insufficient length. The heavy bombers had specific requirements to be met; otherwise, there could be catastrophic results. The runways had to be straight and a certain distance, and the ground had to be firm enough to support the enormous weight of a large plane carrying bombs, fuel, and a crew of ten. If an airfield met all these criteria, it was categorized as a Class A airfield. This name was apropos because each airfield had three intersecting runways that looked like the letter A from the air.

Because Kimbolton did not meet these requirements, the Commander of the 91st Bomb Group, Colonel Stanley T. Wray, was asked to inspect another nearby Air Force base called Bassingbourn. His order was to determine if that base would be more suitable for the 91st Bomb Group and their B-17 planes. Commander Wray took one look at Bassingbourn, with its beautiful brick buildings and other amenities lacking at Kimbolton, and ordered the entire 91st to transfer immediately without first asking formal permission from his superiors.

Not only was the base more appealing from its closer proximity to London, but it had been constructed in 1938 and was exceedingly more comfortable, with its permanent brick buildings with central heating. The base also had barracks for enlisted personnel, which starkly contrasted with the Nissen huts at Kimbolton. Unlike Kimbolton's muddy fields, a common characteristic of the wartime bases, landscaped grounds with curbed roadways complemented the setting.

Most importantly, Bassingbourn had already been reconstructed into a Class A airfield, a top-selling point. Last, its closer proximity to London was the icing on the cake. Wray contacted his staff and ordered them to prepare for immediate relocation. On October 14, 1942, the 91st moved itself and its equipment to Bassingbourn—in one day without haste.

Once they were all settled in, the 91st was allowed to stay, but the top brass were not happy with Stanley T. Wray's actions, even though he pleaded that he misunderstood the order. Nevertheless, he got his country club, and, undoubtedly, he believed the end justified the means. Wray ended up retiring as a Major General, demonstrating that the Air Force never held that bold move against him for too long. At the same time, it was beneficial for all the young airmen at Bassingbourn to have such a quick-acting commander. Hopefully, the crews appreciated the extra comforts Bassingbourn allowed between their missions, provided they were lucky enough to return to base safe and sound.

Bassingbourn Air Force Base. The caption reads: "A B-17F Fortress aircraft of the 91st BG, 8th Air Force executing a low fly-over during a demonstration at Bassingbourn, England, United Kingdom, 1943." Another caption for the same photo reads: "Major Bishop of the 91st Bomb Group buzzes the control tower at Bassingbourn in his B-17 Flying Fortress." Handwritten caption on reverse: "Major Bishop 'Buzz Job' after completing missions."

Control Tower at Bassingbourn. The caption reads: "A B-17 Flying Fortress passes the Control Tower at Bassingbourn." This photo is also pictured in *Airfields of the Eighth Then and Now* by Roger A. Freeman. The caption reads: "On parade at Bassingbourn! L to R are a Piper L-4 Grasshopper, Noorduyn UC-64 Norseman, Republic P-47D Thunderbolt and Cessna UC-78 Bobcat all of station flight. A resident B-17G of the 91st Bomb Group rolls past the control tower while a B-26 Marauder stands by the trees at top right."

— 24 —

The Ragged Irregulars

A "good" landing is one from which you can walk away. A "great"
landing is one after which they can use the plane again.

— A COMMON PILOT SAYING

In 1943, when my father arrived at Bassingbourn, the 91st Bomb Group
was one of forty heavy bomb groups stationed in England. During this
time, the bomb groups began to fly their missions further into the Third
Reich with limited fighter protection.

My father's bomb group, the 91st, sustained frequent casualties and
often received reinforcements from other units to complete their bomb
group formations. Because the leaders had difficulty during this period
of high casualties of putting an entire group into combat, one of the
commanders (most likely Commander Wray) nicknamed the 91st Bomb
Group "The Ragged Irregulars."

The 91st had four Bomb Squadrons: the 322nd, 323rd, 324th, and
the 401st. My father was in the 401st Bomb Squadron. Initially, the
91st aimed to have nine B-17 aircraft assigned to each squadron, making up thirty-six planes in each bomb group. To accommodate all the
aircraft and personnel, each bomb group had its designated air base.
Bassingbourn, home of the 91st, was referred to as Station 121. By 1944,
the bomb groups had almost doubled their number of aircraft, with each

squadron having approximately eighteen aircraft and about seventy-two planes in total.

Each heavy bomber group of the Eighth Air Force played an instrumental role in winning the air war over Nazi Germany. Each had its unique claims to fame. The 91st Bomb Group's outstanding claims to fame included flying 340 missions from 1942 to 1945, flying 9,591 sorties, and dropping 22,142 tons of bombs on European targets. They destroyed 420 enemy aircraft, more than any other group in the Eighth Air Force, and lost 197 B-17s, the highest losses of the entire Eighth Air Force. They were the first to attack a target in the Ruhr on March 4, 1943, and were the early testers and adopters of flak suits.

The 91st led the Schweinfurt mission on August 17, 1943, and was home to the highly acclaimed "Memphis Belle" and the "Delta Rebel 2." The "Nine-O-Nine," another B-17 plane in the 91st Bomb Group, completed 140 missions, more than any other bomber in World War II. Last, the 91st was the first bomb group to complete one hundred missions.

The 91st Bomb Group, and all the other bomb groups in the Eighth Air Force, flew daytime strategic bombing missions. They aimed to destroy industrial targets, aircraft factories, airfields, and oil facilities in Germany and Nazi-occupied Europe. In 1942, their main targets were submarine pens, marshaling yards, and airfields in France. In 1943, they conducted missions into Germany, attacking industrial targets, like aircraft factories and shipyards, and the ball-bearing factories at Schweinfurt.

In 1944, with the arrival of long-range P-51 Mustangs, missions deeper into Germany were possible, and the destruction of the Luftwaffe and aircraft factories became the focus. After the Normandy invasion in June 1944, the 91st performed raids to support the ground troops, including bombing railway yards and tracks. At the point the war ended, the 91st had two uplifting accomplishments—dropping food to the starving Dutch in operation Chowhound and assisting with the evacuations of American POWs in camps scattered across Europe, specifically Stalag Luft I in Barth, Germany.

When daylight strategic bombing was first underway, and the loss rates often reached 10 percent of each mission, Colonel Stanley T. Wray, Group Commander of the 91st Bomb Group Ragged Irregulars, figured out a way to boost morale and lighten hearts. He decided to create the Rigid Digit Award, unique to the 91st Bomb Group. He presented this award to his men for blunders that could have had harmful results. Fortunately, in these chosen instances, they did not. For example, one of the first Rigid Digit awards went to a pilot who ran off the end of a short runway, crashing into a ravine—with Commander Wray in the copilot's seat.

The medal, engraved with the middle finger upraised (giving the bird), would be awarded with much pomp and circumstance to the poor recipient in front of his peers and superiors, helping bring cheer into some exceedingly dark days. The humor of the award served to combat depression and battle fatigue while raising awareness of mistakes. Coincidentally, the medal became so popular that it reportedly was sought after by other commanders as a keepsake. As far as I know, my father never received this award for any adverse actions, and if he did, he kept it silent.

Another colorful story unique to the 91st Ragged Irregulars that helped boost morale and lighten hearts is that they had a mascot, an Irish Setter dog they named Redline. When I looked up the meaning of *redline* in the military, I found out it referred to a red line drawn through a soldier's name for breaking the rules, thus denying his pay. I assumed that is how the 91st Bomb Group mascot earned his name—his color was red, and he worked without pay. However, he earned his keep by bringing friendship and comfort to the young men when they were not flying their missions.

My father's crew had two pictures taken with Redline—one photo shows all six crewmen hovered adoringly around their mascot. The other is the official crew photo with Redline discreetly squeezed in between two of the airmen, barely visible unless one carefully scrutinizes. Redline was also known for staring up in the sky each day when the bomber boys returned from their missions—perhaps especially keeping an eye out for the return of "Bomb Boogie" and her crew.

"Bomb Boogie" Crew Members with Redline—the Irish Setter Mascot of the 91st Bomb Group at Bassingbourn. Pictured left to right: S/Sgt. Dean W. Millward, Waist Gunner; S/Sgt. Norbert F. B. Swierz, Waist Gunner; T/Sgt. Raymond R. Thompson, Top Turret Gunner; S/Sgt. R. D. Hatton, Ball Turret Gunner; T/Sgt. John B. Wenninghoff, Radio. I cannot positively identify the sixth crewman lying down in front. At first, I thought it was my father, S/Sgt. Donald L. Hayes, Tail Gunner, but it appears this aircrew member is wearing an officer's cap, and my father was a sergeant. This photo is also in the book *Flak Houses Then and Now: The Story of American Rest Homes in England During WWII* by Keith Thomas. The caption reads: "A moments relaxation for a crew of the 91st Bomb Group with their Spaniel 'Redline.'"

"Bomb Boogie" Crew and Mascot! Crew Members: Back row, left to right: T/Sgt. John B. Wenninghoff, Radio; Sgt. Dean W. Millward, Waist Gunner; S/Sgt. Donald L. Hayes, Tail Gunner; S/Sgt. R.D. Hatton, Ball Turret Gunner; T/Sgt. Raymond R. Thompson, Top Turret Gunner; Sgt. Silas Williams, Ground Crew; S/Sgt. Norbert F. B. Swierz, Waist Gunner. Front Row, left to right: Lt. Chauncey H. Hicks, Bombardier; 1st Lt. Elwood D. Arp, Pilot; 2nd Lt. Nathan Weltman, Navigator; 2nd Lt. Howard Sherman, Copilot. Look closely, and you will see the 91st Bomb Group Irish Setter mascot, Redline, squeezed in between Weltman and Sherman.

— 25 —

A Plane Named "Bomb Boogie"

High in that hostile alien sphere she flies on, symbol of airpower
incarnate, a haven for the airmen within her . . . a fortress in the sky.

—Peter M. Bowers,
Fortress in the Sky

On the website of the American Air Museum in Britain, under "People," I found my father's name, Donald L. Hayes. He appeared as person 45135 with the following information: "Donald L Hayes: MILITARY | TECHNICAL SERGEANT | TAIL GUNNER | 91ST BOMB GROUP THE RAGGED IRREGULARS Shot down September 6, 1943, in B-17 42-5763 'Bomb-Boogie.' Prisoner of War."

Interestingly, this was the first time I had seen "Bomb-Boogie" in writing. I don't remember hearing my father mention this name or reading it in print. On this same site, under military details, it listed my father's nationality as American, his nickname as Don, his service number, his highest rank of Technical Sergeant, and his role/job as Tail Gunner. Also highlighted were the eight military awards he had earned during the war. The Service category recorded him as a member of the 91st Bomb Group and the 401st Bomb Squadron.

The following section describes his aircraft and crew. Under this category, the heading was: 42-5763 Bomb Boogie / B-17 FLYING FORTRESS. The information that followed was: "Delivered Long Beach 29/12/42; Salina 7/1/43; Homestead 14/2/43; Assigned 401BS/91BG [LL-F] Bassingbourn 9/3/43; Missing in Action 17m Stuttgart 6/9/43 with Elwood Arp, Co-pilot: Howie Sherman, Bombardier: Chauncey Harold Hicks returned via Spain, Ball turret gunner: Russ Hatton (4 evaded capture), Navigator: Nathan Weltman captured in Paris Dec 43, ttg-Ray Thompson, Radio Operator: John Wenninghoff, Waist gunner: Norbert Swierz, Waist gunner: Dean Millward, Tail gunner: Don Hayes (6 Prisoner of War); enemy aircraft KO'd #3, crashed Mons-en-Pevele, near Lille, Fr. Missing Air Crew Report 514. BOMB-BOOGIE."

From this report, I now knew the number and nickname of my father's B-17F Flying Fortress. I learned that the aircraft was delivered to Long Beach and then made its way to Salina Air Base and Homestead Air Base before arriving in Bassingbourn on March 9, 1943. All ten crew members' names and roles, the date the Germans shot the plane down, and where it crashed were noted. The site also highlighted each crew member individually, and when I clicked on their names, more of their military history became available. Drilling down on each crew member, I became privy to how much the young bomber boys endured and how every story was distinct and uniquely powerful.

For example, four of my father's crew members (Hicks, Hatton, Swierz, and Thompson) were initially crew on another plane, called "Old Ironsides," before joining "Bomb Boogie." Enemy aircraft shot down "Old Ironsides," and the pilot was forced to ditch her in the North Sea's freezing waters on June 22, 1943. Luckily, a RAF Air Sea Rescue boat was nearby. Nine of the ten crew members were rescued and returned to duty. Sadly, the tail gunner was killed in action, his body washing up on shore a month later, near Alkmaar, a city in the Netherlands.

The four crew members who would later team up with my father—Hicks, Hatton, Swierz, and Thompson—were lucky to live through this crash. They had survived a landing in the frigid channel, and a British rescue boat, fortuitously, was near the scene to scoop them up. Of course, these young airmen could not foresee they would be shot down twice more within the next few months. As fate would have it, they would be parachuting out of another aircraft named "Bomb Boogie"—once over England and the second time in enemy territory.

At this point, I paused and allowed myself a few minutes of reflection about an airplane nicknamed "Bomb Boogie." My first thought was, why were there no memories of hearing my father mention that name before? I only remembered him talking about B-17s, but never that the name of the plane he flew on was called "Bomb Boogie."

Later, in reviewing some papers he wrote detailing his missions, he called out the name of his plane in one short sentence, "Bomb Boogie shot down over North-East France." These few words didn't seem to portray much emotion. However, compared to other descriptions of his missions, which were factual and to the point, calling his aircraft by its name spoke volumes. This one sentence seemed to humanize his plane; he appeared to be saying goodbye to an old friend, knowing it was the last time they would ever see one another.

"Bomb Boogie" with Flight Crew Ready to Board. The caption reads: "Bomb Boogie on the runway - 24 August 1943 - Bassingbourn, England." My father kept a copy of this picture with the crews' last names scribbled directly on the photo. Most names are no longer legible, but I could decipher my father's name and the radio operator's name. Both are on the far left of the photo heading toward the plane's rear. John B. Wenninghoff (Radio) is nearest to the farthest left propeller, and my father, Donald L. Hayes (Tail Gunner), is close behind him—second from the left.

I was immediately smitten with the sound of "Bomb Boogie"—such a classic name for a B-17 heavy bomber airplane. As I researched other World War II bomber plane names, I became even more convinced of how special that name was—at least, I could say it without blushing. Those young guys had a lot of fun naming their planes and designing the nose art—usually scantily clothed females—to complement the name. They were boys, some still in their teens, about to embark on missions where many would not return. Identifying their planes, however they preferred, was a right well earned.

Usually, it was the flight crew who designated a new plane. In *Plane Names & Fancy Noses*, Ray Bowden summarized that the pilot, being the aircraft commander, invariably had the last word but rarely pulled rank. He stated, "It was usually a joint decision though not always unanimous." As in my father's case, he did not arrive at Bassingbourn until June, almost four months after "Bomb Boogie." Another crew had already claimed the naming rights.

In *Once There Was a War*, John Steinbeck discussed the naming of planes after a rumor circulated claiming all the aircraft names would be removed and substituted with the names of towns and rivers:

> The names are highly personal things, and the ships grow to be people. Change the name of Bomb Boogie to St. Louis, or Mary Ruth of Mobile Memories to Wichita, or the Volga Virgin to Davenport, and you will have injured the ship. The name must be perfect and approved by every member of the crew. The name must not be changed. There is enough dullness in the war as it is.

Reading about all these plane names, I somewhat appreciated my father not flying on the likes of an aircraft called "The Careful Virgin," "Fertile Myrtle," or "Naughty Caroline." Nevertheless, if that had been the case, I am sure I would have acclimated to the title, knowing it was the plane my father and his crewmates depended on to bring them home safe after a harrowing mission. I presumed that was how it was with these planes and the nose art depicting their names; they were unique in their own ways.

No matter the aircraft's designation—"Bad Penny" or "Old Battle Axe"—if it brought you home one time, you believed it would fly you home again. The crew could not help but superstitiously develop a liking for the name and a fondness for the plane.

— 26 —

Tempsford

By the full moon we flew

—INSCRIPTION ON THE TEMPSFORD MEMORIAL

The abundance of air bases in East Anglia proved lucky for my father and many other young airmen in the Eighth Air Force. On his first mission, on their way back to England, their plane, "Bomb Boogie," was severely hit by flak (anti-aircraft fire from guns on the ground) and needed to make an emergency landing.

The pilot did not know if he could safely land the plane at Bassingbourn and gave the order for the crew to bail out shortly after crossing the English Channel. My father and his buddies safely parachuted over England, but one crew member on the plane was too frightened to jump. The pilot, Lieutenant Pitts, heroically stayed with the aircraft and carefully crash-landed it on autopilot on a British Air Force base—one of the first available airfields in sight.

Edward Jablonski, in his book *Double Strike*, described the "Bomb Boogie" incident as follows:

> Another 91st plane . . . was the much-photographed, famed Bomb Boogie. (Its fame rested on the fact that its controls had been so shot up on its first mission so that the pilot, a Flight Officer Pitts, landed the plane by using the automatic pilot alone. Pitts had found

one member of the crew, the engineer, panicking and refusing to parachute out of the plane. Pitts chose to remain with the plane and brought it in for a remarkable, if bouncy, landing at a R.A.F. field. The other eight members of Bomb Boogie's crew jumped to safety over England. This would lend the plane another distinction—for it may well have been the one plane in the Eighth Air Force from which its crew bailed out twice; this would occur in September when the plane was knocked down on the way to Stuttgart).

"Bomb Boogie" with Flak. The caption reads: "A B-17 Flying Fortress (LL-F, serial number 42-5763) nicknamed 'Bomb Boogie' of the 91st Bomb Group." Handwritten caption on reverse: "17/7/43 Tempsford [refers to "Bomb Boogie's" forced landing at RAF Tempsford on this date] MIA 6/9/43."

When requesting permission for an emergency landing, something that happened quite frequently in those days, a Brit monitoring air traffic over the UK would respond by saying, "Hello Yank!" and then guide the troubled American plane to the nearest available airfield. All ten crew members survived that day, the eight who jumped and the two who landed with the plane.

I remember my father saying, "They sent me right back," a few days later on the next mission. In those days, there was no rest for the young bomber boys who flew missions until they were shot down and killed, captured, or lucky enough to complete their quota of twenty-five and go home. My father was twenty-two years old at the time.

Out of curiosity, I researched the name of the British Air Force Base where my father's pilot had to make the emergency landing. It was called RAF Tempsford, and the Allies regarded it as one of World War II's top-secret airfields. Tempsford was home to the RAF 138 and the 161 Special Duty Squadrons, which dropped supplies and agents into Nazi-occupied Europe for the Special Operations Executive (SOE), otherwise known as "Churchill's Secret Army."

They mainly flew customized aircraft called Lysanders. These specialized planes allowed their pilots to fly at low altitudes and touch down on short strips of land to drop off and quickly retrieve special agents and, occasionally, Allied crewmen who had evaded capture. The "Lizzies" were painted dark colors to escape detection and flew at night during the week of a full moon.

Because there was no space for a navigator in those small and agile planes, the pilot relied on skill, moonlight, a map, and a compass—all imperative for successful navigation. The pilots would quickly land on fields secretly marked out by several torches—their special passengers squeezed into the aircraft's rear cockpit. The agents, sometimes wearing specially designed padded clothing, would exit the plane onto the field after it briefly touched down. Agents also parachuted out if the situation allowed, sometimes at dangerously low altitudes.

The pilots from Special Squadrons 138 and 161 (also nicknamed the "moon squadrons") dropped off over 1,000 agents into Nazi-occupied Europe. They also recovered hundreds of special agents, Resistance workers, military personnel, and refugees dangerously needing to return to England and escape the Nazis, who were fast on their heels.

It is incredible to read stories about these brave pilots and the men and women whom the moon squadron pilots flew from the Tempsford airfield, some never to return. I had previously heard about special SOE agents, such as Andree Borrel, Lise de Baissac, and Violette Szabo. Still, many heroes, such as the French Resistance members and other Resistance fighters in Nazi-occupied territories, were dropped off or brought back, whose narratives will never be known. It would be impossible to discover all the names and stories of these countless brave individuals. Most guarded their secrets, if they survived, their entire lives.

One story that stood out was of a Resistance worker whose name remains unknown. In an article in the July 14, 1945, edition of the newspaper *The Evening Standard*, James Stuart, one of the moon squadron pilots, described the details: "One French agent was caught by the Gestapo, who broke his feet in torturing him. He managed to escape from them and we picked him up and brought him back to England. He could not of course make a parachute landing again, but he insisted on returning to carry on with his work in France. So we took him over. He was a brave man."

Countless brave men and women were committed to a cause they believed was bigger than themselves. Records demonstrated that approximately 3,000 Allied soldiers escaped and evaded capture during World War II. Roughly three Resistance fighters, and sometimes their families, lost their lives for every soldier saved. The newspaper article stated, "Tempsford is just a hamlet in rural Bedfordshire. Its inhabitants mostly work on the land, and none of them knew it but Tempsford held one of the big secrets of the war."

Today, in Tempsford, several plaques and memorials honor and validate the secret agents who flew out of this covert airfield: 1) the Gibraltar Farm Barn, near the remnants of the old airstrip, where the agents would pick up the equipment they needed for their dangerous missions; 2) St. Peter's Church in Tempsford, which houses a book of remembrance that lists 623 airmen from the 138 and 161 moon squadrons killed during the war; 3) the Tempsford Museum & Archives in the village of Tempsford, which holds an extensive collection of photographs, papers, maps, uniforms, and aircraft parts associated with RAF Tempsford; and 4) the Tempsford Memorial just outside the church, which memorializes the women who served as secret agents, the RAF aircrew who transported them, and the Allied secret service members killed in the war.

The memorial displays the names of seventy-five known women

agents. Twenty-nine of these women were arrested, sixteen were executed, and three died of illnesses while imprisoned. One committed suicide using a cyanide pill before being captured.

When I first decided to investigate the RAF Air Base where my father's plane crash-landed at the end of his first mission, I had no idea it would take me down this fascinating path. One could spend months or even years exploring the stories associated with this clandestine RAF air base, one of Britain's biggest secrets. I promised to add Tempsford to my list of priority places when I travel back to East Anglia—a pilgrimage to honor all the fearless men and women who believed so strongly in freedom, to the point of sacrificing their lives under the most horrific circumstances.

— 27 —

The Crew

An "esprit de corps" and close comradeship developed among
men joined together in doing a job that was dangerous,
often deadly, but necessary, and doing it well.

—KAPLAN AND SMITH,
One Last Look

Now knowing the names of my father's crewmates, I thoroughly familiarized myself with their backgrounds, including their roles on each
mission. On the American Air Museum in Britain website, a picture
captured the crew alongside their aircraft, "Bomb Boogie." My father, at
one time, had an original copy of this photo. It has since disappeared, but
not before someone in our family, my mother or one of my siblings, made
prints for everyone. This photo of my father and his crew has been in
my living room for years. I had never examined it in detail until recently.

I now studied the crew members, putting names to all their faces. They
appeared to be a tight-knit group. All were smiling like someone just told
a good joke—except the pilot and copilot, who seemed to be putting on
their serious faces. Also pictured was a member of the ground crew. From
several stories I have read, it appeared the ground crew never received the
attention they thoroughly deserved.

After each mission, these mechanics would work endless hours into
the night to ensure "their" bombers were ready to go out early the next
morning and bring "their" crews back safely. They would start this process anew as soon as the bombers and crew returned later in the day or

early evening. A good ground crew was essential to the mission's success and a necessary part of the team. I was gratified to see that the ground crew member was included in this photo, albeit slightly in the back row, peering over the top turret gunner's shoulder.

My Father's Photo of Crew Members in Front of "Bomb Boogie." Crew Members: Back row, left to right: S/Sgt. Dean W. Millward, Waist Gunner; S/Sgt. Donald L. Hayes, Tail Gunner; S/Sgt. R. D. Hatton, Ball Turret Gunner; T/Sgt. Raymond R. Thompson, Top Turret Gunner; Sgt. Silas Williams, Ground Crew; S/Sgt. Norbert F. B. Swierz, Waist Gunner. Front row, left to right: T/Sgt. John B. Wenninghoff, Radio; Lt. Chauncey H. Hicks, Bombardier; 1st Lt. Elwood D. Arp, Pilot; 2nd Lt. Nathan Weltman, Navigator; 2nd Lt. Howard Sherman, Copilot.

The Eighth Air Force routinely took pictures of all the aircrews with their aircraft. Fortuitously, the Army Air Corps had the wherewithal and foresight to ensure this single act happened—simplistic compared to everything else. After the war ended, it was a treasure for each airman to have these pictures to remember a time that most people could not relate to or were trying to forget. I know my father kept his photos safe with him his entire life. I wish I had asked him at some point to pull them out of the drawer and go over them with me in detail. Not because I needed to know who these young men were, although now I would appreciate hearing stories about their personalities, but most of all, to show him that I cared and was interested.

After arrival in Europe on June 3, 1943, my father, Staff Sergeant Hayes (tail gunner), was most likely transferred to another location where he was briefed and updated on the ETO before being assigned to a group. He arrived at Bassingbourn on June 25, 1943, the same day as his pilot, Lieutenant Arp; his copilot, Lieutenant Sherman; Technical Sergeant Wenninghoff (radio operator); and Staff Sergeant Millward (waist gunner). The five made up five of the crew pictured in the official photo in front of their plane.

Four additional crew members from the ditched "Old Ironsides" crew made nine—Technical Sergeant Hicks (bombardier), Staff Sergeant Hatton (ball turret gunner), Staff Sergeant Swierz (waist gunner), and Staff Sergeant Thompson (top turret gunner). The navigator, 2nd Lieutenant Weltman, made up the tenth crew member. These ten airmen eventually joined up to compose the principal ten-man crew pictured in front of a plane called "Bomb Boogie." They did not all start together, but, ultimately, the stars aligned, and they all united for their official crew photo on August 31, 1943, their third to last mission.

The "Bomb Boogie" crew pictured in their official photo only flew their last three missions together as an entire group. However, a few flew every mission together, like my father and John Wenninghoff, the radio operator. My father also flew with Lieutenant Arp, the pilot, on all his missions, except the fateful first. And as my father's missions increased, so did the same crew members' participation on each flight. After they parachuted out of their aircraft and survived their first mission, with "Bomb Boogie" miraculously remaining exquisitely intact, they continued solidifying as a team. They were thrown together by the prevailing circumstances—Ragged Irregulars becoming more regular with each mission. There was nowhere else to go but up.

I am sure they had highs and lows, with some missions more straightforward and synchronized than others. I never heard the excruciating details of each mission other than the freezing cold temperatures, but one story stood out.

According to one of my sisters, my father swore it was so cold up there in the plane that the crew members would bring buckets of cream, leftover or "borrowed" from breakfast. After high school and before he enlisted, my father worked at Franklin Creamery in Brockton, Massachusetts. He had learned something about making ice cream, and I trust he played a significant role in initiating those "buckets of cream" escapades. And yes, when they returned home safely, there would be *iced cream* for all—an exquisite example of the indomitable American spirit.

— 28 —

The Dailies

Often forgotten is the work of tens of thousands of non-combatant clerks and record keepers whose jobs were to capture the administrative minutia of the process of war on paper.

—The 91st Bomb Group Memorial Association

The Daily Reports, otherwise known as the "Dailies," were the day-to-day records of the four individual squadrons that made up the 91st Bomb Group. These reports chronicled each squadron's missions and movements from inception through the war's end.

An introduction to the Dailies and a tribute to those who wrote them are featured on the 91st Bomb Group Memorial Association website: "From our viewpoint today, the Second World War was a black-and-white pageant of men and machines battling across or above a grainy, forgotten landscape. War is a narrative voiced by calm, analytical announcers who examine the past from an academic distance. Their efforts, while doubtless tedious at the time, provide an outstanding backdrop against which the war plays out in practical terms."

And what a fantastic backdrop the Dailies proved to be. The information garnered in these daily reports is bountiful, and one can literally feel transported back in time. I read all the Dailies for the 401st Squadron from the start of the war to the finish. By the time I concluded, I had begun to recognize names and felt a connection to so many of these young men who, at first, were only typeset names on a page.

For example, there was the account of an airman who survived his plane crashing in the English Channel, staying in the water for thirty minutes until British sailors rescued him. After his rescue, his superiors granted him leave to go to the English countryside at Moulsford Manor to rest and recuperate. He returned to duty, only to have what appeared as a mental breakdown.

The author of the Dailies described the details under the heading "Casualties" as follows: "Mission in Action—Sgt bailed out of plane over St. Omer. For no apparent reason he left his post and ran through the ship hollering for the crew to bail out, whereupon he himself left the ship from door in the waist. Remainder of crew did not follow. Aircraft was not in any trouble at the time, but the flak was bursting close to the aircraft."

I couldn't help but wonder what happened to this poor fellow, so I looked him up on the American Air Museum in Britain website. I was relieved to find that he was captured without injury and spent the remainder of the war in the same POW camp as my father. His personal page stated he was a leader in the POW camp, so it appeared he survived the war physically and hopefully mentally.

Unfortunately, during this time, there were insufficient means of identifying when this brave young man and others like him needed a little more rest and recuperation (R&R) before these incidents were bound to occur. As noted in *The Anatomy of Courage* by Lord Moran, the author stated, "Courage is will-power of which no man has an unlimited stock, and when in war it is used up, he is finished. A man's courage is the capital that he is always spending. The call on the bank may be only the daily drain of the front line or a sudden draft threatening to close the account."

According to Lord Moran's description, it seemed a person only had so much courage stored up before it became depleted. How do you detect when courage is down to its last pennies, and the soldier is becoming overrun by fear or needs to be reenergized before continuing his duties? What are the early signs and symptoms to identify an impending crisis, and as Lord Moran pointed out, "In time to rest a soldier who was not wearing well, that he might once more quit himself like a man."

More than likely, there was not enough time to rest sufficiently during this period in history, and with limited manpower in those early war years, when one soldier rested, others did not.

The military granted leaves to the men after a traumatic incident, such as ditching their aircraft in the North Sea or witnessing their fellow crewmates die or suffer injuries. In the Dailies, some airmen were granted short leaves to Moulsford Manor, one of sixteen country homes or "flak houses," as the men sardonically referred to them. These country homes housed the airmen for R&R from the stress of active duty—such as flying missions and the daily experiences of witnessing their buddies leave on raids and not return.

The airmen were granted a one-week rest during their twenty-five to thirty mission tours to escape the horrors of war, and sometimes more if the situation was deemed necessary. The American Red Cross ran the homes, and a resident medical officer provided care or medical advice. Scanning all the Dailies from 1943, I did not observe that the Army Air Corps ever granted my father a pass to Moulsford Manor. He was most likely not at Bassingbourn long enough, and parachuting out over England on his first mission did not fall under the category of requiring R&R. He had just arrived.

Continuing to examine the 91st Bomb Group Dailies, I was convinced that none of the squadrons held as much detailed, concise, and colorful information as the 401st Dailies, my father's squadron. The author of these Dailies was Captain F. G. Davison. He wrote the Dailies for 1942 and 1943; then it was turned over to another record keeper from 1944 to the end of the war in 1945. There is a noticeable difference between Captain Davison's notes and that of the other scribes, as far as the formatting, the amount of information he included, the attention to detail, and the apparent pride and gusto he poured into what could have been a mundane job. He clearly loved his duty and the young airmen he wrote about daily.

From the first day the 401st Bomb Squadron was activated, on May 16, 1942, at MacDill Field in Tampa, Florida, to Captain Davison's last entry on December 30, 1943, I felt transported on the same life-changing journey these young men had embarked on. In these Dailies, it was evident that they started as a young, fledgling group of boys, full of promise and eager to begin their missions. They progressed to a group of seasoned airmen quickly introduced to the terror of war and all too wary of the dangers ahead each day as they boarded their planes and took off into enemy territory.

In 1942, the 401st Squadron Dailies commenced with a light tone. The captain filled his entries with descriptions of the friendly towns, good food, parties, and sports activities the 401st experienced before embarking to the European Theater.

The May 31, 1942, entry described the group getting settled at MacDill Field:

> Usual excitement of getting acquainted and finding out their special duties with some flying by the pilots—most of them being checked out on B-17s. Nice base—good food—nice surroundings, war at its best, here's hoping the rest of it will be half as nice.

On June 22, 1942, the squadron was transferred to Walla Walla Army Air Base in Washington.

> Life starts at Walla Walla, Washington. It's a nice little town with many beautiful residential sections. As quarters were not finished all officers secured their own billets off the post, and were extremely fortunate to find rooms with the better families of the town. The Enlisted men were housed in new barracks—were moved around quite a bit, but finally settled down to a regular round of activity. Squadrons maintained their own mess halls and how those boys were fed. We officers ate most of our meals with them and raised quite a howl when we were forced to eat at the Officer's Mess when it was completed the latter part of our stay there. A few Beer Busts were had and appreciated by all those present and missed by those who stayed away.

Oh, those halcyon days; if only the 91st Bomb Group, 401st Bomb Squadron, would have been able to stay in Walla Walla. But then one would also have to wish if only Germany would have remained inside Germany.

Captain Davison goes on to describe the daily activities that primarily consisted of training in preparation for their overseas assignments. On August 23, 1942, he wrote:

> The best of friends must part for awhile—Air echelon departs for its
> staging duties and to get those new airplanes we've been promised;
> See you later boys!!!

Over the next month, he described the Ground Echelon departing on the *Queen Mary* and eventually arriving at the air base in Kimbolton, England, on September 13, 1942. The first planes of the Air Echelon arrived on October 6, 1942. The following note expressed the excitement of the first big new birds arriving at the air base:

> They sure looked good to us and were welcomed by the ground crew.
> Such loving care no new planes ever received as was lavished on them
> by their respective crews—new life in the squadron.

Shortly after that, a brief paragraph stated that one of their new planes (one out of thirty-six) crashed en route from Gander to Prestwick, Scotland, flying through the fog and killing all but two aboard. All the crew names and their roles are called out in detail. This incident was the first tragedy described in the captain's notes and a harbinger of many more to come. After this incident, I observed a noticeable shift in the captain's writing tone—more matter of fact and filled with the required, essential details, but minus many of the striking observations and light-hearted, colorful descriptions displayed previously.

On October 14, 1942, the captain recorded the swift move from Kimbolton to Bassingbourn in the Dailies:

> The organization moved from Kimbolton to Bassingbourn with
> the 91st Bomb Group. The move was made by truck convoy over
> a distance of 30 miles and time of arrival was 1830 hours. The Air
> Echelon brought over their planes.

There was no mention of the haste this move entailed, ordered by Commander Wray at the spur of the moment. For Captain Davison, the scribe of the 401st Bomb Squadron, it was a relatively staid description and most likely intentional in its brevity, describing such a monumental (and somewhat unauthorized) event.

On November 8, 1942, a note is capitalized describing the 401st squadron's first mission:

TOO MUCH EXCITEMENT AROUND FOR THE
SQUADRON GOES ON ITS FIRST MISSION. TARGET
ABBEVILLE, FRANCE. SQUADRON SUPPLIED
FIVE AIRCRAFT.

There are no reported casualties on this first mission. As the missions got underway, Captain Davison developed the following format for each day he transcribed the happenings of the 401st Bomb Squadron: Date, Personnel Changes, Ground School information, how many aircraft the squadron supplied for the mission, the identifying number of the aircraft, altitude at target, bombs on target, and a brief description of the mission, providing there was something he considered out of the ordinary or a situation that warranted further explanation.

On some missions, he described the claims the gunners made about shooting down enemy aircraft. Another section gave all the crew members' names, including their roles and if they received credit for the mission. He included information on whether a plane had to abort the mission and the reason why.

In 1942, the 401st Squadron only flew two missions—one on November 8 and one on November 9. I noticed that on November 9, Stanley T. Wray flew with this mission to Saint-Nazaire, France. The 401st put up two of the fourteen planes that made up the mission, and Colonel Wray led the bomb group on a plane called "Kickapoo."

No aircraft were lost for the 91st Bomb Group, but several crew members were seriously injured, and one bombardier was killed. Captain Davison recounted the mission:

> This raid was commonly called the suicide raid as it was at low altitude instead of high altitude and subjected the Group to both light and heavy flak. The aircraft just pushed through one barrage after another and everyone feels that the Group was fortunate to come through with its aircraft.

The Dailies also described all the ground school activities when the men were not flying—such as link training in flight simulators, airplane recognition, skeet shooting, and target identification. I also noticed a "Lecture on Sex Morality" that the Army Air Corps required everyone in the squadron to attend every few months. The materials were blunt and covered everything a soldier would need to know about safe sexual habits. The military required their men to be on their best behavior with their host nation and stay out of trouble. Most importantly, the AAF could not afford their men to be out on leave for any amount of time with sexually transmitted diseases. In the 91st Bomb Group, that would be sufficient reason to be awarded a Rigid Digit Medal—something that did occur.

However, staying out of trouble was probably easier said than done. These young men were in a new country loaded with young English girls and far away from home. Everyone was looking for a good time in a period of history when times were unpredictable. This loose spirit was coupled with the strong possibility that one might not be around to enjoy another day. The airmen lived life to the fullest; there were dances at the bases, parties in the villages and the pubs, and adventures in the big cities, such as London, provided they were lucky enough to get passes for a few days.

Even the Dailies highlighted some of these diversional activities:

> October 27, 1943. SOCIAL: Squadron held dance at Aero Club on the Base with Molesworth Band supplying the music. WAAFs from Henlo and civilian girls were guests. Had chocolate ice cream much to the delight of everyone. Party hours 2000 to 2330 hours.

Thousands of men entered into relationships with British women despite the lectures and reading materials created to educate and warn the airmen about the dangers of not conducting oneself carefully. Many married, some had children, and thousands of "war brides" returned to the US after the war. I cannot comment on my father's behavior except to say he was a good Catholic boy and probably spent most of his spare time at the chapel at Bassingbourn—and I will half-jokingly leave it at that.

The 1943 Dailies were not as upbeat as the 1942 Dailies when the missions were first underway. The action intensified, and the casualties began to mount. The mood in the Dailies became more serious in what must have seemed like an overnight occurrence. The captain now became occupied detailing the casualties and fatalities that occurred mission after mission—men and planes that did not return to base.

Reading through the 1943 Dailies, I highlighted the missions that

"Bomb Boogie" flew and my father's missions. In the Dailies, I found "Bomb Boogie" had arrived in Europe almost four months before my father. She was delivered to Bassingbourn on March 9, 1943, and flew a total of twenty-three missions. A beautiful, colorful drawing of "Bomb Boogie" appears on the cover page of *B-17 in Action*, written by Larry Davis and illustrated by Don Greer. She is pictured alongside the "Memphis Belle," unloading their bombs on Wilhelmshaven, Germany, on March 22, 1943, a few months before my father arrived in England. Although "Bomb Boogie" is drawn flying next to the "Memphis Belle," this was inaccurate as the two planes were in different parts of the formation that day. Still, a lovely rendition by the artist of two magnificent aircraft.

My father kept notes on all his missions that he wrote after the war ended. Reading through the Dailies, I discovered that he took off on a total of thirteen missions. Two of the thirteen missions didn't count, possibly due to mechanical issues; therefore, the crew did not receive credit. Perhaps, for this reason, my father only included eleven missions in his written accounts. "Bomb Boogie" was the only plane my father flew on once he landed in England, and she became his new home away from home.

All my father's missions were thoroughly described in the 401st Dailies. That was the beauty of the Dailies. Anyone with a loved one who served in the Army Air Corps flying bomber planes can access these daily reports. Reading through the Dailies, it was possible to travel back in time and take a peek into the incredible experiences these young men endured daily. Of course, the amount of information captured depended upon the scribe, and the 401st Bomb Squadron of the 91st Bomb Group had one of the best.

— 29 —

A Good Pilot

*And I am not afraid. My plane may be shot away; But I shall
not fall, For I have wings—Wings not of wood or steel or stuff,
But wings of a firmer kind—Wings God gave my soul.*

—Major George Earl Preddy Jr.,
American World War II Ace Pilot

While reviewing information about my father's first fateful mission,
I uncovered an interesting story. In the Dailies, I noticed that the
same pilot, Lieutenant Pitts, flying "Bomb Boogie" on July 17, 1943
(my father's first mission), had to make another emergency landing in
England on July 26, 1943, nine days later. However, he was flying a different plane that day, not "Bomb Boogie."

The Dailies described the situation:

> Aircraft #679 had severe engine trouble just before reaching the
> enemy coast. Lt. Pitts, the pilot, deciding that the safety of his crew,
> ship, and himself, depended on staying with the formation for pro-
> tection, elected to do just that. Ordering the crew to jettison the
> bombs and salvo all loose equipment, he managed to stay with the
> formation for a while but gradually dropped back. His aircraft then
> began to receive constant and concentrated attacks from enemy air-
> craft for over an hour. But due to skillful flying, he was able to evade
> destruction, bring his aircraft safely across the channel, and land at
> an English base on the coast.

Out of many, this pilot's escapade was an incredible narrative peppered throughout these daily reports. The most astonishing part of this account was that this same pilot was the one who crash-landed "Bomb Boogie" at RAF Tempsford one week earlier. Lieutenant Pitts was getting to know the RAF Air Force bases more than he fancied. And the British were becoming all too familiar with this "Yank" pilot with a propensity for harrowingly making it over the English Channel.

Nevertheless, I was not quite finished exploring pilot Pitts's escapades and wondered how the rest of his flying career unfolded. So, traveling back to my old source, the American Air Museum in Britain website, I punched in his name under the People category. I gasped when the information came up on the page. That young, skillful pilot was shot down over Germany and was killed in action (KIA) on November 3, 1943, to Wilhelmshaven, in B-17 #4230805, along with six of his crew. The remaining three survived and became prisoners of war. It was his twenty-first mission—so close to going home for good.

Using the plane's serial number, I looked up more information on the aircraft Lieutenant Pitts was flying that fateful day. Another crew delivered the plane to Bassingbourn on September 24, 1943, only about a month earlier—a brand-new aircraft that had only flown two missions. Someone had named that plane "Bomb Boogie's Revenge." Since Lieutenant Pitts was the only pilot to fly this plane since it arrived at Bassingbourn, it seems he claimed naming rights, perhaps in honor of the original "Bomb Boogie" that had gotten him home without harm only a few months prior under the most hazardous of circumstances.

Sadly, "Bomb Boogie's Revenge" could not fly him and his crew back to base on that tragic November mission in 1943. When I read the Dailies, the squadron sent out six planes that day, and only three returned. Thirty men in the 401st Bomb Squadron were killed or became prisoners of war. The other three 91st Bomb Squadrons had minimal casualties. Regardless, I am sure it was one of the more somber days for the Ragged Irregulars group, having lost a good pilot who, time after time, had brought several of these young airmen back to the safety of Bassingbourn.

During my father's time in the Eighth Air Force, the summer and early fall of 1943, attrition rates were high, with only a few bomber crews making it to their twenty-fifth mission. As the war progressed, with the help of improved technology—specifically fighter planes that could fly longer distances—these numbers began to decrease. By the war's end, the Eighth Air Force would claim 47,000 casualties (about half of the USAAF losses), with over 26,000 deaths. While these numbers are high, they might not have caught my attention as they do now, painfully aware that each number represents a story—like the good pilot and most of his crew going down in flames over the skies of Nazi Germany.

— 30 —

Little Friends

*Like Shepherd Dogs protecting a flock, fighters hover above, below
and on the flanks of bomber formations to ward off attackers.*

—*AAF* The Official Guide to the Army Air Forces

During the last few months of 1943, over 2,000 men of the Eighth Air
Force had been killed in action. On August 17, 1943, the Eighth lost
sixty Flying Fortresses on one raid alone—the infamous Schweinfurt-
Regensburg mission. Their crews, 600 men, were either killed in action
or taken prisoner, with only a small percentage that managed to evade
capture. In a follow-up debriefing, as the commanders discussed what
needed to change, one young man in the group yelled out, "We need
better damn fighters!"

During those initial years of the war, especially in 1943, when my
father flew his missions, the Eighth Air Force suffered some of its highest casualties. "The bomber will always get through" was the thought of
the top brass; however, this proved wrong. The bombers needed protection against the German Luftwaffe. At the beginning of the war,
British and American fighter planes—the Spitfires, P-38 Lightnings,
and P-47 Thunderbolts—did not have the range to escort the bombers
into Germany.

As the bombers flew missions deeper and deeper into the Third Reich,
their "Little Friends" could only accompany them a limited distance until

they ran low on fuel and had to turn around to make it back to their bases. The German fighter pilots knew this and would wait until the fighters turned back before attacking the heavy bombers. At this point, the bombers would fly unaccompanied to their target and back, sustaining most of their losses. On the way back, the bombers, when in range, would be met again by their fighter escorts on the final leg of their journey home.

At the time, Air Force Commander Curtis LeMay became increasingly disturbed about these high casualty rates and was determined to develop more robust tactics. He concluded that the bomber planes needed to fly in tight formations (known as combat box or staggered formations) and could not veer from their formations as they neared their targets. In the past, the bombers would leave the formation, performing evasive maneuvers to escape enemy fighter planes. However, the Air Force commanders noticed that these maneuvers left the rest of the group unprotected.

Evasive maneuvers close to the impact point also decreased the precision of the bombs reaching their targets accurately. From here onward, bombers would fly "straight and level," usually under the control of the bombardier (and eventually one lead bombardier) for the last five to ten minutes approaching the target. LeMay often flew on the missions with his airmen and ordered anyone leaving the formation to be court-martialed. Tough tactics for a challenging situation paid off with fewer casualties until the primary solution would arrive—the long-range escort fighter planes.

In November 1943, the first effective fighter planes with extended range capability arrived in the ETO. They were called the P-51 Mustangs. These fighter planes were faster and could fly the longer, vital distances deep into Germany and back again. Living up to their expectations, the Mustangs were crucial in escorting bombers to deep-penetration targets such as Berlin.

A new commanding officer also led the Eighth Air Force, with General Doolittle replacing General Eaker. General Doolittle changed tactics significantly, allowing the P-51s to range ahead of the bombers, not maintaining close contact. This allowed the fighters to engage the Luftwaffe at a distance, lowering casualties among the bombers. Once free of escort duties, upon returning, the fighter pilots were instructed to hit any target of opportunity on the ground.

By early 1944, this effectively destroyed the Luftwaffe's capability, turning the tide of the air war to favor the Americans and their Allies to the point that they were unopposed by the Luftwaffe at the time of the Normandy invasion. Unfortunately, it was a little too late to help my father, the "Bomb Boogie" crew, and countless other crews and planes shot down by enemy fire in 1942 and most of 1943. But, at last, help was on the way for all the remaining bomber boys that followed.

Similar to how the heavy bombers were rendered vulnerable when injured or flying out of formation, the fighter pilots were limited in terms of how many seconds of ammunition they could carry. I often wondered about their tactics and the dog fights during the bomber raids. At first, I thought they were showing off, but then I learned that a fighter plane only had about thirty seconds of ammunition; it had to be used sparingly, and it had to be right on target. As soon as they ran out of ammo, they were sitting ducks, and their experienced foes could easily recognize the situation.

General Doolittle summed up the skills needed to be a fighter pilot as follows: "To become an ace, a fighter must have extraordinary eyesight, strength, and agility, a huntsman's eye, coolness in a pinch, calculated recklessness, a full measure of courage—and occasional luck!" And he might have added a P-51 Mustang! Other than that, it was easy peasy.

In 1942, when the Americans entered the war, the British were bombing only at nighttime. Having tried daytime precision bombing and sustaining heavy losses, the RAF had decided to change their strategy to attack only at night. They also adopted "area" or "carpet bombing"—bombing large areas without a clear distinction if their bombs exploded on military and civilian targets. Another reason that prompted the British to "take off their white gloves" and pursue carpet bombing was when the Nazis relentlessly began nightly raids over their beloved London and other cities not known primarily for being military targets. Hence, the British delivered more of the same back to Germany—random nighttime bombing over cities with dense civilian populations and military targets alike.

When the Americans first arrived in England, leaders in Britain insisted they should adopt nighttime bombing with the RAF. Ira Eaker, the Eighth Air Force Bomber Commander, argued that the Americans would bomb during the day, and the British could continue to strike at night. In truth, Ira Eaker found nighttime bombing distasteful—indiscriminately bombing civilians, churches, and homes. He argued for strategic bombing—missions during the day with clear views of the military targets. He said, "We will do things our way."

At the Casablanca Conference in January 1943, this argument came to a head between Churchill and Eaker. When Eaker adopted the words "round-the-clock bombing," Churchill liked that phrase, which settled the dispute.

Another reason Americans were notably confident daytime bombing would succeed is that they had arrived with their B-17 Flying Fortresses equipped with twelve .50-caliber machine guns and the Norden Bombsight—a top-secret instrument that supported precision bombing. The Americans touted that the Norden Bombsight was so accurate that the bombardier could drop a bomb into a pickle barrel from 20,000 feet. However, this did not prove to be entirely correct. Nor was the instrument top secret as the Germans had received information in advance from a spy posted in the US who had worked on the project.

One of the advantages of the Norden Bombsight was that it synchronized with the automatic pilot function. In *One Last Look*, a pilot summarized the process: "You flip on your automatic pilot, and the switch coupling it to the Norden Bombsight, and wherever your bombardier aims his bombsight is where the plane flies. As a pilot, all you do is hold a constant airspeed and altitude . . . and the bombardier controls all the rest." In theory, the Norden Bombsight allowed the bombardier to drop bombs more accurately by continually calculating the conditions as the bomber approached the target.

The bombardier pre-set specific inputs such as bomb type, altitude, and airspeed. He would get a drift angle from the navigator's drift meter, see the target through the lens of the sight and make adjustments accordingly. The process and incredible calculations necessary were much more intricate than described here, but it operated quite well in perfect conditions. However, under combat conditions, with flak rocking the aircraft, smokescreen or clouds obscuring targets, and changes in wind direction between the high altitude and the ground, bombing with the Norden Bombsight had less than desired precision and sometimes missed targets entirely.

This inaccuracy of the Norden Bombsight during combat demanded that the Air Force develop other complementary tactics. At the beginning of the war, each bombardier was responsible for aiming and dropping his bombs independently. To create improved accuracy, the Air Force developed the lead bombardier procedure. The Air Force commanders picked highly trained crews to be in the lead bomber role, in charge of aiming and dropping their bombs first. Then the rest of the bombers would follow suit.

In *One Last Look* by Kaplan and Smith, Frank Nelson, a lead navigator in the 487th Bomb Group, described the process as follows: "The group lead crew performed all the navigation and timing for the arrival over the Impact Point. Also, there was a lead crew for each squadron. Each squadron dropped its bombs when its lead ship dropped."

"Bomb Boogie" With Her Bomb Doors Open. The caption reads: "Approaching the target, the bomb-bay doors are opened electrically. The bombardier is over his sight. He and the pilot are guiding the big plane on the 'bomb run.' This is the crucial point of a bombing mission. This plane, the Boeing B-17 Flying Fortress 'Bomb Boogie' is attached to the 91st BG Europe."

"Bomb Boogie" Dropping Her Bombs. The caption reads: "Boeing B-17 airplane dropping incendiary bombs over Germany." This same photo is also included in the book, *The Ragged Irregulars of Bassingbourn.* The author, Marion H. Havelaar, writes his caption: "'Bomb Boogie,' training its bomb load. Careful observation reveals the ball turret gunner sighting through the open bomb bays checking the release of the bombs for the pilot."

After dropping their bombs, they would head back to England, praying they would not be hit by flak or shot down by enemy fighters. The planes were often so shot up and crippled that they depended on the fighter escorts to meet them after target and protect them from attacks. The pilot had to make tough choices—aim to stay with the formation, drop to a low level, try to make it to a neutral country such as Sweden or Switzerland, give the order to parachute out, or attempt to make a forced landing. The pilot actually had one other choice—to gamble that the plane would make it over the channel, and he could safely land it in England.

With this last choice, the crew would lighten the weight, even dropping the ball turret and flak jackets. They might also have to ditch in the North Sea with hopes of a quick rescue in the frigid waters. Not until they crossed the English Channel and reached England were they able to relax a bit—but they still had to hope they could land safely.

Often, they brought back their planes so beat up, flying with one out of four engines still functioning, that the crew on the ground wondered how these magnificent birds ever made it home. The B-17s were not indestructible but often withstood massive barrages. They undoubtedly lived up to their beloved nickname—Flying Fortresses.

By 1944, the heavy bombers, on their way to their targets, blanketed the daylight skies, and the contrails of their fighter escorts scattered the heavens. This incredible sight was a tremendous morale boost to the people in occupied Europe. A friend whose mother was with the Dutch Resistance in the Netherlands said he remembered her saying how uplifting it was to see the thousands of American bombers passing overhead, knowing the war against Germany would end someday. This same friend's father, a forced laborer in a factory in Germany, said he looked up one day and counted exactly 1,080 bombers (thirty groups of thirty-six bombers) flying overhead. He exclaimed, "They stretched for as far as I could see! I knew then that I would be liberated someday. I love America."

It was fascinating that this type of aerial warfare my father engaged in could only have occurred during the span of World War II. The dropping of the atomic bomb on Hiroshima and Nagasaki to end the war in the Pacific instantly made large-scale battles fought in airplanes obsolete. My father and other young men like him were in uncharted territory at an extraordinary time in history. They were just doing their jobs and perhaps had glimmers of their special roles. Still, decades later, the uniqueness of these air campaigns remains dazzling and almost incomprehensible.

—31—

The Missions

The amazing thing about it to this reporter is how these boys fly day after day with the nonchalance of a high school kid driving a Ford down Olive Street.

—Virginia Irwin,
American Journalist during World War II

From his June 3, 1943, arrival date in England to September 6, 1943, my father completed additional training and flew bombing missions in his B-17 plane nicknamed "Bomb Boogie." As previously noted, each B-17 aircraft had ten crew members: the pilot, the copilot, the navigator, the bombardier, the flight engineer/top turret gunner, the radio operator, and two waist gunners, the ball turret gunner, and the tail gunner.

My father was the tail gunner, and, as the name implied, his designated area was in the plane's tail, where he operated two .50-caliber machine guns. The tail gunner on a B-17 was not near the other crew members, except during takeoff and landing when, due to safety reasons, they were stationed in the radio compartment with the other gunners.

In *A Tail Gunner's Tale*, author Gerald E. McDowell described a tail gunner's feelings:

> As I think back, it sure was lonely back in the tail position. To get there, after passing the tail wheel, I got down on my hands and knees and crawled some 10-12 feet or more to the tail gun position. I had

twin .50s on a pivot mount, twin canisters of .50 caliber ammo, and 500 rounds on each side of me. Also, twin oxygen systems in case one were blown away, as they were sometimes. A piece of armor plate about eighteen inches wide and perhaps three-eighths of an inch thick was directly in front of my chest and tapered so I could reach around it to operate the old "fifties." I sat on a "bicycle" type seat, kneeling right in the back of the armor plate as I viewed the sky through a piece of two and three-eighths-inch battle plate glass directly in front of me. This gave a perfect line on the iron grid sight mounted outside. The very thick crystal-clear glass would stop machine-gun bullets, even a 20mm cannon shell hitting from a wide angle. So, you feel safe as combat would allow, but isolated from the crew if you should need help for some reason, such as being wounded.

I had heard stories of tail gunners losing their oxygen supply and dying back in the tail, unbeknownst to the rest of the crew. My father also had tales of passing out on one mission due to a lack of oxygen. Luckily, he prevailed, perhaps by good radio communication and another crew member realizing there was an issue and fixing the problem. If the situation couldn't be rectified, the pilots would have to quickly descend to lower altitudes or even abort missions due to oxygen supply problems. In addition, flights were extremely cold at those high altitudes, and I recall my father saying how freezing his hands would become handling the guns.

A typical day in my father's life at Bassingbourn proceeded as follows: The airmen were either completing their training, flying on missions to Germany and Nazi-occupied Europe, or having a day off between missions. If they were assigned to fly a mission, Air Force personnel would wake them before dawn. They would be served a hearty breakfast and then go to the briefing room to hear about the day's mission. The aircrew would then separate, with each undertaking specific briefings and duties. Bombardiers would get familiarized with the target and approach using aerial photos and then pick up the Norden Bombsight to install in the aircraft. Navigators would get updates from intelligence about what flak areas to avoid and a weather update. Radiomen would be briefed on the day's frequencies and codes. Gunners would check their .50-caliber guns and install them in the aircraft.

All would get dressed in their special gear for the frigid temperatures at high altitudes and pick up their parachutes, flak suits, escape kits, and maps—leaving all personal items behind. With everything in order, the crew would go out to their plane and wait until the control tower gave the okay to start their engines and head off for the mission: "Gentlemen, you are cleared for takeoff—and good luck," was the typical tower greeting. When they returned, they would go to the briefing room and debrief.

As previously mentioned, my father flew thirteen missions (receiving credit for eleven) from England to Germany and Nazi-occupied Europe. Of my father's eleven credited missions, there are three that stand out: the first mission, when he had to parachute out over England, the seventh mission when he flew on the Schweinfurt-Regensburg raid, and the eleventh and last official mission when he was shot down and parachuted out over Nazi-occupied France. Perhaps each mission had its significance for my father, but these three missions seemed the most notable when reading about them in his personal notes.

Earlier, I briefly described the story of my father's first mission when he parachuted out over England. His seventh mission was when the Air Force decided to strike two cities simultaneously—Schweinfurt and Regensburg. This mission was a memorable day for my father; he wrote a one-page summary of the day entitled "Synopsis of Schweinfurt-Regensburg Mission." In his notes, he stated that he had "vivid recollections of that lucky 7th."

He wrote, "On August 17, 1943, the USAAF and the German Luftwaffe slugged it out over Europe in the bloodiest and costliest air battle of WWII" (to that date). The Eighth Air Force lost sixty B-17 bombers that fateful day. The 91st Bombardment Group (BG) had sent out twenty-four planes: eighteen in the 91st BG formation and six as part of the 101st composite group.

In his synopsis of the mission, my father's recollection of the day went as follows: "Twelve out of the original 18 were shot down, two ditched in the channel, and three were so crippled with battle damage they were forced to land at other bases on their return from the mission. My pilot aborted the mission over Germany."

In his book *Double Strike*, Edward Jablonski tells how "Bomb Boogie" ran into mechanical problems once deep into the Third Reich, and the pilot had to turn around because they had lost oxygen supply. Jablonski summarized the plight of "Bomb Boogie" and her crew during the Schweinfurt-Regensburg mission using direct quotes from my father describing the event:

> But on August 17, Bomb Boogie developed oxygen trouble. Tail gunner Don Hayes recalls that as a rather memorable, but for his crew relatively uneventful, mission. "We got almost to the German border (over France) when we had to abort. As I recall one engine was acting up, the ball turret was acting up and one of the crew members (waist, I believe) couldn't get oxygen. What had occurred was that the oxygen system simply went bad and would not function in the cockpit at all and low in the ball turret position; pilot Elwood Arp had no alternative but to swing around, descend to a breathable altitude and head back home." Then as Hayes would recall, "we landed back at Bassingbourn and waited . . . and waited for the others to return." Arp had set their Fortress down at 1423 (after unloading the bomb load in the Wash [a bay on the North Sea]); they would have a long wait before the others returned—those that would.

Once again, my father drew the lucky straw. This was not the case for all of his buddies at Bassingbourn, who had set out early that morning never to return. After each mission, the control tower would count the planes as they flew back later that day. Even the villagers got into the habit of counting the planes that would go out in the early morning hours and then count them up again when they returned later in the day. On August 17, 1943, sixty planes in the Eighth Air Force did not make it back to base. "Bomb Boogie" was one of the fortunate ones to make it home to Bassingbourn.

I often wondered how my father felt that evening while waiting for his buddies to return. Did he feel relief that he had returned to the base unharmed? Was it devastating to him that all the other planes, each with ten crew members, never returned? Was he scared that on the next mission, that would be his fate?

— 32 —

Captured by Krauts

*Kraut: Older Slang: Disparaging and Offensive. A contemptuous
term used to refer to a German, especially a German soldier.*

—MERRIAM-WEBSTER DICTIONARY

On my father's eleventh and final mission, his plane was shot down by
German fighter planes and flak over Nazi-occupied France. All ten
crew members were able to parachute out and survive. Four of the
crew members managed to evade capture and eventually returned safely
to England with the help of the Resistance.

Six crew members, including my father, were captured and sent to
POW camps until the war ended. My father's parachute landed him on
a German fighter base in Reims, France, and he had no chance of escaping. When he finally hit the ground, he was surrounded by Germans,
pointing their guns at him. He surrendered and became a prisoner of
war. In his notes, he wrote, "Welcome committee on hand to greet me
before the silk settled."

Maybe my father was lucky once again—captured by soldiers and
landing in France. German civilians were outraged that the Allies had
bombed their cities, losing countless civilian and military lives. It was not
uncommon for Germans to shoot airmen in the sky or for civilians, both
men and women, to kill the young men when they touched the ground by
any means available to them. I have read stories of the German farmers

even pitchforking airmen to death. Imagine, after all the bomber boys had undergone in terms of daily survival to be captured and ultimately pitchforked by a Kraut.

Those words sound derogatory and undoubtedly not politically correct for this modern age. But war is war, and that was one of the words the American soldiers called the Germans during World War II—Krauts, Jerries, and other names. Kraut was used mainly by American soldiers and less by British soldiers, who preferred Jerry or Fritz. My father always called the Germans Krauts, specifically referring to the German prison guards he faced while he was a prisoner.

When he said the word *Kraut* back then, it seemed okay. It appeared he was separating the German people under the Nazis from the Germans before and after the war. There was a definite distinction. When I spoke with my grown son about calling Germans Krauts during World War II, he had never heard of the term. He asked, "What did the word signify?" I informed him it was because the German people were perceived to eat lots of sauerkraut. He said, "That's it?" I said, "Yep, that's it."

I recently had a friend who went back to Germany to visit friends and heard stories from their perspectives on being a German citizen during World War II. One family showed my friend family photos in her living room of innocent-looking German boys with blue eyes and blond hair who had attended Hitler Youth indoctrination schools, as was the practice at the time. They spoke of having no choice but to go along with the Nazi propaganda; otherwise, the Nazis would kill entire families.

My friend heard firsthand from survivors in Germany about the shame of living with this part of history. It reminded me of the red door exhibit at the Dutch Resistance Museum in Amsterdam. Which door would you have chosen? Still, somehow an entire nation got behind a man who promised a better tomorrow for the "Fatherland"—a future without Jews and other countries getting in the way. And they came incredibly close.

In the beautiful book *Belonging* by Nora Krug, she illustrated a poignant story of her family's involvement with the Nazi Party and her life struggle, generations later, to come to grips with *Heimat*, the German word for the place that first forms us. Unrelenting and tremendously brave, she asked her family and friends difficult questions, feeling guilt by association and aware that the answers might cause her more shame and pain. She traveled back to Germany, her birthplace, to understand why individual family members became involved with the Nazi Party—an uncle signing up in his teens and a grandfather joining at a later age.

She described why it was imperative she journey back into the past in the following sentences: "No matter how hard I look, a nagging sense of unease won't disappear. Perhaps the only way to find the Heimat that I've lost is to look back, to move beyond the abstract shame and ask those questions that are really difficult to ask—about my hometown, about my father's and my mother's families. To make my way back to the towns where each of them is from. To return to my childhood, go back to the beginning, follow the breadcrumbs, and hope they'll lead the way home."

In a way, she reminded me of my story, trying to uncover my father's history during World War II and the painstaking research it takes to unravel the past. She asked the same soul-searching question that I have often asked myself, "How do you know who you are, if you don't understand where you come from?" But that is where the comparison ended. She told a story of a German woman reckoning with her history and birthplace while I was uncovering and celebrating my father's contribution to fighting for freedom. I was proud of his participation in World War II. Admittedly, I was sometimes ashamed of his actions during my growing-up years, but never about his war years.

PART SIX

PRISONER
OF WAR

— 33 —

Missing in Action

*We were merely young men accepting our times. Some of
us fancied the role we played; others did not. In any case,
we did not go off into the sky shouting hosannas.*

—Elmer Bendiner,
The Fall of Fortresses, Navigator, 379th Bomb Group

When a pilot realized he could not save his plane, he would give the order to bail out. If there was enough warning or he still thought there was a chance to keep the aircraft aloft, he would first prepare the crew by communicating an alert: "Put on your chutes and stand by." Sometimes the situation was hopeless, and the scene unfolding became highly chaotic. The young crew frantically scrambled about to find their parachutes, trying to figure out which escape route they could exit. Often, there was no time to prepare as their final scenes unfolded and the plane with its crew fell to the ground.

After the Germans shot down my father's plane, the pilot explained the event months later after he had evaded capture and reached safety:

> On our way to target, number three engine was hit and the oil sump knocked out in a fighter attack. The oxygen bottles were turned into sieves. When I could not feather the prop, for lack of oil pressure, I said, "Put on your chutes and stand by; we're going down to cover." The waist gunners, who may not have caught the last two words, jumped immediately. We reached cloud cover at 5000 ft, but the

fighters came in again as soon as we emerged. Number two engine was hit, the controls were cut, and fell back in my lap. I gave the bail-out order, set up the automatic flight control equipment and destroyed the radio equipment.

My father, alone and deep in the plane's tail section, was able to parachute out and escape the damaged aircraft. While reading about "Bomb Boogie" in the book *Plane Names & Fancy Noses*, I was astonished to see a paragraph describing my father's firsthand account of that fateful day as the crew abandoned ship and parachuted out of their plane. The book's author, Ray Bowden, recounted how the mission to Stuttgart, Germany, on September 6, 1943, proved disastrous for the Eighth Air Force, particularly for the 91st Bomb Group. The absence of extra fuel tanks caused many planes to ditch into the North Sea due to the lack of fuel experienced on the return trip. It was thought that "Bomb Boogie" was one of the B-17 planes having to ditch, but not so:

> Don Hayes, tail gunner on the ship, and other crew members had already bailed out. Don's recollection of events was of the plane being hit in the first Fw190 pass over northern France when a 20mm shell exploded in the No. 3 engine, forcing her to fall behind the formation. Continued fighter attacks caused more damage and two flak bursts added to the mayhem, cutting intercom communication through the ship. Don attempted to crawl through the plane to assess the situation but ammunition boxes had jammed against the door preventing his movement. The crew began bailing out and he saw five chutes pop open below before he, too, decided to abandon the plane. He and others who had left the ship came down near Reims. Most were quickly rounded up and sent to POW camps, but three [*sic*] men including Lt. Arp (the pilot) managed to evade capture and eventually make their way to Spain.

When a plane goes down, and the crew does not return home, Air Force personnel back at the base immediately file a Missing Air Crew Report (MACR). Army Air Force headquarters required the air bases to submit these documents within two days after the aircraft and aircrew failed to return from their mission. Reports varied, but a typical,

complete file, including my father's MACR, consisted of a Missing Air
Crew Report, an Installed Weapons Report, an Eyewitness Report, and
the Map of Route Taken.

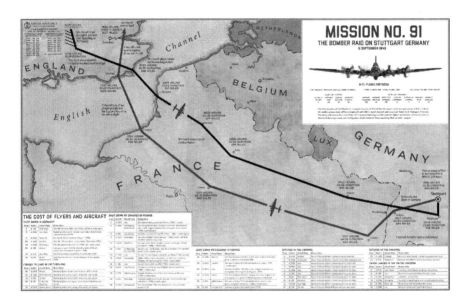

The Bomber Raid on Stuttgart, Germany. This was my father's last mission. "Bomb
Boogie" was shot down over northern France on her way to target on September 6,
1943. Three of the crew members bailed out near Reims, France. "Bomb Boogie"
continued north for approximately 125 miles, ultimately crashing down in Mons-en-
Pevele near Lille, France. The remaining seven crew members parachuted out just
before the plane crashed. The Eighth Air Force sent out 338 B-17s from sixteen
bomb groups on this fateful day. Forty-five aircraft were destroyed, and hundreds
of men lost their lives or went missing—proving it to be one of the more costly
missions of World War II.

The report's first section included the crew names, roles, ranks, serial
numbers, and specifications about the air base they flew out of and their
intended destination. Details about location, weather conditions, and
visibility at the time of the crash were also recorded, if available. Type of
aircraft, serial number, and engine information completed this section of
the report. Next, the Installed Weapons Report was a separate page and
listed all the weapons on board, along with their serial numbers.

The Eyewitness Report included stories from returning airmen who had witnessed the attack. Ideally, it included location at the strike time, hit by flak or fighters, how many parachutes opened, and how many crew members escaped. In my father's MACR report, the Eyewitness Report, recorded by a member of another nearby aircrew, described the strike:

> At 0840 hours, 16,000 feet, at 49°30' N, 03°35' E, A/C No. 763 was last seen going down under control. Two yellow-nosed FW-190s attacked formation at 3 o'clock. After this attack, our A/C fell out of formation, jettisoned its bombs, and headed slowly down. A/C was last seen going into clouds. As many as 6 chutes were reported seen, and a few crew members reported seeing some crew members of A/C No. 763 making delayed jumps.

Last, the complete MACR report included the Map of Route Taken. Directional arrows on the map outlined the navigation route the "Bomb Boogie" crew would have taken to Stuttgart and back had she not been hit by fighters and flak near Reims, France, on the way to the target. A black circle on the map indicated the last position of the downed aircraft. According to the coordinates given in the Eyewitness Report, "Bomb Boogie" was last sighted near Laval-en-Laonnois, France, about twenty-five miles northwest of Reims. Shortly after that, the pilot gave the order to bail and set up the automatic pilot.

It was somewhat sad to trace "Bomb Boogie's" path as she limped her way northwest approximately 125 miles until she finally crashed in the small village of Mons-en-Pevele, near Lille, France. This time around, the autopilot was not capable of landing her safely. Luckily, all the crew members managed to parachute out of the aircraft at various points, all ten parachutes opened up, and all ten survived their plane being shot out of the sky.

My father's MACR report was in two parts. First, the staff at Bassingbourn submitted an initial report of the crash on September 6, 1943. Second, military personnel presented a supplemental statement a year later, on September 19, 1944. The supplemental MACR report consisted of four individual interrogation statements from the four crew members who evaded capture. The Military Intelligence Service documented their stories upon returning to England seven, eight, and twelve months later in March 1944, April 1944, and September 1944.

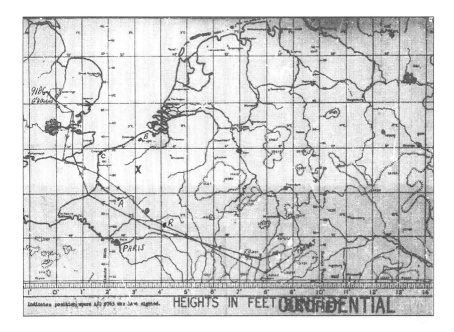

Map of Route Taken. The bottom of the map states: "Indicates position where A/C 763 was last sighted." The small black circle surrounded by another indicates where the plane was last sighted—near Laval-en-Laonnois, per the Eyewitness Report. The "X" north of where the aircraft was last seen shows the approximate spot where "Bomb Boogie" crashed in the village of Mons-en-Pevele, France. Additional bearings are: P=Paris, A= Amiens, France, C=Calais, France, B=Bruges, Belgium, and R=Reims, France.

The supplemental MACR documents submitted after the four crewmen returned and gave interviews held fascinating and disturbing new details. The first part of the document consisted of the information reported in March 1944 by crew member Chauncey Harold Hicks, the bombardier. Upon returning to England, he said he heard that one man went down with the ship and was believed to be the tail gunner. The paragraph under the title "Hearsay Information" stated, "Natives near the scene of the crash informed Hicks that one body was found in the plane and it is the opinion of source and others of the crew that it could only have been Sgt. Hayes, Tail Gunner."

Another report by the pilot, Elwood Arp, obtained in April 1944, stated that all crew members bailed out, and all chutes opened. "Pilot, co-pilot, top turret gunner, ball turret gunner on ground. 2 waist gunners bailed out early. One went down with the ship-believed to be Tail

Gunner." The third report by the copilot, Howard Sherman, did not mention information about the tail gunner's status, just question marks around my father's name and an MIA notation.

The last report obtained in September 1944 by Russ Hatton, the ball turret gunner who also evaded capture, stated the French reported they found a body in the aircraft after it had crashed. Hatton additionally noted that the Germans had removed the aircraft engine and hauled it away on trucks. The supplemental report's final section validated that four crew members evaded capture, and six crew members were POWs. Not until the last paragraph, at the bottom of the page, did the report confirm my father survived the crash: "Tail gunner was reported dead; proved false."

It is an indescribable feeling to unwittingly read your father listed as a body, dead in the aircraft. I wonder what all his crew thought when they believed my father, the tail gunner, was the only one out of the ten crew members to go down with the plane. Were they disturbed, or was there no time to think about losses? Was each crew member consumed with their thoughts of escaping and returning home alive? I never asked my father if he knew about this crash report, nor did I have the opportunity to meet any of his crewmates and ask them any of these questions.

So after carefully reviewing the final MACR documents, the following statements describe in sequence what transpired on that fateful morning of September 6, 1943, to "Bomb Boogie" and her crew on their way to target in Stuttgart, Germany.

At 0840 hours over northern France, traveling at 16,000 feet elevation, "Bomb Boogie" was attacked by two German fighter planes (Fw 190s) at three o'clock (on her mid-right side). They knocked out her number three engine and damaged the oxygen supply. The pilot told the crew, "Put on your chutes and stand by; we're going down to cover." According to the pilot, the two waist gunners may not have heard the last two words and bailed out immediately somewhere over Laval-en-Laonnois, France, the coordinates given in the Eyewitness Report.

A few minutes later, according to my father and reports by other crew members, the plane was hit by flak, cutting intercom communication throughout the aircraft. Shortly after that, my father was forced to assess the situation on his own after seeing a few parachutes open and amid the absence of an intercom system and the inability to communicate with other crew members. Trapped in the tail (blocked by scattered ammunition boxes) and unable to travel to the front of the plane to assess the situation, he also decided to bail out using the rear exit door. By that time, the aircraft was over Reims, France.

In the meantime, in what must have been a very chaotic situation, the pilot decided to stay with the plane and try to return to base. He took the plane down to cloud cover at 5,000 feet, reaching a breathable altitude—no longer having oxygen capability—hiding from the fighter planes in the safety of the clouds. According to the pilot, fifty minutes later, at 0930 hours, and around fifteen miles near Lille, France, they ran out of cloud cover, and the German fighter planes came in immediately for an attack from the rear, knocking out the number two engine and all the air controls. The pilot previously had ordered the ball turret gunner to be pulled into the aircraft, fearing the number three engine would explode. Essentially, this left the plane's rear empty and vulnerable, with the waist gunners and tail gunner already gone.

At this point, the pilot gave the order to bail, and the remaining seven crew members successfully parachuted out of the crashing plane. The radio operator was captured immediately, the top turret gunner evaded capture for three days, and the navigator evaded capture for two months. The remaining four crew members managed to evade capture for seven to twelve months, eventually making it back safely to England.

Additional documents called Escape and Evasion Reports were compiled for the four crew members who evaded capture. These documents described how the four young airmen initially evaded capture, traveled south through France, across the Pyrenees into Spain, and eventually back to England, aided by the French Resistance and Basque citizens. The reports are fascinating; decades later, they still portray the terror everyone involved in these journeys experienced.

The components of the Escape and Evasion Reports were structured and concise. The evader answered a series of questions followed by a free-form essay that described the evasion experience. Air Force personnel reviewed each report and made notations in the margins grouping the data into the following categories whenever possible: description of the crash, delays jump to specified feet, the situation at landing, first help, details that could be helpful for future aircrews, and journey arranged. The summary of these reports yielded valuable lessons and was shared with the airmen back at base, who could likely be in the same plight.

The young crew members seemed to have had comparable experiences, depending on who greeted them when they touched the ground. Four of the six who ended up in POW camps were captured immediately by German soldiers with no chance of escaping. Another, the top turret gunner, was captured three days later. One of the six, the navigator, initially managed to evade but was ultimately caught in Paris two months later. He ended up at Stalag Luft I POW camp. The Nazis sent the others to Stalag 17B. As previously mentioned, my father landed on a German fighter base in Reims, France, surrounded by German soldiers pointing their machine guns at him. He did not have a chance at escaping.

The stories were strikingly similar for the four crew members who evaded capture. All managed to land in farmland in the middle of beet, bean, and turnip fields. All commented that they had purposely delayed opening up their parachutes, following previous instructions, and that these delays were essential for survival. Opening up a parachute too soon exposed the airmen for more extended periods, allowing trigger-happy enemies a chance to shoot them in the sky. It also allowed Germans on the ground ample time to meet and greet them when they finally landed.

The pilot described a harrowing experience with his jump from the plane and trouble opening his chute: "I went out the nose hatch at 4000 ft and delayed my jump to 1500 ft. When I pulled the rip-cord, the chute did not open. I immediately pulled out the pilot chute and the rest billowed out automatically. I was still counting chutes when I bounced on a plowed field. I rolled over and got up without being bruised."

The copilot described his jump: "I bailed out through the bomb bays when the pilot gave the order. We were then at 4000 feet and I delayed my jump to approximately 800 feet, which is longer than I had intended and made a perfect landing. Those who had left before me were still up in the air. I came down in a beet field in which 25 people were working."

And the bombardier's description was, "The pilot gave the order to bail out. I went out the nose at about 4,000 feet, counted seven and pulled the rip-cord. My parachute jerked roughly. I hit hard in a turnip patch and twisted my ankle."

The airmen were immediately greeted by the French farmers and civilians, who quickly removed their parachutes and hid them in the fields. Pilot Arp describes his first contact with help: "I was still wearing my harness when a peasant grabbed my hand. As I was led away a farmer pulled off my chute. We traveled quickly along the hedgerows for a quarter of a mile and I was left with a man who had already collected two crew members."

After hitting down hard in the turnip field, the bombardier described his first contact with help: "About 30 people came up and helped me off with my parachute. They asked me if I was English and all wanted to kiss me when they found out I was American."

The Germans were already searching for the airmen in their motorcycles, trucks, cars, and on foot. The crew members found various hiding spots with the French farmers' help, some hiding in the fields as the Germans patrolled the area and later in barns with Germans staying in the same house. The copilot and pilot even hid in trees for two days.

"There were 40 in the patrol," the pilot later described in his report, "and they searched the fields for three days. They walked through the weeds carrying tommy guns and continually kicked at the earth. All the French in the area were questioned."

Not long after they had landed and initially hid in the fields, a French woman came out with a basket to pick beans. "The basket contained food and civilian clothing," said Pilot Arp. "She worked diligently and calmly until we had all changed and been fed. She told us, as she took them, that our leather jackets reflected the sun and had made it easy for her to spot us in the fields at a distance." Her advice was an example of the pertinent information the airmen would later pass on to help future airmen in the same predicament.

After three days of hiding, all the reports related the same story, which concerned the next step. Their French saviors took them to a place or person where their "journey was arranged." Nothing more was said or transcribed; that information seemed so top secret that it could not even be written in a confidential government report.

Several interesting comments about the journey's route were expressed without mentioning people or specific places. They all contained the following similar details. The course was south across the Pyrenees to Spain. It was six or seven months before they made the crossing, but it took three days when they finally set out on the trip. They traveled in the snow all the way. All four complained that they had foolishly given up their GI shoes, thinking they were conspicuous.

"During the crossing, I would have gladly given a hundred dollars for a pair of GI shoes," the pilot said. "The French shoes had pasteboard soles and my heels were frostbitten." They all complained of being very hungry and having little to eat on this segment of the journey.

When they returned to England, the crew members also provided tips that the airmen should keep their GI shoes and pay attention to the helpful lectures on parachute jumping. They emphasized that the airmen needed to communicate with the patriotic French farmers that they could not stay with them for long periods.

The copilot, Howard Sherman, summed it up in his last statement: "When you are staying with patriotic farmers, who have not yet contacted more organized help, make it clear to them that you wish to return to duty as soon as possible. They become so fond of airmen, that they always want them to 'stay for the invasion.'" The invasion would be almost a year away, but in the French people's minds, there seemed to be no doubt that the Americans would soon arrive.

The people in the Nazi-occupied countries looked to the Allies as their saviors. But in many ways, the ordinary citizens demonstrated unbelievable courage and bravery. They risked their lives and families if the Nazis caught them helping the Allied soldiers. Yet, they did not hesitate to help, fully knowing the consequences. The Resistance workers and other ordinary citizens chose the possibility of torture and death rather than living under an evil regime's subjugation.

In John Steinbeck's remarkable short novel, *The Moon Is Down*, he powerfully demonstrated the triumph of ideas and the people's power in the face of a brutal occupation. At the end of the book, there is a quote by the mayor of a small occupied town. As he marches to his execution, clairvoyantly, he declares to the occupying commander, "The people don't like to be conquered, sir, and so they will not be. Free men cannot start a war, but once it is started, they can fight on in defeat. Herd men, followers of a leader, cannot do that, and so it is always the herd men who win battles and the free men who win wars. You will find that is so, sir."

Hence, the Resistance. Forever resistance—and victory—for people longing to be free.

— 34 —

Stories from Camp

None of us would have said it aloud, but we all knew that persevering was about more than survival; it was an act of defiant faith.

—NED HANDY AND KEMP BATTLE,
The Flame Keepers

On September 6, 1943, my father became a POW for twenty-two months until the war ended in May 1945. Once the Germans captured the American airmen, the protocol was to transport them to Frankfurt, Germany, where the main transit/interrogation camp, Dulag Luft, was situated.

After a period of interrogation, which averaged about one week, the Germans sent the airmen to a designated POW camp. Per routine, my father would have been transported first to Frankfurt for interrogation before being sent to his final destination. Perhaps, at Dulag Luft, he met up with the rest of his crew, all undergoing interrogation before their POW camp assignments.

As I was reading stories about POW experiences at Dulag Luft, I gleaned that the captured airmen passed their time in solitary confinement in small cells with no windows and minimal food. Generally, the interrogations would begin after a few days of the downed airmen being locked up. The interrogators would ask the soldiers about their missions, how many planes were in their squadrons, what group they were from, and a barrage of other questions.

During such interrogations, the Air Force had trained the airmen to provide only their name, rank, and serial number, as required under the terms of the Geneva Convention. When the chief interrogator realized he could not extract further information, he might inform the soldier that he already knew everything about him. He would then spew out all the details he was privy to, hoping to catch the airmen off guard and obtain additional facts.

In *A Tail Gunner's Tale*, Gerald E. McDowell said, "There was no doubt that the living conditions here at Dulag Luft were expressly designed to lower morale and cause mental depression. Yet most of us successfully withstood the harsh treatment and refused to give any information to the Germans other than name, rank, and serial number."

In 1943, the year my father would have been at Dulag Luft, thirty-five to forty primary interrogators questioned the 8,000 or so prisoners that passed through the camp walls. The Luftwaffe interrogators had their specialty areas—either fighter or bomber expertise. Of all the interrogators, there was one German who stood out. His name was Hanns Scharff, referred to as the "Master Interrogator at Dulag Luft."

His specialty was with fighter pilots, so I am unsure if he would have interrogated my father and crew. At any rate, he was skillful at discreetly getting information from the crew members without them realizing they had divulged anything of importance. He treated his prisoners with respect and dignity using psychological, not physical, techniques, making them drop their guard and converse with him even though they were trained to remain silent.

One POW commented, "Hanns could probably get a confession of infidelity from a nun." However, not all interrogators employed the powers of psychology. Some resorted to brute threats, torture, and even execution—definitely not part of the terms outlined in the Geneva Convention.

In 1942, the beginning of the American daylight bombing campaign over Nazi-occupied Europe, the Germans shot down, captured, and interrogated the first American airmen. On July 21, 1942, the USAAF published a guide called "Instructions For Officers And Men Of The Eighth Air Force In The Event Of Capture." This three-page document was presented to every member of the Eighth Air Force and summarized the following: What Information Should Be Given To The Enemy (Name, Rank, and Serial Number only), What The Enemy Will Try To Find Out From You, How The Enemy Will Try To Learn These Things from You, and How You Can Defeat The Enemy.

The document emphasized that the airmen must remain silent and warned of eavesdropping, including microphones hidden everywhere by their German captors. Information stressed that the enemy would try to wear the airmen down by prolonged interrogations or catch them off guard by flattery, casual conversations, and feigned sympathy. "It is good to be patriotic, but you can best prove your patriotism by keeping silent." And another reminder, "The enemy will not treat you nicely and offer you drinks because he likes you. He is after information to use against us."

My father never spoke about being interrogated, and I could not help but wonder how it went for him. Did he only give his name, rank, and serial number, following his training and the guidelines in the Geneva Convention, or did he succumb to other types of pressure?

Knowing my father and his simple tastes, I don't believe he would have been tempted by creature comfort offers such as food or warm clothing, nor would he have intentionally betrayed his fellow crew members. I would like to imagine he would have withstood harsh treatment for his country and the Eighth Air Force. That was his nature. However, he loved his cigarettes, drink, and winning at poker, mostly when the bets were high. Those would have been the weaknesses that a wily interrogator would have figured out—but maybe those habits were not as fully developed then as they were in his later years.

After the Germans determined an interrogation was complete, their captors assigned the young men to prison camps. For the most part, the Nazis designated airmen to Luftwaffe-run camps under the German Air Force administration. They transferred the Army Air Corps officers to camps such as Stalag Luft I or Stalag Luft III, and the rest of the aircrew to Luft camps primarily for sergeants. As my research uncovered, my father ended up at Stalag 17B in Krems, Austria, situated at the base of the Alps.

Stalag 17 was the fictional prison camp in the TV series *Hogan's Heroes*. When we watched that program together as kids, which my father loved, he repeatedly mentioned that true prison life bore no resemblance to the TV show's portrayal. The real Stalag 17B was one of the worst of all the POW camps. Two sets of double barbed-wire fences about eight feet high and ten feet apart surrounded the prison, with guard towers positioned at each corner and intervals in between. The prisoners became overly familiar with the warning wire, the inner fence closest to the prisoner barracks because the German guards had orders to shoot, without warning, any prisoner touching this fence.

The guards operated the towers 24/7 with machine guns and searchlights. They also patrolled the camp on foot, often accompanied by ferocious German Shepherds. When I was young, I came home with a stray German Shepherd dog. My father, an animal lover at heart, never bonded with that animal. He allowed me to keep my new pet, but now I wonder if that German Shepherd ever conjured up disturbing memories of his prison camp days. If so, he remained silent.

My father's new prison camp, Stalag 17B, contained over 30,000 prisoners from the occupied countries, primarily Russians, Poles, Slovaks, Serbs, Italians, and French. Upon entering the prison gates, the American POWs passed next to this group of distinct nationalities, immediately observing the results of the subhuman treatment they endured at the hands of their captors. And once settled, although their barracks were divided by barbed wire, the Americans were situated close enough to these other POWs to witness the ongoing atrocities they suffered, most notably the Russian prisoners.

How overwhelming it must have been to confront the other prisoners' miserable conditions as they first passed through the prison gates, especially after their recent traumatic experiences. The airmen had parachuted out of crashing planes, survived endless hours of interrogation, and traveled on cramped boxcars for hours with no food, water, or bathroom facilities. The first sight of these starving and wretched prisoners in their new POW camp must have seemed too much to bear.

One of the Foreboding Guard Towers at Stalag 17B. Prison guards in the towers were manned with machine guns and stood watch over the prisoners 24/7. Any POW touching the warning wire could be shot without warning. The German guards posted signs stating the following: ANYONE TOUCHING OR CROSSING THE WARNING WIRE WOULD BE FIRED UPON IMMEDIATELY WITHOUT WARNING!

Ned Handy, in his book, *The Flame Keepers*, described his first experience entering Stalag 17B:

> There were barbed wire enclosures on either side of the street that bisected the compounds. We passed thousands of scarecrows, a haunted gallery of mostly Slavic faces, silent witness to malnutrition and suffering. They watched us with doll's eyes sunk into their skin-tight skulls; some mouthed words we could not understand while others stood in blood-and-sweat stained garments and stared. Our own anxiety ensured that we barely acknowledged them as we continued our march toward the far end of the camp.

The reception on the American side of the compound was quite different. The longer-term prisoners would greet the new soldiers by running up to the gates, yelling welcomes, asking for news from the home front, and ardently searching the new arrivals' faces for any signs of familiarity. There would be yells like, "Welcome home, fellas," "The new Kriegies!" or "When is the war going to be over?"

With answers back like "Soon," "It's almost over," and "Not too much longer," cheers would erupt from the seasoned prisoners. The camaraderie, humor, and positive attitude demonstrated on the other side of the wire heartened the new airmen, at least as they initially entered their present lives as POWs.

This welcome to the brand-new POWs was one example of the triumphant American spirit the Germans had been unable to squelch. These freshly arrived prisoners would make mental notes to follow this positive example for the next group of new arrivals at Stalag 17B, with numbers that eventually totaled just over 4,000 Americans.

When the Americans first entered the POW camp's main gate, the guards escorted them to a building where their pictures were taken. Their mug shot was filed away with their name, rank, serial number, and unique POW number. The prison guards would retrieve these files periodically to keep track of the prisoners, although escapes were rare, and there were not too many places they could hide. In addition, the POWs received a new set of dog tags engraved with their POW number with commands to keep this identification on them at all times. I never discovered my father's POW number, although I imagined he remembered it all his life.

Stalag 17B Main Gate. This was the POWs' first entry to life behind the wire.

After these steps were completed, the Germans deloused and shaved the prisoners' heads and made them stand naked, waiting for their clothes to come out of the cyanide ovens—about six hours later. The prison guards next assigned the POWs to their barracks. And, if the reality of their future existence behind "the wire," as the prisoners referred to their camp, hadn't already set in, now, taking inventory of their dismal surroundings, it suddenly hit hard.

All the hardships they would endure until the war ended became strikingly real. In *The Flame Keepers*, the authors described initial feelings when entering the compound's enormous outer gate:

> Our field of vision was narrowing moment by moment and soon enough, all that would matter to many of us within these wires would be survival, day by day. Men whose lives had encompassed the whole world would have to learn that the only thing of importance now would be rogue bits of carrot or potato, a pack of cigarettes or a D-bar, the haven of sleep if you could find it. Even the strongest among us would be slipping their skins with no idea what that new skin would look like.

Separated from the other prisoners, the Americans occupied five compounds, each measuring 175 yards by 75 yards and containing four double barracks 100 by 240 feet. The Germans built the barracks to accommodate 240 men, but at least 400 men crowded into each barrack after the first few months of occupancy. Due to the overcrowded conditions, the prisoners slept in bunk-type beds stacked three high with two to three men in each space—curling up close to one another for extra warmth and because there was no other choice. The young prisoners would repeatedly describe how freezing it was in their barracks while Europe experienced some of the coldest winters recorded in decades.

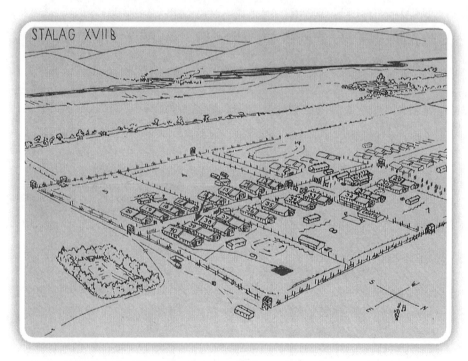

Stalag 17B Barracks Where the American Prisoners Were Detained. The Americans occupied five compounds, each measuring 175 yards by 75 yards and containing four double barracks 100 by 240 feet. The double barracks were labeled "A" and "B" and separated in the middle by six wash basins. My father was detained in barrack 39A, in compound nine of the American sector. Original sketch by Ben Phelper, a POW at Stalag 17B.

Barrack 36A in the American Compound at Stalag 17B. This is the barrack where Bill Doubledee's (author of the Stalag 17B website) father was detained—a few barracks away from my father's barrack. The caption he wrote reads: "Photo of Barracks 36A (the one my father was in) taken by a prisoner with a camera he got by bribing a German guard."

In the book, *Not Without Honor*, Steve Carano, a POW at Stalag 17B, described in his journal what they all had to endure. "The winter here was intolerable, mud which came up over our ankles after every little rain. Cold! I never thought a place could be so cold."

I know my father hated the cold for the rest of his life, moving from the East Coast, where he had once enjoyed skiing and ice skating, to sunny California after the war ended. As kids growing up, we would beg him to take us to the snow, but he never would, explaining that it was not that big of a deal. Finally, one winter, after endless pleading, he drove us for a few hours until we first sighted snow. He let us out of the car for about ten minutes, then back in the car and home to our overly heated house. We now had seen snow, and that was that.

Overall, the living conditions at Stalag 17B were deplorable. There was no heat, no hot water, and inadequate toilets and bathing facilities. The "mattresses" were straw-filled burlap bags that attracted fleas, lice, and mites. The Germans allowed the POWs one cold shower once a month, and the latrines were outside the barracks but not accessible after lights out.

Besides the cold, food was the other significant hardship on young men's minds every waking moment. The diets consisted of thin broth with rutabaga and sometimes a few other scraps of carrots, potatoes, and cabbage floating around. The prisoners would serve themselves, one dipper per man, along with one slice of brown bread laced with sawdust. Occasionally there would be cooked barley, raisins, and prunes.

The POWs depended on regular deliveries from the American Red Cross to keep them alive and letters and packages from home to boost their spirits. Many men would have starved to death if not for the food in the Red Cross parcels. That was a story told over and over by the survivors. Alternatively, the International YMCA contributed to the men's mental well-being by supplying wartime journals with pencils, recreational equipment, and educational materials. Although it was not their coveted food, these items kept the POWs occupied and helped to nourish their psyches.

Perhaps the most crucial reason the POWs at Stalag 17B would survive their imprisonment was the overall strong morale in the camp, despite all the poor physical conditions and mental factors of being behind the wire. This positive morale could be attributed to the camp's leadership and how the POWs self-organized their reporting structures. Stalag 17B undeniably had outstanding leadership, further confirmed from Army and Air Force accounts and stories from the POWs after the war ended.

In Stalag 17B, a young airman named Kenneth J. "Kurt" Kurtenbach was voted in as the "Man of Confidence." His chief role was to liaison between the German officers, the prison guards, and the American POWs. In addition, he helped advocate for any rights the POWs had according to the Geneva Convention. It was instrumental that he spoke some German and was a natural and fair leader that the airmen could look up to and depend upon to help them out in grave situations. Thanks to Kurtenbach and other leaders, there was an organizational structure in place at Stalag 17B that kept the POWs in line when everything could have been much worse.

In Stalag 17B, POWs stated that the men in the camp seemed to focus on the positives of their experiences, not on the negatives. To pass the time, the Americans devised activities to occupy their days. They taught language classes, read books, organized baseball games, played cards, and held boxing matches. "We created a theater called the Cardboard Playhouse. We would put on shows; we even had an orchestra," stated one of the former POWs in an interview years later.

Besides the prisoners' activities and projects, the other task that kept the young men occupied was the endless roll calls that the German guards would conduct daily. The roll calls averaged one hour, but sometimes they could take three hours or longer with the men standing outside in the bitter cold while the guards counted and read them warnings. The men could always anticipate the first roll call each morning around 8 a.m., but any additional calls were up to the guards and sometimes arranged to aggravate their prisoners.

The roll call word in German is *appell*, and the guards would yell to the prisoners, "Appell, appell," hurrying them along to stand outside in formation. My father, when he tried to hurry us kids up, primarily for school or church, would always say, "Temple, temple." I think that was his interpretation of tempo, tempo, or "hurry up" in German. I guess he experienced difficulty hearing, or maybe he just lacked a genuine desire to learn German correctly.

Roll Call—Appell. Roll call at Stalag 17B, otherwise known as *appell* in the German language. The prisoners assembled outside every morning, sometimes in freezing temperatures, and frequently more often throughout the day and evening if the guards felt it warranted—for whatever reason.

Even though there were over 4,000 Americans in Stalag 17B, I am sure that my father and Kurt Kurtenbach's paths probably crossed many times during the twenty-two months he was in the camp. It turned out that Kurtenbach was a tail gunner on a B-17 plane called "Wulfe-Hound" shot down in northern France on December 12, 1942. He evaded capture for thirteen days until the Nazis caught him on Christmas Day in the train station in Dijon, France.

Kurtenbach spoke a bit of French and some German, so he may have felt more equipped to travel in Nazi-occupied France, progressing south on his way to Spain. However, he traveled with another crewmate, the ball turret gunner, who spoke neither German nor French. The name of that gunner was George N. Dillard, otherwise known as Toby.

Crew Photo of George N. Dillard (Toby) and Kurt Kurtenbach. The caption reads: "FARRAR CREW–360th BS. B-17F Yardbird #41-24602 (PU-A) (original crew assigned 360BS: 03 Feb 1942 - photo: 14 Oct 1942). Back row, left to right: 1Lt. John W. Farrar (P), 2Lt. Joseph E. Trojan (CP), 2Lt. Rictor H. Auman (N), 2Lt. Jack W. Stewart (B). Front row, left to right: M/Sgt. Mike Cimbalos (E), T/Sgt. Kenneth C. Hassler (E), Sgt. George N. Dillard (WG), S/Sgt. Kenneth J. Joe Kurtenbach (TG)."

I am not sure if the language issue was why the Germans noticed them; there could have been many reasons, but in the end, the Gestapo captured Kurt and Toby in the train station after they were questioned and unable to present proper documentation papers. They both were arrested and sent to prisoner of war camps. Kurt became a leader and pillar of strength in Stalag 17B for the men who needed that in their lives. Toby became my father's bunkmate and best friend in the camp. Their friendship continued long after the war ended.

While in prison, the camp leaders occasionally smuggled in radios or built radios from scratch, tuning in to the BBC whenever possible. News from the outside world, especially victories for the Allies, was uplifting for the men, and the camp leadership disseminated positive information whenever possible. Additionally, the POWs trained in a secret code language mailed out letters to covert organizations in the States. In return, they received coded messages and packages distributed through regular mail. The Germans scrutinized all correspondence, both outgoing and ingoing, but never deciphered the coded messages.

In an article written by Joseph R. Kurtenbach, the grandson of Kurt Kurtenbach, he explained the following:

> Kurtenbach appointed Staff Sergeant Joe Dillard . . . to be his Chief of Security or "Big X." Dillard had been trained in the code language that POWs used to communicate with the military's secret organization devoted to freeing prisoners, known as MIS-X. As a trained code user (CU), Dillard was able to send coded letters in order to obtain escape aids such as compasses, maps, coffee, cigarettes—and especially money. Once at Stalag 17B, Kurtenbach, who had also received C.U. training in London, communicated with the War Department in order to inform the US of the camp's existence and request further instructions.

An article by Kenneth J. (Kurt) Kurtenbach in the May 1988 edition of the 303rd Bomb Group Association's *Hell's Angels Newsletter* clarified his choice for Chief of Security: "Matters were in such a state of flux at this time there was not really a cohesive escape committee. This came later at Stalag 17-B when I chose Sgt. Joe Dillard, a most capable person, as Chief of Security. A most cool-headed person, as impeccably dressed as possible under those conditions, and one of the older prisoners from Luft III that had transferred in."

So apparently there were two Dillards at Stalag 17B, my father's

friend Toby Dillard and crewmate of Kurtenbach's, and another gentle-
man named Joe Dillard, a.k.a. "Big X." Although my father never talked
about these clandestine activities happening in the camp, it must have
made life behind the wire a little more interesting being in the company
of all these brave leaders.

One significant danger the men faced every day, other than their physical hardships, was the mental dangers always lurking in the background.
POWs later reported it was necessary to stay occupied and not dwell
on one thought too long, whether it was your mom's favorite dessert or
dreaming of escape or life back home. They emphasized the need to look
after each other and report a friend who seemed sad or acted a bit off.

Once notified, leadership would put the POW on a suicide watch.
There were stories of men not coping, mentally snapping, and running to
the barbed wire where they would be shot immediately, without warning.
Luckily, those tales were few; overall, the men functioned the best they
could, day in and day out—at least outwardly.

Often, to survive, the prisoners needed a sense of purpose. Some
POWs rumored there was a flame keeper in Stalag 17B—a prisoner
who made it his job to keep a fire burning continually. He was the first
one up in the morning to light the flame and the last one at night to
ensure it was still burning. In that simple act, he watched out for his
fellow prisoners. This behavior and the random acts of caring by other
prisoners kept up morale and provided hope that they would survive
their captivity.

Ned Handy, in his book *The Flame Keepers*, declared: "We needed the
same kind of resolve in this hellhole of a camp. It was as if we too were
flame keepers, keeping alive for ourselves all that was right and good
about America."

A Catholic chaplain named Father Kane also consoled the prisoners
and delivered services regardless of denomination. The POWs creatively
built a chapel out of the Red Cross boxes where the Father would say
daily Mass and serve communion. In *Not without Honor: The Nazi POW
Journal of Steve Carano*, edited by Kay Sloan, there is a section of the
book dedicated to Father Kane that describes the spiritual guidance he
provided to the POWs in Stalag 17B: "His sermons and stories helped

build morale among the soldiers, sometimes bearing a mystical message about the power of faith."

My father was a devout Catholic and rarely missed Sunday Mass; there was a high probability that he adhered to this routine during his life as a POW. It was gratifying to know that Father Kane provided guidance and helped the captured men overcome the daily struggles and depressive moments that pervaded life behind the wire.

Counterbalancing all the systems the men put in place to keep their mental state healthy, other factors proved detrimental and undermined the work camp leadership struggled daily to achieve. Although I never heard my father voice this, one of these factors was how the War Department showcased the plight of the POWs back in the States. In what seemed to be almost a propaganda effort or formal policy not to worry the folks at home, the government portrayed that their boys were treated well by the Germans during their captivity.

Therefore, many Americans believed that the soldiers were relatively well fed, played sports, and received regular Red Cross parcel deliveries to supplement the meals at camp. Life seemed almost tolerable. In the book, *No Ordinary Time*, Doris Kearns Goodwin wrote, "The Office of War Information, established by Roosevelt in the spring of 1942 to coordinate the dissemination of war information, had so sanitized the war experience that few people on the home front understood what the war was really about."

As a result, occasional stories surfaced of men receiving letters from girlfriends and even their parents, calling them cowards, or referring to how good they had it in the camps while the real men were fighting the war. I am happy to say that my father never felt treated this way and, hopefully, most of the men did not either. Perhaps these letters from home were a ripple effect of the War Department's overall strategy, no matter how well meaning, with its less than accurate portrayal of the prisoners of war.

An added determinant contributing to low morale was how some of the POWs viewed themselves. A few men felt they had not contributed enough to winning the war, and now they were prisoners, not doing their share. Some men felt guilty because they were shot down on their first mission or remorseful about missing their enemy targets. Others felt at fault for being caught and unable to escape and evade capture, like some of their fellow airmen. A pilot later talked of his shame of bailing out before the rest of his crew, even though he had given the bail-out order and assumed everyone had escaped before him.

And at times, letters and packages from home did not help or reflect the actual conditions the men were undergoing. For example, precious parcels sent from well-intentioned families sometimes contained items of no use to the POWs, such as neckties or toothpicks. After the war, the POWs learned that the War Department had mistakenly instructed the public that they needed these items. Americans also believed their loved ones continued to receive standard packages from the Red Cross in the war's final years. However, this could not have been further from the truth, especially as food became scarcer for everyone, including the Germans.

Another factor that lowered morale in the camps was the uncertainty of what the Germans had in store for the Allied prisoners. The Nazis had already devised a plan for the Jews in the extermination camps and other nationalities in forced labor camps. Still, plans for the Allies varied, particularly as the war escalated and drew to an end. Mounting casualties for the Germans influenced how they treated the Allied prisoners.

After a devastating airstrike, which leveled the city of Dresden, Hitler demanded executions of all the Allied airmen in POW camps. He was talked down by his Luftwaffe commanders citing fear of reciprocity. Rumors of the Nazis' plans to kill the POWs, some later proving to be accurate, circulated continuously through the camps. I recall my father mentioning execution stories after the war, but I'm unsure if he knew of this potential horror while he was a prisoner. I remember how he believed the execution order was accurate and how lucky he felt he survived being a guest of the Third Reich.

While in camp, POWs were oblivious to extermination camps, such as Mauthausen, about eighty-five miles from Stalag 17B. In this case, ignorance was bliss because the captured airmen could have done nothing to help. While in camp, the Americans already witnessed the horrific treatment the Russians and other nationalities endured, interned just across the dirt path on the other side of the barbed wire. If the Americans thought they had it bad, they could glance that way and realize treatment could be worse. In his journal, Steve Carano beautifully summarized the situation:

> We do not complain—that was long ago. Elsewhere there are many who are lying in muddy holes in the ground. There are some who look up at the rain, but do not feel the rain on their faces. Why should we complain? We are only in exile. We still have the sky and a dream.

As with most of my father's POW stories, everything seemed woven on a positive note, and he recounted most with a humorous bent. I heard many times about the campmate who could not eat anything if it had a hair in it, so all of the other guys would say they saw a hair and then eat his meager ration.

Or the story about one of the men who kept an ocelot. And there was always the worm soup story, stating there were more worms in the soup than anything else. He told this tale with ample humor, although those worms were probably the main staple mixed in with the scarce rutabagas, potatoes, and cabbage.

I also remember him talking about playing baseball, mainly throwing a ball and playing catch. He never mentioned brutal guards or being sad. He kept that and many other stores to himself. Even with a saving grace of humor and practiced positivity, twenty-two months is a long time to be behind the wire. There must have been days when he just sat around and daydreamed of when it would all be over.

— 35 —

The Barbed-Wire Front

In this war American POWs, like their British counterparts, would no longer be considered passive victims, grounded and inoperative. The POW was to think of barbed wire as his new "front."

—LLOYD R. SHOEMAKER,
The Escape Factory

Fort Hunt, Virginia, nestled in a beautiful wooded area on the west bank of the Potomac River just twenty miles from Washington, DC, held some of World War II's biggest secrets. The citizens in the nearby city of Alexandria, Virginia, believed Fort Hunt was nothing more than a POW camp for captured enemy soldiers. They never uncovered that much more was going on inside the compound gates.

Two intelligence organizations were located on this site—their secret location was known only as PO Box 1142. Here, the American Military Intelligence Service, operating within the War Department, housed two select units, solely referred to as MIS-Y and MIS-X. MIS-Y was established in April 1942, a few months before MIS-X, and its primary mission, in addition to operating a POW camp, was to interrogate German POWs thought to have valuable information that could aid the war effort.

In the book, *The Escape Factory*, Lloyd R. Shoemaker described the following scenario:

> The city of Alexandria believed that Fort Hunt was strictly a POW camp. It did not know that it was an information-gathering

center . . . where POWs thought to know something of importance were interned. It did not know that "cooperative" German POWs were being flown from England in darkened airplanes, picked up in the windowless buses that moved mysteriously through town, and brought to Fort Hunt to be "milked" for information.

The other covert unit headquartered at Fort Hunt, known only by the initials MIS-X, was responsible for initiating and overseeing all American escape and evasion efforts in enemy territories. So ultra-secret was this organization that the US Congress, most military leadership, and most POWs never knew about its existence.

After the war ended, the Army ordered the buildings where MIS-X operated demolished, all equipment destroyed, and all records obliterated. Anyone involved with MIS-X had sworn oaths of silence. These oaths were not broken until almost five decades later when the military declassified information related to MIS-X and opened up its records— those that had been allowed to survive. It was remarkable that MIS-X personnel guarded their secrets more carefully than even those associated with the atomic bomb project. Some never gave up their secrets, taking them to their graves.

When the Eighth Air Force began making arrangements to move to England in 1942, the US Air Force Commander, Major General Carl Spaatz, met in London with British Intelligence. In his debriefings, he became aware of MI9, the top-secret department under British Intelligence in charge of assisting servicemen with escape and evasion efforts. Impressed with everything MI9 had accomplished, General Spaatz convinced the United States to follow suit. By October 1942, MIS-X was up and running, modeled after the success of MI9.

Upon its inception, MIS-X divided itself into five operational areas: interrogation after evasion, correspondence, POW locations, training and briefing, and technical. The new unit was given the responsibility to 1) instruct aircrews on evasion of capture; 2) provide instructions on escape, including escape from POW camps; 3) provide education on proper conduct after capture, including information on the rights of prisoners under the Geneva Convention; 4) obtain information from POWs during captivity via codes; 5) assist in the preparation and distribution of escape kits and other necessary equipment such as radios; 6) plan and carry on correspondence with POWs by codes and teach those codes to selected personnel; and 7) maintain a close liaison with the British MI9 branch conducting similar operations.

Of all these missions, two especially were significant for the young men fated to be POWs: training selected airmen to become code users and the technical aspects of preparing and distributing secret equipment behind the wire.

The entire process of training and becoming a code user (CU) was fascinating. When the MIS-X intelligence officers, known as briefers, first trained US servicemen on escape and evasion techniques, they were secretly selecting a few men from each squadron to be trained as code users. Each trained CU was given a code name and instructed, if captured, to notify their camp commander that they had been trained in CU and possessed the ability to establish and maintain contact with the US War Department. The CU would then write a letter to a family member and send it out via the regular mail process, but within the letter would be a coded message. The CU was not privy to how that letter would be intercepted, only confident that somehow it would reach the appropriate destination back in the States.

Only the most trusted personnel were selected to be trained code users, even within MIS-X ranks. In *The Escape Factory*, Shoemaker described the success of the code user program: "By the war's end, however, this system had become so efficient that MIS-X briefers had taught 7,724 military personnel the letter codes, and MIS-X was able to maintain constant communication with American POWs in virtually every German POW camp. And so selected were these code users that not one ever broke security."

Equally as fascinating was the technical aspect of MIS-X. Early in its organization, MIS-X put out the call within the military ranks for trained craftsmen, not specifying a job description or any other details about the request. Military personnel who answered the call and met qualifications learned to become technical experts in their new espionage role. They devised methods of hiding escape equipment such as maps, compasses, and other escape aids in hollowed-out game boards, baseballs, decks of cards, shoe brushes, and shaving equipment. With the equipment often came warnings beforehand via coded letters informing the POWs to expect a delivery and how to find the secret loot. The equipment within the parcels was so well hidden that the POWs often needed these instructions to locate the items.

The MIS-X technicians fine-tuned their craft to such perfection that most of these escape items could pass undetected under the strict scrutiny of the German guards and into the eager hands of the waiting American POWs.

MIS-X knew the importance of not sending secret items via the Red Cross. They did not wish to jeopardize the integrity of the organization the POWs depended upon to stay alive. Two fictitious organizations were created: the War Prisoner's Benefit Foundation and Servicemen's Relief. MIS-X would mail their escape and evasion supplies to the captured Americans through these newly created pseudo philanthropic groups. Each organization would send parcels containing food, clothing, and recreational materials. The food parcels would not include any hidden escape aids, but MIS-X would load the clothing and recreational packages with escape aids expertly hidden within their contents.

In *The Escape Factory*, an entire chapter was devoted to Stalag 17B and the leaders trained in CU who communicated with MIS-X throughout their years behind the wire. In their efforts to actively participate in the barbed-wire front, Kurt Kurtenbach, the Man of Confidence in Stalag 17B, organized the over 4,000 Americans in the camp into groups of 1,000 men. Each group elected a person to represent them on the newly formed escape committee.

As previously noted, a man named Joe Dillard was the chair of this committee and was given the designation BIG X. His duties included organizing all CUs in Stalag 17B to coordinate their communications, selecting other POWs to widen the correspondence network, and training them in CU to keep up with increasing workloads. Life seemed exceedingly busy in the POW camp with organized escape attempts, monitoring incoming packages, hiding the contraband within the camp, coding correspondences coming in and out, and just daily survival. As MIS-X and the War Department intended, Stalag 17B and the other American POW camps became diligent and active fronts behind the barbed wire.

With MI9, MIS-X was instrumental in numerous prison camp breaks, including helping with the Great Escape at Stalag Luft III. In the end, MIS-X was credited with helping thousands of American prisoners around the globe to escape and to evade capture. It has been called one of America's most secret intelligence agencies ever created. And as quickly as it appeared, it disappeared. As if it never existed.

I am unsure if my father ever knew about MIS-X—at least, I never heard him mention this top-secret organization in conversations. Even though his bunkmate, Toby, was a crewmate and close comrade to Kurt Kurtenbach, the American leader at Stalag 17B, he may not have been in that inner circle of code users and security organizers—or maybe he was, and he kept it secret. At any rate, I remember my father mentioning that his family always mailed him playing cards, balls, and other games while he was a POW. Were these items loaded with clandestine cargo? And now I wondered how he and Toby ever became bunkmates? Was it because they had similar interests and similar responsibilities? It was an intriguing thought, and now I speculated if my father was ever trained as a CU? If so, he was one of those that took this secret to his grave.

— 36 —

The March

I hate war as only a soldier who has lived it can, only as one who has seen its brutality, its futility, its stupidity.

—General Dwight D. Eisenhower,
Supreme Commander of Allied Forces in Western
Europe during World War II, 34th US President

Toward the end of the war, from January 1945 to May 1945, prisoners in POW camps on the eastern borders of Nazi Germany were forced to march west. No one foresaw Hitler's decision to evacuate all the POW camps close to the advancing Russian Army—neither the Allies nor the German guards within the camps.

The evacuations occurred suddenly and without warning or time to accumulate additional Red Cross parcels, extra clothing, and medical supplies. The first departures took place in January and continued for the following five months until the war ended. To make matters worse, the winter and spring of 1945 had some of the coldest weather conditions recorded in decades, with temperatures often below freezing.

The reasons for the evacuations appeared varied and somewhat uncertain. In mixed reports, the Germans expressed fear that the POWs remaining in their camps would fight against them once they were liberated by the Russians. Other accounts stated that Hitler wanted to use the POWs as bargaining chips to stay in power and escape punishment by the soon-to-be victorious Allies.

Hitler's need for leverage appeared even more apparent as the Allies advanced deeper into the Third Reich, discovering firsthand the German atrocities toward the Jews and other prisoners of the state. However, contrasting statements asserted that Hitler had no intention of negotiating a surrender. In *The Last Escape* by Nichol and Rennell, they claim: "In truth, Hitler gave scant thought to the Allied prisoners within his borders. He did not care about them one way or the other. His whole vision of the world was collapsing and he would not bargain with their lives because he had no intention of bargaining at all."

Additional stories ludicrously declared that the Germans did not want the Russians to liberate the POWs, as Germany hoped the Allies would join them in the fight against Russia. And still, other communications conveyed how the Nazis wanted to hold the prisoners hostage in cities that the Allies continued to bomb.

In his book, *Kriegie,* Kenneth W. Simmons, a POW at Stalag Luft III, recounted the following words he reported hearing firsthand: "Under the direct orders of Hitler the German Air Force has been ordered to march us to Berlin. We are to be held in the city as hostages to prevent further bombings from the Allied Air Force."

Luckily, the Germans did not carry out that order due to negotiations between the camp leaders and their captors. Whatever the reasons behind the ordered marches, it was a dangerous time for the POWs, both in terms of the uncertainty and the physical hardships they were forced to endure.

The Forced March for Stalag 17B began on April 8, 1945. This is when the American compound gates swung open, and 4,000 malnourished, war-weary American airmen were released to start their long journey toward freedom. The POWs marched hundreds of miles in the snow with inadequate clothing, minimal food, and often no shelter above their heads during the night. Many young men suffered from disease, frostbite, malnutrition, and hunger. Tragically, some died along the way. Those prisoners too sick to make the journey stayed behind and were liberated by the Russians on May 9, 1945.

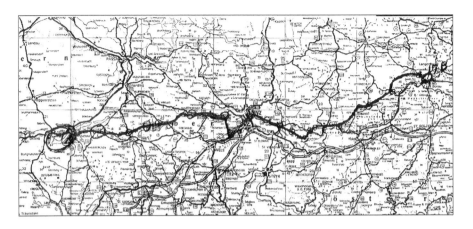

Stalag 17B Forced March. Highlighted is the route the American prisoners in Stalag 17B traversed from Krems, Austria, to Braunau, Austria. Stalag 17B is circled on the far right of the map, and on the far left is a circle indicating the POWs' final endpoint in the Weilhart Forest in Austria. The march began on April 8, 1945, and took eighteen days. The POWs covered a reported 281 miles in freezing conditions, often without shelter, little food, and adequate clothing.

Kurt Kurtenbach, the camp's appointed leader, described the emotions of that day when the prison camp doors opened. In an article he wrote after the war ended, Kurtenbach said, "The exhilaration of going down the infamous hill into Krems cannot be described. Down through the narrow alleyways of the city and out into the open country we went, along the Danube and heading West and to home."

During the march, the German guards divided the POWs into eight groups, each consisting of 500 men. Every group had an American leader in charge and German guards with dogs. At the end of each day, the POWs slept in open fields, barns, and vacated buildings, if available. They had little food besides the Red Cross parcels issued at the start of their journey and what they managed to scrounge in villages along the way.

Back on the road early each morning, the Americans began to see increasing numbers of German vehicles. For the first time, they witnessed Jewish prisoners from nearby concentration camps also forced to march west. These prisoners resembled living skeletons scantily clothed in striped prison garb with yellow stars.

I will never forget the tone of my father's voice when he described these Jewish prisoners. He would say, "We had it bad, but nothing like the Jewish people." The emotion and terrible sadness in his voice when he told these stories were palpable. I will never forget how he sounded when he described the atrocities he had witnessed at the young age of twenty-four.

In *The Last Escape* by John Nichol and Tony Rennell, a POW described the Nazi barbarity he witnessed as the Germans forced him to march west. He recounted how the prisoners caught sight of a group of about 2,000 Jews leaving Auschwitz during the war's final days, "whose pitiful state was beyond all human belief." The POW went on:

> As we slowly moved by them, I looked at their faces. I looked in vain for . . . anything in their faces showing they were aware of us or anything. There was nothing. The treatment, the weather, had sucked the life out of them. Their heads like skulls, their eyes large, luminous, and staring, all the same, not a flicker of feeling, like dead men but still alive. It still wrings my heart to think of them. I have tried but my words are inadequate to describe what I saw in those faces.

After eighteen days and 281 miles, the American POWs from Stalag 17B arrived at their designated destination in the Weilhart Forest near Braunau, Austria, on April 25, 1945. The men had no housing available upon their arrival and cut down trees to build temporary shelters. On May 3, 1945, the US 13th Armored Division liberated the POWs in their makeshift camps. Six days later, on May 9, the Americans were evacuated to France on C-47 transport planes—the start of their long-awaited journey home.

Building Shelter in the Weilhart Forest. Once they arrived at their destination, the POWs created temporary shelters by cutting down trees and building makeshift huts as there was no housing available. On May 3, 1945, the POWs were liberated by their fellow Americans.

— 37 —

The Escape

Courage is fear holding on a minute longer.

— GEORGE S. PATTON,
US Army General during World War II

At some point during the march from Stalag 17B to their new camp, my father chose to escape. I still vividly remember him saying, "They were marching us to another camp, and the guy in front of me turned around and said he was going to roll down the hill, and did I wanna follow him?"

I am not sure if they had discussed this plan ahead of time or if it was a spur-of-the-moment decision without time to thoroughly weigh the risk, benefits, and consequences of their actions. The POWs outnumbered the guards and dogs during the march, but the Germans would shoot or turn the dogs loose on any prisoners caught trying to flee. Being so close to the end of the war, most POWs decided to stay with the group rather than escape. Not my father.

I often wondered what was going through his mind at the time. Was he so sick and tired of being a prisoner that the thought of freedom was too overwhelming to resist waiting it out a bit longer? Was he uncertain when the war would end and did not realize how close he was to being liberated by the approaching American troops? Did the experience of seeing how the Germans treated the Jewish people and other

234 Finding Bomb Boogie

nationalities make him fear that he could meet the same fate? Whatever the reasons, the lure of escaping and the feeling of being free outweighed the "safety" of staying with his group.

My father described how he and his buddy eventually met up with a group of Russians who shared their food with them and kept them safe in a forest located most likely in Austria. He would often repeat how much he loved the Russians. Those actions and memories would endear him for life to this group of people. I am unsure if these Russians were soldiers or forced laborers in POW camps who had fled their captors.

I cannot remember those details or how far he was into the march before escaping. I will speculate that it was likely after two weeks since he said he spent two weeks with the Russians and, after that, the US Army arrived and liberated the POWs. Though there are no written records nor verbal stories to prove it, it is likely that my father eventually met up with the Americans after his time hiding in the forest, hopefully soon after the war ended in Europe on May 8, 1945.

Perhaps, he even reunited with his buddies from Stalag 17B and was flown back to France on the same C-47 transport planes. Once back in France, most airmen were transported to Camp Lucky Strike or one of the other Recovered American Military Personnel (RAMP) camps in northern France to recuperate and wait for their voyage back to America.

PART SEVEN

HOMEWARD BOUND

— 38 —
Demobilization

America was built on courage, on imagination, and an
unbeatable determination to do the job at hand.

—HARRY S. TRUMAN,
33rd US President

Upon liberation, my father transitioned from being a prisoner of war (POW) to a Recovered American Military Personnel (RAMP). The US Army established several holding areas for RAMPs that my father would have been transferred to while he convalesced and waited for a troopship to take him home. These holding sites were called cigarette camps and city camps, after popular cigarette brands and names of American cities.

The cigarette camps varied in size, accommodating around 2,000 to nearly 60,000 soldiers, with their numbers increasing as the war ended. The largest cigarette camps were the "Big Three"—camps Philip Morris, Old Gold, and Lucky Strike. The Army chose the names of cigarettes and cities for security purposes, anticipating that anyone eavesdropping or listening to radio traffic would think cigarettes or city names were being discussed.

The camp names also provided some degree of comfort to the soldiers eagerly awaiting transport home. Familiar American city names conjured up warm thoughts of life back in the US, and cigarette brands promised the luxury of an endless supply of tobacco. My father most likely stayed at Camp Lucky Strike, one of the main cigarette camps for repatriated soldiers and liberated POWs at the war's end.

Most of these temporary US "tent cities" were built around Le Havre's port in northwestern France. Le Havre was the prime location for these shelters because it had the only functioning port in western France big enough to handle the large ships carrying the troops back to America. The area also had a landing strip long enough to accommodate the transport planes flying soldiers from all over Europe to these final departure sites.

At first, the US military organized the tent cities to house the Americans following D-day. Later, they became a point of entry for nearly all the soldiers arriving in the European Theater. At the war's end, these sites transformed into repatriation centers for the weary and exhausted men anxiously awaiting their voyage back to America.

When the RAMPs arrived at the sites, they would be deloused and offered showers and new uniforms. They would also receive medical examinations and medical care as needed. Many RAMPs suffered from malnutrition and disease and required hospitalization at the field hospitals on site. In the hospitals, the medical staff would provide the men with medications and fluids and place them on strict feeding regimens—initiating a longer recovery process that would continue for several months when they returned to the States.

By the end of the war, the field hospital at Camp Lucky Strike had expanded from 350 to 1,500 beds. I imagine my father may have occupied one of these beds, remembering his stories about being severely malnourished.

Debriefing would begin after the RAMPs settled in and received their immediate care requirements. Military personnel in charge would ask them about their last missions, missing crew members, their experiences during captivity, and their treatment at the hands of their captors. During the debriefings, the military used the intelligence gathered from these newly freed soldiers in courts-martial, war crime proceedings, or follow-ups to locate missing Americans.

For many RAMPs, these debriefings stirred up traumatic experiences and triggered raw emotions. Some men reported that military personnel in the camps directed them not to share their negative experiences with the folks back home, including any atrocities they had witnessed. In the book, *A Tail Gunner's Tale,* the author described his experience at Camp Lucky Strike as follows:

> We were strongly reminded that under military law, when we got home we were not to reveal or discuss with anyone anything about POW camp, treatment there, or any atrocities we saw or were involved in. I don't remember a time limit on this, but it was probably for as long as you were in the military, I presumed. Most of us didn't want to talk about it anyway, for who would understand what had happened.

Cigarettes played a prominent part in the culture of World War II. They were in the Red Cross parcels and were used to bargain for other items. And the cigarette camps—the holding areas that offered soldiers safety, clean clothes, hot cooked meals, showers, and a ticket home—were named after them. It is no wonder many men smoked during World War II and became addicted for their entire lives—men like my father.

— 39 —

The Crossing

Home Alive By '45

—Slogan, Operation Magic Carpet

When World War II ended, over 8 million Allied soldiers around the globe, primarily in the European and Pacific theaters, required transportation back to America. Operation Magic Carpet—the campaign to bring all the troops home—was accomplished in about eighteen months.

In Europe alone, over 3 million soldiers required repatriation back to the States, starting in June 1945 and concluding in February 1946. In the Pacific, the process began on September 6, 1945, four days after V-J Day, and ended on September 1, 1946. While the goal was to bring all the troops home by Christmas of 1945, some soldiers would have to wait an additional nine months before their transport back to the States.

In the ETO, the Navy did not participate in the initial movement of troops across the Atlantic, with the war in the Pacific still active. Therefore, in the beginning, the job fell to the Army and Merchant Marine, which immediately converted 300 Liberty and Victory cargo ships into transports. Luxury passenger ships such as the *Queen Elizabeth* and the *Queen Mary* also took part in the operation, along with hospital ships, aircraft carriers, battleships, and twenty-nine converted troopships for war brides.

241

Travel back to the US was far from luxurious. Conditions on the ships had to be adapted to accommodate a large number of passengers. Soldiers were crammed into small areas to get as many soldiers home as quickly as possible, sometimes in bunks five levels high. Once back on American shores, transportation had to be arranged to take the men to their assigned redistribution stations. Some soldiers needed to be admitted to hospitals to recover from war injuries. And in the case of the POWs, in addition to possible war injuries, they needed time to recuperate from months of starvation and other diseases.

The military determined eligibility for repatriation and the "right" to earn passage home by a score assigned to each soldier called the Adjusted Service Rating Score (sometimes referred to as the Advanced Service Score) or ASR score. The number of points you earned during your military service determined how quickly you could be repatriated back to the US. Points were given for years of service, years of service overseas, the number of medals, and the number of dependents. You needed a score of at least 85 to be considered eligible for the first crossings back to the US. My father's score was 124, making him among the first on a long list to earn passage home.

My father's discharge papers noted that he left Europe on June 14, 1945, and arrived in the US on July 1, 1945. These dates indicated it took him approximately seventeen days to journey across the Atlantic and dock on US soil. I remember him telling me how he sailed on a large ship carrying troops back home. I vaguely remember that he said the ship was the *Queen Mary*. Still, I cannot confirm the accuracy of that memory, as the Army intentionally destroyed all records of troop crossings after the war ended.

I imagine my father had plenty of time to hone his poker and gambling skills while in the POW camp. Consequently, the only story I can recall about his return voyage was that he played a lot of poker. He won quite a large sum of money—in the thousands. However, before the sea voyage was over, he lost all of it—not by playing cards, but stolen while he slept, maybe after a few drinks and a deep slumber. Easy come, easy go.

— 40 —

Repatriation, Rejuvenation, and an Honorable Discharge

I don't mind being called tough since I find in this racket it's the tough guys who lead the survivors.

—Curtis E. LeMay,
Eighth Air Force Commander, 1942–1944

Before World War II came to an end, the US military had the foresight to create Redistribution Stations in the US in preparation for the masses of soldiers returning to the States. In 1943, the Army established redistribution stations in Atlantic City, New Jersey; Miami Beach, Florida; and Santa Monica, California—ideal spots where resort hotels and beaches offered facilities for relaxation and recreation.

Later, in 1944, three additional redistribution stations (Greensboro, North Carolina; Santa Ana, California; and San Antonio, Texas) were activated, set up on training command installations no longer in use.

Still remembering the after-effects of soldiers returning from World War I and even recalling lessons learned from the Civil War, the US Army knew they needed to address the needs of their battle-fatigued soldiers who had served their country well. The primary purpose of creating these redistribution centers was to establish a place where soldiers could rest, recuperate, and convalesce in hospitals if their conditions required advanced medical care. The redistribution centers allowed the young men space to decompress and readjust back to stateside life in comfortable surroundings.

According to one historian, "Rest was stressed in the programs during a time prior to the recognition of such a thing as Post-Traumatic Stress Disorder (PTSD), which back during WWII was referred to as 'combat fatigue,' 'battle neurosis,' or 'combat stress.'"

My father arrived back in the US on July 1, 1945. At some point, as indicated on his Discharge Record, he was transported to AAF Redistribution Station #1, situated in Atlantic City, New Jersey. Before the war started, Atlantic City was a tourism hot spot known for its elegant hotels, countless restaurants, theme park, and amusement pier dating back to 1898.

In 1942, this thriving resort town was converted into a US military base, first functioning as a basic training center for Army Air Corps and Coast Guard recruits. In 1943, Atlantic City shifted from a training base to a redistribution center for returning servicemen. A large hospital in Atlantic City called Thomas England General Hospital and several other convalescent units treated soldiers suffering from war injuries, diseases, and malnutrition. Soldiers returning from the war spent time in Atlantic City to heal, rest, and reunite with loved ones before officially being discharged into civilian life or assigned further military appointments.

Regardless of where my father recuperated, the treatment was most likely the same in all the redistribution centers that offered advanced care. After malnutrition and starvation, food had to be started slowly. During World War II, when the US Army began liberating concentration and POW camps, they realized that many people suffered complications, sometimes even death, when food was introduced too quickly. As previously noted, this phenomenon later became known as Refeeding Syndrome. I remember my father saying how, at first, he could only eat mashed potatoes for several weeks before another bland food was introduced. My father, Irish to the core, always loved his potatoes, so I imagine he was not too bothered by this strict and careful diet.

If my father had to spend time in a hospital recuperating from the effects of the war, Atlantic City was the place to be, especially as a young soldier on the road to recovery and regaining strength. I imagine him eventually walking the boardwalk and eating a hot dog dripping with mustard—something he probably dreamed about multiple times during his years of starvation in a Nazi POW camp. Maybe he also would have taken a ride on the Ferris wheel surrounded by his buddies, who were also on the mend and eager to restart their new lives.

World War II Veteran

Let every nation know, whether it wishes us well or ill, that we shall pay any price, bear any burden, meet any hardship, support any friend, oppose any foe to assure the survival and the success of liberty.

—JOHN F. KENNEDY,
35th US President

fter almost three months of convalescing, my father was ready to say goodbye to the Army Air Forces and start the next chapter of his life. On September 22, 1945, he signed his separation papers, sealed the documents with his thumbprint, and was issued his Honorable Service Lapel Badge and Button, informally known as the "Ruptured Duck." My father then collected his travel pay and headed home.

After discharge, the Army permitted soldiers to wear their uniforms for up to thirty days after separation—time enough to transition to civilian life and buy new clothes. The Honorable Service Lapel Badge, showing an eagle inside a ring, was placed over the right breast of the uniform worn at discharge. It served as proof to the military police that its wearer was not absent without leave.

Each soldier also received a small gold button (sometimes referred to as a pin) to wear on the left lapel of their new civilian clothes to proudly display to their fellow Americans that they were honorably discharged. The young soldiers nicknamed the discharge badge and button the Ruptured Duck because they thought the eagle bore more resemblance to a duck spreading its wings in flight—depicting their own hurried flight or rupture from the military.

The Honorable Service Lapel Badge and Button (Pin). The Honorable Service Lapel Badge and Button, otherwise known as the "Ruptured Duck," pictured an eagle inside a ring, spreading its wings, ready to take off in flight. The badge was sewn onto the right breast of the uniform worn at discharge and served as proof that its wearer was not absent without leave. The gold button or pin was worn on the left lapel of the soldier's civilian clothes to show their fellow Americans that they were honorably discharged. The Army awarded my father the Ruptured Duck badge to wear on his uniform and the pin to wear on his new civilian clothes after he signed his separation papers and was honorably discharged.

Honorable Service Lapel Badge.

Honorable Service Lapel Button.

In addition to his WWII Honorable Service Lapel Button, the Army Air Forces awarded my father five additional medals: the Air Medal (for the first five missions) with one Oak Leaf Cluster (one cluster for each additional five missions), the American Defense Service Medal with Star, the American Campaign Medal, the Good Conduct Medal, and the European-African-Middle Eastern Campaign Medal with Star. The US military created the World War II Victory Medal and the Prisoner of War Medal later after the war ended, raising my father's total medal count to eight. My father never showed us his medals; he may have lost track of them at some point, but the Army recorded them on his Discharge Record—proof despite their absence.

Nevertheless, my father did not leave the Armed Forces empty-handed. On his separation day, the Army granted him travel pay in the lump sum of $19.10, enough to take the bus home. The Army also issued him a military paycheck for all his accumulated paid time while a prisoner of war—a total sum of $10,708.82 (equivalent to about $155,000.00 today). A nice comfortable amount to start his new civilian life.

My father officially separated from the Armed Forces on September 22, 1945, five years, one month, and fifteen days after he enlisted. I imagined he left Redistribution Station #1 in Atlantic City and headed straight home to Brockton, Massachusetts, to see his family and friends for the first time in over five years. When he closed the Army door behind him, I envisioned that he was only looking forward—filled with anticipation and excitement about what lay ahead.

Part Eight

LOOKING FORWARD

— 42 —

Life after the War

When you look fear in the face, you are able to say to yourself, "I lived through this horror. I can take the next thing that comes along."

—ELEANOR ROOSEVELT

A t some point after his Honorable Discharge, my father took advantage of the GI Bill. One of the benefits of the bill paid for veterans to attend college. He applied to Fresno State and the University of Southern California. He chose Fresno State because Fresno was where his POW buddy Toby was born and raised. He attended four years of college at Fresno State, majoring in history and journalism.

While at college, my father also enjoyed playing baseball and was on the ice hockey team. His ice-skating years as a young boy in New England came in handy in his college years. He kept up his friendship with Toby and his family while in Fresno and often talked about the delicious food at the Mexican restaurant Toby's family owned, named Estrada's.

After my father graduated from Fresno State, he landed a job at an advertising firm in Stockton, California. His primary role was to create a magazine called *Tideways*, highlighting farming activities around the Stockton Delta region. In my father's high school yearbook, a quote next to his picture stated he would pursue a future business career. Thanks to the GI Bill, his yearbook quote came to fruition.

American Prisoners of War Silver Dollar. Released by the United States Mint in 1994. The commemorative coin features an eagle with a broken chain on one leg, flying through barbed wire toward freedom. My father's friend and POW bunkmate, Toby, gave each of these coins to his grown children fifty years after the war ended and ten years after my father passed away. Toby's oldest daughter shared this memory with me and gifted me with her coin—further solidifying the bond between two lasting POW friends and their families.

American Prisoners of War Silver Dollar (United States Mint image).

American Prisoners of War Silver Dollar (reverse side).

At the age of thirty, after graduating from Fresno State and working for a few years, my father met my mother, and they were married on January 27, 1952, at Saint Mary's Church in Stockton, California. My mother was a registered nurse working at the County Hospital. A native of Puerto Rico, she had traveled to the US with a group of nurses and lived in the hospital's nurses' building. One evening she and a few other nurses decided to go to the Army base to a dance, where she met my father. He often said she was a wallflower, and he felt sorry for her and asked her to dance. However, I don't think that was the case. I think he took one look at her, and that was it.

For her, it was the same. After a few months, they were married. She was twenty-four years old, and my father was thirty. Nine months later, I came along, and then all of my four siblings, one year after another.

My father also took advantage of his veteran status to take out a VA loan and purchase our first home in 1952 for just under $10,000. There were so many wonderful memories growing up with Mom, Dad, and us five kids. But scattered in between all these happy childhood recollections were sometimes actions by my father that were difficult to deal with and incomprehensible to a young daughter who looked to him for love, nurturing, and safety.

— 43 —

The Battles Continue

We must always remember that it is the things
of the spirit that in the end prevail.

—John Gilbert Winant,
US Ambassador to the United Kingdom during World War II

So many positive qualities come to mind when I think about my father. He was intelligent, funny, handsome, self-deprecating, and kind-hearted. He was religious and never missed Sunday Mass, and I never heard him say a bad word about anyone. He was honest and taught us values, especially to be truthful and proud of our democracy. He treated all of us kids the same and did not play favorites. He was interesting and seemed to know everything about everything. I loved being around him.

My father worked hard and did everything he could to ensure we had a roof over our heads and three meals a day. He cooked all our dinners, made our school lunches, and drove us to class in the mornings. Most of all, he made us laugh with his corny jokes that we repeat to this very day.

Where are you going, Dad?"

"Crazy, wanna come?" would be his reply.

He would put all five of us kids in the station wagon and take us down to the neighborhood public swimming pool in the hot summers, and we would swim for hours. His favorite game was putting us on his back and diving with us underwater into the deep end of the pool. He always took his time coming up for air, and we would pinch his back, silently begging him to rise to the surface. Once on top of the water, he would laugh and laugh. He loved that game, and so did we, although there were times when we thought maybe he was purposely trying to drown us.

After our fun adventure, he would bring us home, cook dinner, make sure we had baths, were dressed in our pajamas, and brushed our teeth. Then he would tuck us into bed. My parents worked full-time, but my father continued to work when he got home, performing household duties. At the same time, my mother rested in another room or engaged in her other hobbies, primarily sewing.

It was my father whom I remember being exceptionally present in our lives—until he wasn't. I can't recall when I realized he had a drinking problem. He didn't drink every day, and it might be months or years before he took a drink. He could have a few drinking episodes close together and then not indulge again for an extended period, maybe a few months, perhaps a year. But when he did drink, it was always upsetting and often destructive.

In my life, I have learned that there are all types of alcoholics. Some alcoholics can drink every day and still carry on. They are what you call functioning alcoholics, although issues are always at the heart of it. My father was not a functioning alcoholic. Like all alcoholics, he was powerless over alcohol. And maybe more powerless than most.

Later, I came to recognize that if he took just a few sips of alcohol, his entire countenance would change, and his personality would follow. You could all but see him slip into another skin and his soul leave his body. He became a different person, not the father I depended on to keep me safe, not the father I trusted. And once he had one drink, it led to another and another until he often became unconscious. It was not within his power to stop.

His favorite pastime when drinking was to drive, and throughout his life I worried, as did all my family, that he would injure himself and another innocent person unfortunate to be in his path. He never did harm himself or anyone else, but the worry was always there.

The cars he drove were not so fortunate. In the morning, we would sometimes wake up to see my father had made it home in one piece, but not so his vehicle. His car would be parked on the street, totally smashed. And then the neighbors would start asking questions, mostly our nosy neighbor next door. I remember trying to cover up for my father at an early age when the prying neighbor would track me down and start asking questions.

He would begin with queries like, "What happened to your father's car?"

And I would answer, "I don't know," and then run off before he could ask anything more.

The most humiliating part was when a short article in the town newspaper described an incident with my father's full name in bold print. Then the questions would start again in the neighborhood and also at school. I still remember clearly to this day an incident when I was in grammar school. I was playing on the rings with one of my girlfriends, and she told me her family read an article in the newspaper about my father getting arrested for drunk driving. I quickly informed her that it was not my father, that it must be another man with my father's exact name. She kept insisting, and I kept denying it. I remember that little girl's name to this day, and I remember the queasiness in my stomach when she unrelentingly brought up her rhetorical questions.

I never spoke about my father's drinking problem to anyone practically my entire life until much later, after marriage and kids. And we never talked about it at home. We were ashamed, and, besides, it was so much easier to forget about it when our father was sober and returned to the loving, gentle person he was when not under the spell of alcohol.

After a drinking episode when he had done something terribly wrong, he was so remorseful, so ashamed, and uncharacteristically reserved. It would be weeks before he overcame his depression and became the father we all knew and loved. I remember feeling sorry for him at an early age, but shame and anger came with my sorrow.

This is why I felt relief when he finally passed away. I would not have to worry about him drinking and driving and possibly hurting himself and others, which was a real everyday concern. I think this is why I just made myself stop thinking about him when he died. Come to find out, he was always there inside of me, but I lacked self-awareness. I didn't even know I had not thought about him in over thirty years until I did think about him again. I was oblivious.

I believe that is why I was so emotional at the beginning of this journey, and the tears ran freely. When I questioned why I was so distraught, I realized there were many reasons. I was crying for the young man I never knew about, part of the Greatest Generation and who made countless sacrifices during the war without question. I was crying because I never realized my father's complete story while he was still alive. But I was also crying because I felt guilty that I did not show more compassion. There were parts of my father that I did not understand.

Knowing his war history, I wonder if I would have felt differently about him when he was alive. Would I have been more forgiving, more understanding, less angry? Would I have been more helpful, more supportive? Heck, I was only a young girl; I did not know how to deal with him and his problems.

— 44 —

Understanding, Acceptance, and Resolution

I think one day you'll find that you're the hero you've been looking for.

—JIMMY STEWART,
Actor and World War II Bomber Pilot in the Eighth Air Force

The process of applying for VA benefits to aid with my mother's escalating health care costs was a gift in so many ways. If not for this process, I probably never would have consciously allowed my father back in my life nor researched his World War II history. I would never have allowed myself to acknowledge that human beings are intricate and many-layered and that not everything is black and white. Ultimately, I would never have learned to understand and accept my father's shortcomings and eventually come to the realization that he loved us but suffered from a disease that he could not surmount.

Although my father never outwardly showed signs of depression or post-traumatic stress disorder (PTSD), I can't help but think he may have experienced this disorder, primarily because of the traumatic situations he was exposed to during World War II, especially being a POW for almost two years. In those early years after the war ended, PTSD was not an official diagnosis. The Army knew soldiers experienced stress during the war, and they called it battle fatigue, shell shock, or soldier's heart.

While the Army recognized this syndrome and created redistribution centers for their war-weary soldiers, long-term care, medication, and psychotherapy were not the norms. Not until years later, sometimes forty years later, after veterans had raised their families and retired from their jobs, could they take a breath, recognize, and talk about their situations.

I had heard stories of POWs who never felt quite normal when they returned home, although they desperately wanted to return to the life they knew before the war. And though they could not blame all of life's troubles on their imprisonment, the experience certainly changed them, often mentally and physically.

The symptoms they experienced were varied. Some relived their trauma through nightmares and flashbacks, while others felt shame or guilt about the event. Others reported feeling on edge, startled by loud noises, angry or irritable, and acting out in unhealthy ways, such as smoking, abusing alcohol, or driving aggressively—my father, a classic example.

In the case of the POWs, their exposure to traumatic events was prolonged and repetitive and occurred in a place where they perceived little or no chance of escape. Even if a harmful incident did not happen directly to them, they were trapped in a situation where they experienced secondary trauma on an ongoing basis. My father spoke about witnessing the plight of the Jewish people during his forced march, but he also observed firsthand the trauma he and his fellow POWs endured while imprisoned.

Although he never spoke of it, there were POWs in Stalag 17B who had lost limbs and suffered from severe burns and disfigurement. Some of the young men died from their war injuries or from diseases they contracted while in camp. They were also subjected daily to deplorable living conditions, including harsh treatment by the prison guards. Some inmates were on suicide watch and several were executed while trying to escape. The list goes on and makes one believe that no one came back from a POW camp quite the same person.

One of my friends, whose father spent almost three years as a POW, confided that her father returned from the war a damaged man. She said that he suffered from recurring nightmares, and the sound of an unexpected loud noise could set him off on a tirade. Not until her father joined an Ex-Prisoner of War Organization, decades after the war had ended, did his nightmares subside. She lamented that she wished he would have found this organization earlier because, perhaps, he would have been a better father.

The absence of the Armed Forces and society to formally recognize that PTSD was a serious medical issue and, therefore, the subsequent lack of support programs resulted in additional hardships for the World War II veterans and their families. Many veterans, throughout their lives, used alcohol to self-medicate and forget their painful memories. I am not claiming that what my father went through in World War II caused him to abuse alcohol. But at the same time, I cannot entirely rule it out as one of many contributing factors.

Throughout this process of learning my father's story, I educated myself about alcoholism. I now fully understand and accept that it is a disease. Alcoholism, like other diseases, can be caused by genetic, environmental, social, and psychological factors—similar to other chronic conditions, like diabetes or heart disease. I learned that alcoholism needs to be diagnosed, a treatment plan must be put in place, and the alcoholic must adhere to that treatment plan to stay healthy. Otherwise, like any other chronic, debilitating illness, it becomes a downward trajectory leading to more sickness and eventually death. And it is not just the alcoholic's worsening decline at stake, but all those close to the alcoholic who witness the pain and suffering and the roller coaster ride of highs and lows; they also become victims of the disease and require proper support to care for themselves.

Finally, I have learned not to be ashamed to talk about alcoholism and to admit that my father was an alcoholic. There are no healing benefits to keeping it secret because, in doing so, a person closes off all avenues of help, of which there are many. Today, if I could meet that little girl in the schoolyard, the one who informed me about my father's arrest for drunk driving, I would be able to say, "Yes, that was my father in the paper. He has a disease, but he is trying to get help so he can get better." I am now hopeful that when you are truthful and open your heart, others also open theirs.

I don't know if my father ever fully embraced the fact that he was an alcoholic. I don't remember him going to Alcoholics Anonymous (AA) meetings, where you say your name at each meeting, followed by "I'm an alcoholic." If so, he would have found a support group of other men and women with the same disease at these meetings, sharing similar stories and offering help to the others around them. He possibly would have found a particular person he looked up to who would be his sponsor. This person would have provided ongoing encouragement and companionship during my father's rough times when he felt down and desperately wanted to bury his troubles in a bottle. My father never had this type of support. Sometimes you seek a sponsor; other times, you are lucky, and a sponsor finds you. Unfortunately, a caring sponsor never entered my father's life, or he never opened up himself to this gift. In this regard, his good fortune ran out.

Similarly, my mother never embraced any assistance to help her cope with all the challenging situations. Al-Anon, a group for spouses, children, and friends of alcoholics, was not in her repertoire. My mother did everything possible to keep matters secret rather than seek help until events spiraled out of control and secrecy was impossible. She became codependent, and together, their marriage survived, but with many ups and downs. In some ways, I think they still loved one another, but they appeared trapped. Life continued, and their kids seemed to be the glue that kept the marriage together. In the end, we all survived because our parents were two good people who loved each other and loved their children, despite all the heartaches.

My father passed away at the age of sixty-five. I want to believe he led a full life, growing up on the East Coast with a supportive family, joining the Army Air Corps, fighting in World War II, and moving to the West Coast to attend college. He married, raised a family, and lived long enough to see his children marry and meet a few of his grandchildren. And yet, sixty-five seems young in many ways. I know he had made plans on how he wanted to spend his final years that never came to pass.

I was at my father's bedside when he passed away. Initially, he was admitted to a medical unit in the VA hospital for treatment for his lung cancer. However, his condition worsened after contracting pneumonia during his hospital stay, necessitating his transfer to the intensive care unit (ICU). In prior years, when I worked as a critical care nurse, a colleague once told me that when a loved one dies in a hospital, especially in an intensive care unit, this moment in time will not be how you remember them. Instead, you will eventually forget this distorted image and think of your loved ones as they were in their everyday lives before entering the hospital. However, at least for me, this theory has proven inaccurate.

I've found it difficult to forget the ventilator breathing for my father when he could no longer do so on his own. Trying to block out images of his numerous intravenous lines providing medications and fluids, the foley catheter draining his urine, and the arterial line monitoring his blood pressure have been equally challenging. The multiple blood draws, the endless suctioning of secretions, and the painful procedures he endured continue to be lasting memories hard to erase.

The ICU at the VA hospital was a wide-open room with no walls between bed spaces. In this large ward, all the patients were easily visible unless a curtain was drawn around the bed for privacy when the hospital caregivers deemed it necessary. In this hectic place, each patient seemed every bit as sick as my father. The nurses, doctors, and other medical personnel never seemed to stop moving or have slow periods where they could sit and catch their breaths. If they were seated, it was to write their never-ending notes in the bedside charts.

Amid all this chaos in what turned out to be my father's final hours, I held his hand and softly said, "Dad, we're going to the cafeteria for a cup of coffee. We'll be right back." He became distressed and seemed exasperated that we were leaving him at this particular moment. Reassuringly, I told him we wouldn't be gone long. In retrospect, I wonder if he was aware that the end was drawing near and he was afraid he might die alone.

My mother and I returned less than an hour later, during change of shift. As the nurses communicated their hand-off reports from the corners of the room, they looked up and acknowledged us but immediately returned to their conversations. As my mother and I settled in on either side of my father's bed, I looked up at the cardiac monitor and noticed that his heart rhythm was more irregular and erratic than before we went to the cafeteria. He was experiencing considerably more premature ventricular contractions—dangerous heartbeats that potentially could lead to a lethal turn of events.

As I studied the heart monitor, I noticed that the nurses had silenced the alarms, so they were unaware of his deterioration. His heart rate quickly turned into a cardiac rhythm which I knew was incompatible with life, and his arterial line monitor reflected a blood pressure that was slipping away. Still, the caregivers had not noticed.

At that point, I walked over to them and pointed to the monitors. They quickly rushed into action calling a code that gathered the doctors and the rest of the nurses, respiratory therapists, and hospital staff to my father's bedside. I couldn't bear to witness what would happen next—the cardiac compressions, the defibrillation, more invasive lines, and uncomfortable treatments.

Calmly, I urged them to stop and not continue with the code. A few of them looked at me, and one doctor quietly asked if I was saying they should not resuscitate.

"Yes," I answered. "Do not resuscitate." I silently prayed, *Please, just let him die peacefully*. Many years later, I remember my mother saying she had let my father slip away. While she was on the same page as I, she was passive. I was the one who actively let him slip away.

Over the years, I've revisited this scene and watched the entire scenario play out in my mind. I didn't want to put my father through all those painful, invasive treatments when his chances of surviving his lung cancer were slim. I honestly believed it would just be delaying the inevitable and prolonging his suffering. Still, some part of me questioned if we gave up too quickly. On some level, I wonder if I just thought life would be easier for me and everyone else without him.

In my father's brief chronicle of all his missions, the last word he wrote was *KAPUT*. He spelled it out in capital letters. The previous sentence in the chronicle was "Bomb Boogie shot down by fighters, flak over France." My father used this word to describe that his missions were over and that he was captured and officially a prisoner of war. *Kaput* is derived from a German word, which in English colloquialism translates to indicate the end, finished, done, over. So, this is the word I think of as my father's story draws to an end. KAPUT.

Regrettably, I wish my father could have known that his contribution to World War II would have been recognized as heroic. Maybe that would have made him more content and lessened the pain. Perhaps that would have given him the strength to fight his individual issues head on. Learning my father's World War II story, while acknowledging and accepting that he also fought his own internal battles long after the war ended, has been a powerful journey. Finally, I have found that *within my father* was always the hero I had been looking for.

My father was not perfect. He had his weaknesses, and his share of personal struggles, like most of us do in our lives. But when our freedom was threatened, he rose to the challenge and demonstrated a resiliency and courage to be admired. Through his actions, he showed he had the "right stuff," and I will forever choose to remember those qualities about him.

And so, this is KAPUT, the end of my memoir about finding my father's World War II history. And like the flame keeper in Stalag 17B who kept the fire burning for all his fellow POWs, I now have preserved my father's story in writing to spark a rekindling of his life, especially his war years, for all who read it.

Acknowledgments

First and foremost, I would like to thank my husband for continually providing encouragement and support and believing in my project. You were the first to proudly tell anyone who would listen that I was writing a book—before I even acknowledged it myself.

I would like to express appreciation to all my family for inspiring me to write this story. Our future generations will always know that our father—your grandfather, your great-grandfather—answered the call when the stakes were high, and our democracy was threatened. My deepest thanks especially to my dear siblings, Michael, Donna, Naomi, and Von, who recognized the importance of sharing our family stories—the good and the less good.

One aspect I did not anticipate when writing my father's story was re-establishing long-lost connections to extended family, particularly my cousin Cathy Clark. I thank her for sharing her father's (my uncle Johnny's) military memoir a few years after I started my research. Cathy, I will always be grateful to receive those papers that confirmed my father's accounts were accurate.

Another facet of researching my father's WWII history was initiating contact with the family members of his crew, primarily his pilot's son, Doug Arp, and the family of his radio crewmate, John Wenninghoff. You were invaluable in identifying photographs and providing additional documents and stories and I treasure our connections. Our fathers would be proud.

A heartfelt thank you goes out to family members of my father's POW campmate and longtime friend Toby, who answered my calls and were willing to share stories. Like the POWs themselves, who felt that sometimes only a fellow POW would understand what they went through, a similar emotion exists for family members of POWs. A built-in bond and a mutual understanding occurred when we also shared our stories. Thank you family members for your willingness to be so open.

Beta readers are people you trust to read your *baby* when you have no idea if it is worth reading. I want to acknowledge the following people—my beta readers—who read my first drafts and provided encouragement and constructive feedback: Dan Buick, Naomi Aradi, George Aradi, Donna Tenuta, Mike Hayes, Von Hayes, Jill Hersh, and John O'Connor. Although you did not know it then, any signs of disinterest probably would have put a big dent in my belief that my project was worthwhile. Thank you again for honestly expressing interest.

To Rebecca Youngblood Vaughn, an author herself and a member of the 91st Bomb Group Memorial Association, to whom I timidly gave the first draft of my manuscript. Rebecca provided thoughtful and considerate feedback, primarily to include lots of photos and to revise, revise, and revise some more. Thank you again, Rebecca, for your time and detailed suggestions.

I would also like to show my appreciation to Amanda Sargisson for helping me get started with my first book for my family only—for all her technical advice and graphic design help. Seeing my first finished product gave me the confidence to start a second.

To Gary Hall, a fellow member and longtime editor of the 91st Bomb Group Memorial Association (BGMA) newsletter, whose grandfather died on a bombing mission during WWII and whose zeal to discover his story was inspirational. Gary, I admire your perseverance and dedication to preserving the history of all those who served in the 91st Bomb Group.

The invaluable assistance of my primary fact-checker, Mick Hanou, President of the 91st BGMA, deserves special recognition. I thank Mick for being an incredible historian with fantastic attention to detail. His mother and father were living in Nazi-occupied Europe during WWII, and when his father looked up in the sky and saw exactly 1,080 bombers flying overhead, I did not doubt it. It's genetic. The amount of time and thought Mick provided to my manuscript was phenomenal. My story would have been incomplete without his help.

I want to thank Val Burgess, World War II POW Historian and

Speaker and Executive Director, Wars' Voices, who reviewed the POW portions of my manuscript. Your dedication to preserving the voices of POWs is commendable and does not go unnoticed.

I wish to show my appreciation to Kimberly Guise, Senior Curator and Director for Curatorial Affairs at the National WWII Museum in New Orleans, for meeting with me and encouraging me that my project was worthwhile. Also, for organizing a WWII online POW course in conjunction with Arizona State University, which I attended, the first of its kind to recognize the hardships and strengths of all POWs worldwide during World War II.

Much gratitude goes to my fabulous editor. How often have I imagined myself saying those four words—*to my fabulous editor*? So a considerable acknowledgment goes to Sandra Wendel, my editor and author of the book *Cover to Cover,* a book I read cover to cover and knew she was the one for me. Thank goodness she felt the same.

I am deeply indebted to all the Flame Keepers—primarily the bomb group memorial associations, especially the 91st Bomb Group Memorial Association (BGMA) and the 8th Air Force Historical Society (AFHS), and the World War II museums, especially the National WWII Museum in New Orleans, the National Museum of the Mighty Eighth Air Force in Georgia, and the American Air Museum in Britain. Lest we forget.

Praise goes to all the families who did the research and put together websites—those excellent repositories of information—to honor their veterans, especially Bill Doubledee for creating his Stalag 17B website to honor his father. Without his research, I would never have seen my father's name with his correct POW camp listed in print.

I am so grateful to the United States Department of Veterans Affairs for their comprehensive and ongoing support for all our veterans. The plethora of programs they offer to veterans and families is exceptional. I will never forget that my project started with their offer to help a family of a World War II veteran.

Finally, I recognize anyone who has ever said *my father was in World War II, but he never wanted to talk about it.* I hear you and have faith that one day you will find your veteran's story if you have not already. You are the future flame keepers.

Above all, I acknowledge my father and veterans like him who gave their all when called upon. Dad, you were right all along. Nothing in life is free.

Notes

PART I: LOOKING BACK

CHAPTER 1: A True Veteran

3 **In his book, *The:*** Tom Brokaw, *The Greatest Generation,* Random House, 2004, 11.

CHAPTER 2: Veterans Day

6 **They were known as**: "The 90th Infantry Division During World War II," United States Holocaust Memorial Museum, Washington, DC, https://encyclopedia.ushmm.org/content/en/article/the-90th -infantry-division.

6 **It states, "Every day**: "WWII Veteran Statistics: The Passing of the WWII Generation," National WWII Museum, updated September 30, 2021, https://www.nationalww2museum.org/war/wwii -veteran-statistics.

7 **The US Department of**: Katherine Schaeffer, "On 75th anniversary of V-E Day, about 300,000 American WWII veterans are alive," Pew Research Center, May 8, 2020, https://www.pewresearch .org/fact-tank/2020/05/08/on-75th-anniversary-of-v-e-day-about -300000-american-wwii-veterans-are-alive/.

7 **These veterans are in**: "WWII Veteran Statistics: The Passing of the WWII Generation," National WWII Museum, updated September 30, 2021, https://www.nationalww2museum.org/war/wwii -veteran-statistics.

8 **He said, "Tell a**: "On 'SNL,' Congressman Crenshaw Accepts

Pete Davidson's Apology," NPR: All Things Considered, November 11, 2018, https://www.npr.org/2018/11/11/666767906/on-snl -congressman-crenshaw-accepts-pete-davidsons-apology.

CHAPTER 3: VA Benefits

12 **The VA informed me**: Dee Zimmerman, "Veterans Day November 11: A Veterans Experience, World War II Veteran Max Bergen," *Clark County Press*, Neillsville Wisconsin, November 8, 2017, https://wiclarkcountyhistory.org/clark/news/OldDays/2017 _11_8.htm.

13 **The Detaining Power listed**: "Display Partial Records: World War II Prisoners of War Data File, 12/7/1941–11/19/1946," National Archives, https://aad.archives.gov/aad/fielded-search .jsp?dt=3159&cat=WR26&tf=F&bc=,sl#.

PART II: SETTING SAIL

CHAPTER 4: Preparation

18 **Reading about Stalag Luft III**: "Stalag Luft 3 1942–1945," Muzeum Obozow Jenieckich, https://muzeum.zagan.pl/en /stalag-luft-3/.

18 **The Luftwaffe—the name**: Ibid.

19 **Fifty men, more than**: Paul Brickhill, *The Great Escape*, Amereon House, 1950, 178.

19 **This prison camp was**: Susanne Rieger and Gerhard Jochem, "A Brief History of Nuremberg POW Camps," 32nd Bomb Group, last updated December 1, 2001, https://www.b24.net/powNuremberg Camps.htm.

19 **In 1939, the camp**: Ibid.

20 **In late 1944 and**: Ibid.

20 **In the winter and**: Ibid.

21 **Stalag Luft III's march**: John Nichol and Tony Rennell, *The Last Escape: The Untold Story of Allied Prisoners of War in Europe*, Viking Penguin, 2003, 73.

21 **In the Sagan area**: "Stalag Luft 3: American Prisoners of War in Germany," prepared by Military Intelligence Service War Department,

July 15, 1944, compiled and presented by Greg Hatton, 392 Bomb Group, https://b24.net/powStalag3.htm.

21 **After arriving in Spremberg**: Ibid.

21 **From there, they were**: Ibid.

21 **This segment of the**: Ibid.

CHAPTER 5: Everyone Has a Story

24 **He fought in the**: Charles B. MacDonald, *The Battle of the Bulge*, Weidenfeld and Nicolson, 1984, 11.

CHAPTER 6: On His Heels

29 **We learned that the**: "The 'House Prison' at Gestapo Headquarters in Berlin: Terror and Resistance 1933–1945," ed. by Topography of Terror Foundation, updated 2007, https://www .topographie.de/en/the-hoistoric-site.

29 **At the time of**: "Berlin 1933—The Path to Dictatorship," Topographie Des Terrors, updated 2013, https://www.topographie.de /en/publications/detail/berlin-1933-the-path-to-dictatorship.

36 **While I waited for**: Muzeum Obozow Jenieckish, "Stalag VIIC and Stalag Luft 3 P.O.W. Camps," museum pamphlet obtained September 2018, https://muzeum.zagan.pl/en/stalag-luft-3/.

36 **By 1945, the camp**: Ibid.

36 **As previously mentioned, Stalag**: Ibid.

36 **In Stalag Luft III**: "Stalag Luft 3: American Prisoners of War in Germany," prepared by Military Intelligence Service War Department, July 15, 1944, compiled and presented by Greg Hatton, 392nd Bomb Group, https://b24.net/powStalag3.htm.

36 **Apart from one another**: Nichol and Rennell, *The Last Escape*, 66.

39 **Peter asked us if**: "Records Relating to the Katyn Forest Massacre at the National Archives: Summary of Events," National Archives, last reviewed November 25, 2022, https://www.archives.gov/research /foreign-policy/katyn-massacre.

39 **He told us that**: Katarzyna Utracka, "The Katyn Massacre— Mechanisms of Genocide," *The Warsaw Institute Review,* May 18, 2020, https://warsawinstitute.review/issue-2020/the-katyn -massacre-mechanisms-of-genocide.

CHAPTER 7: Nuremberg, Amsterdam, and Back to Base

43 **In 1934, Albert Speer:** "Former Nazi Party Rally Grounds," museen der stadt nurnberg Documentation Center, museum pamphlet obtained September 2018, https://museums.nuernberg.de /documentation-center/.

43 **Between 1933 through 1938:** Ibid.

47 **Based on Red Cross estimates:** "Netherlands Forced Labor— WWII," https://www.documentatiegroep40-45.nl/dwangarbeid_oud /indexenglish.htm.

47 **Of the 140,000 Jews:** JCH Blom, "The Persecution of the Jews in the Netherlands: A Comparative Western European Perspective," *European History Quarterly*, 19 (3): (July 1989): 333–351.

CHAPTER 8: My Generation

49 **A baby boomer is:** Sandra L. Colby and Jennifer M. Ortman, "The Baby Boom Cohort in the United States: 2012 to 2060," *US Census Bureau*, Issued May 2014, https://www.census.gov/history/pdf /babyboomers-boc-2014.pdf.

PART III: UNRAVELING THE TRUTH

CHAPTER 9: Starting from Scratch

57 **I was shocked to:** "The 1973 Fire, National Personal Records Center," National Personal Records Center, last reviewed October 8, 2021, https://www.archives.gov/personnel-records-center/fire-1973.

57 **Firefighters arrived on the:** Ibid.

57 **The fire crews poured millions:** Ibid.

57 **After almost five days:** Ibid.

57 **Due to the extensive:** Ibid.

57 **When all was said:** Ibid.

58 **The estimated loss of:** Ibid.

58 **According to information on:** Ibid.

58 **After firefighters completely contained:** Walter W. Stender and Evans Walker, "The National Personnel Records Center Fire: A Study in Disaster," *The American Archivist* 37, 4 (October 1974): 521–549,

https://www.archives.gov/files/st-louis/military-personnel/NPRC
_fire_a_study_in_disaster.pdf.

58   **A quote from the**: Kerri Lawrence, "Archives Recalls Fire That
Claimed Millions of Military Personnel Files," *National Archives
News*, last reviewed August 20, 2019, https://www.archives.gov/news
/articles/archives-recalls-fire.

Chapter 10: What I Heard

62   **Later, I concluded that**: Nichol and Rennell, *The Last Escape*,
preface xi–xii.

Chapter 11: Where to Start?

63   **During this process, I**: The National WWII Museum, New
Orleans, https://www.nationalww2museum.org/ and American Air
Museum in Britain, http://www.americanairmuseum.com/.

Chapter 12: What Camp?

65   **"Only when sharing your**: Nichol and Rennell, *The Last Escape*,
preface xiii.

65   **As I searched for**: "POW Camp Listings," The National
Ex-Prisoner of War Association, http://web.archive.org/web
/20061128041920/www.prisonerofwar.org.uk/camp_list.htm/.

65   **About 100 centers held**: "Guests of the Third Reich: American
POWS in Europe," The National WWII Museum, https://
guestsofthethirdreich.org/home/.

66   **The number of POW camps**: Eric Lichtblau, "The Holocaust Just
Got More Shocking," *New York Times,* March 1, 2013, https://www
.holocaustchild.org/2013/03/nyt-the-holocaust-just-got-more
-shocking/.

66   **On the United States**: "Holocaust Encyclopedia: Nazi Camps,"
United States Holocaust Memorial Museum, Washington, DC,
https://encyclopedia.ushmm.org/content/en/article/nazi-camps.

66   **I came up with**: H. M. Mehanna and colleagues, "Refeeding
Syndrome: What It Is, and How to Prevent and Treat It," *BMJ* 336
(June 26, 2008): 1495–8.

67   **There were essentially four**: "POW Camp Listings," The National

Ex-Prisoner of War Association, http://web.archive.org/web /20061128041920/www.prisonerofwar.org.uk/camp_list.htm/.

67 **Stalags, short for *Stammlager*:** Ibid.

67 **A Stalag Luft was:** Ibid.

67 **Dulags, short for *Durchgangslager*:** Ibid.

67 **The following are the:** Ibid.

68 **After opening in 1940:** "Kriegsgefangenen Lagers: Home of the 'Kriegie' Airmen," 392nd Bomb Group, https://www.b24.net /powCamps.htm.

68 **The camp reopened in:** Ibid.

68 **In 1943, American POWs:** Ibid.

68 **In my search, I:** "World War II—Prisoners of War—Stalag Luft I," Stalag Luft I Online, http://www.merkki.com/.

68 **Under one of the:** "Research Tips," Stalag Luft I Online, http:// www.merkki.com/macr.htm.

70 **The site opened to:** "Kriegsgefangenen Lagers: Home of the 'Kriegie' Airmen," 392nd Bomb Group, https://www.b24.net /powStalag4.htm.

70 **The camp was for sergeants:** Ibid.

70 **Stalag Luft V in Halle:** Christine Schmidt van der Zanden, "Buchenwald/Halle," Holocaust Encyclopedia United States Holocaust Memorial Museum, https://encyclopedia.ushmm.org /content/en/article/buchenwald-halle.

71 **This camp was built in:** "Kriegsgefangenen Lagers: Home of the 'Kriegie' Airmen," 392nd Bomb Group, https://b24.net/pow Camps.htm.

71 **In June 1943, Stalag:** Ibid.

71 **In July 1944, as:** Greg Hatton, "The Heydekrug Run," 392nd Bomb Group, originally printed in AXPOW Bulletin August 1989, https://www.b24.net/storiesHatton.htm.

71 **What these prisoners experienced:** Ibid.

71 **Claude Watkins, an American:** Claude Watkins, "A Prisoner of the Luftwaffe," 392nd Bomb Group, https://www.b24.net/pow StoriesClaudeWatkins.htm.

72 **Noteworthy at this camp**: Nichol and Rennell, *The Last Escape*, 183–184.

72 **By 1943, Stalag Luft III**: "Stalag VIIIB/344 Lamsdorf: History," Prisoner of War Online Memorial and Museum, https://www .prisonersofwarmuseum.com/camps/stalag-viiib-344-lamsdorf/.

72 **The Germans had built barbed-wire**: Ibid.

72 **Toward the end of**: "Ken Brown & the Stalag XIB (357) Memorial," 207 Squadron Royal Air Force History, last updated January 20, 2019, http://www.207squadron.rafinfo.org.uk/stalag_XIB _ken_brown.htm.

73 **By mid-1944, the**: Ibid.

73 **Conditions continued to deteriorate**: Ibid.

CHAPTER 13: Out of Many, One

75 **The 392nd Bomb Group**: Annette Tison and Andy Laing, "Wendling England History," 392 Bomb Group, https://www.b24 .net/wendlingHistory.htm.

75 **I found a link**: "World War II Luft Camps in Germany," 392 Bomb Group, https://www.b24.net/.

75 **It stated, "One of**: Ibid.

76 **It was a camp**: "Kriegsgefangenen Lagers: Home of the 'Kriegie' Airmen," 392nd Bomb Group, https://b24.net/powCamps.htm.

76 **As Germany started to**: Ibid.

76 **Numbers at this camp**: "POW Camp Stalag VII-A," Moosburg Online, last updated April 24, 2022, https://www.moosburg.org/info /stalag/indeng.html.

76 **A total of 150,000**: Ibid.

76 **In October 1943, when**: "Kriegsgefangenen Lagers: Home of the 'Kriegie' Airmen," 392nd Bomb Group, https://b24.net/pow Camps.htm.

77 **By the war's end**: Ibid.

77 **I found 3,220 records**: "World War II Prisoners of War Data File, 12/7/1941–11/19/1946," National Archives, https://aad.archives.gov /aad/free-text-search-results.jsp?cat=all&s=644&bc=sd&q=Stalag +17B&btnSearch=Search&as_alq=&as_anq=&as_epq=&as_woq=.

77 **Everyone listed had the**: Ibid.

78 **The source of this**: "World War II Prisoners of War Data File, 12/7/1941–11/19/1946 (info)," National Archives, https://aad .archives.gov/aad/series-description.jsp?s=644.

78 **"Using copies of reports**: Ibid.

78 **The first section was**: "Stalag 17B Roster American Prisoners of War," National Archives and 1994 Directory of American Former Prisoners of War 1943–1945 Stalag 17B, http://www.valerosos.com /Stalag17BRoster.pdf.

78 **Under the heading read**: Ibid.

78 **It further stated, "The**: Ibid.

78 **The second section of**: Ibid.

78 **The top of the**: Ibid., 720 (p. 22 of PDF document).

79 **The author indicated that**: Ibid., 759 (p. 61 of PDF document).

79 **In the 1990s, the**: "World War II Prisoners of War Data File, 12/7/1941–11/19/1946 (info)," National Archives, https://aad .archives.gov/aad/series-description.jsp?s=644.

79 **When I typed in**: "Welcome to the Borinqueneers Website!" Puerto Rico's 65th Infantry Regiment US Army, http://www .valerosos.com/.

80 **A paragraph went on**: Ibid.

80 **The home page described**: American Ex-Prisoners of War, http:// www.axpow.org/.

CHAPTER 14: Eureka!

83 **I started this website**: William Doubledee, "Stalag XVII B Introduction," last updated January 25, 2020, http://web.archive.org /web/sitemap/stalag17b.com.

84 **"Like all the other**: William Doubledee, "Stalag XVII B: My Father's Diary," http://web.archive.org/web/sitemap/stalag17b.com.

84 **The first file was named**: William Doubledee, "Stalag XVII B: Files-My list of American prisoners held at Stalag XVII B," http:// web.archive.org/web/sitemap/stalag17b.com.

86 **Enclosed is a copy**: Private email message to the author and reply back, November 9, 2018, and November 10, 2018.

PART IV: THE TRAINING YEARS

CHAPTER 15: Enlistment

95 **I learned that during**: Army Air Forces Aid Society, *AAF The Official Guide to the Army Air Forces*, Simon & Schuster, 1944, 356.

95 **I also discovered that**: Ibid., 9.

95 **In 1917, when America**: Ibid.

95 **In 1920, the Air**: Ibid.

95 **In mid-1941, as**: Ibid., 356.

97 **It was interesting to**: "The Birth of the United States Air Force Force," *Air Force Historical Research Agency*, 2022, https://www .afhra.af.mil/About-Us/Fact-Sheets/Display/Article/433914/the -birth-of-the-united-states-air-force/

97 **"All told, US Army**: Ibid.

CHAPTER 16: Fort Slocum, New York

99 **During World War II, Fort Slocum**: "The Army's Century on Davids Island: Cooks, Railroaders and WACs (1922–1946)," Westchester County Archives, 2018, http://davidsisland .westchesterarchives.com/index.php/history/cooks-railroaders-a -wacs-1922-1946.html.

99 **According to the *AAF***: Army Air Forces Aid Society, *Official Guide,* 103–104.

100 **The Westchester County Archives**: "The Army's Century on Davids Island: Cooks, Railroaders and WACs (1922–1946)," Westchester County Archives.

CHAPTER 17: The Republic of Panama

101 **Rio Hato Air Field, also**: "Rio Hato (Cap Scarlet Martinez Airport)," Pacific Wrecks, updated May 2, 2022, https://pacificwrecks.com /airfields/panama/rio_hato/index.html.

101 **Even before the Japanese**: Jon T. Hoffman and colleagues, "Defending the Canal," in "The Panama Canal: An Army's Enterprise," Center of Military History United States Army Washington, DC, 2009, 86–87, https://history.army.mil/html/books /panama/panamacanal/CMH-70-115-1-PanamaCanal.pdf.

101 **Their primary aim was**: Army Air Forces Aid Society, *Official Guide*, 298.

102 **In 1940, when my**: "Rio Hato," Pacific Wrecks.

102 **Later in 1941, squadrons**: Ibid.

102 **The initial fighter planes**: Ibid.

CHAPTER 18: Las Vegas, Nevada

106 **There were ten crew**: Army Air Forces Aid Society, *Official Guide*, 17–18.

106 **The Flexible Gunnery School**: United States Army Air Forces, "Establishment of Schools and Securing of Structures," in *Army Air Forces Historical Studies: No. 31: Flexible Gunnery Training in the AAF*, prepared by Assistant Chief of Air Staff. Intelligence Historical Division March 1945, last modified March 26, 2017, 7, http://www.ibiblio.org/hyperwar/AAF/AAFHS/AAFHS-31/AAFHS-31-1.html.

106 **The school provided training**: *Flexible Aerial Gunnery: Making a Gunner*, US Army Air Forces 1943, 13:05 min., https://archive.org/details/TF1-760.

107 **The film started with a**: *Rear Gunner*, US Army Air Forces Film, 1943.

108 **I also discovered an**: *Flexible Aerial Gunnery: Making a Gunner*, US Army Air Forces, 1943.

108 **At the start, it**: Ibid.

108 **Clearly, it made the**: Ibid.

108 **In one part, during**: Ibid.

108 **A short training pamphlet**: Army Air Forces, *Get That Fighter*, November 1, 1943.

109 **One of the training**: Ibid.

109 **The first page read**: Ibid.

110 **Over 44,000 students eventually**: United States Army Air Forces, "Establishment of Schools and Securing of Structures," in *Army Air Forces Historical Studies: No. 31: Flexible Gunnery Training in the AAF*, 11.

110 **In the year my**: Ibid., 7.

CHAPTER 19: Crew Training

113 **"The training standards established**: W. F. Craven and J. L. Cate, eds., "Combat Crew and Unit Training," in *The Army Air Forces in World War II: VI Men and Planes*, University of Chicago Press, 1955, 605.

113 **The ultimate goal of**: Ibid.

114 **The Second Air Force**: Ibid., 606.

114 **The book entitled *The***: Ibid.

114 **"The crew was the**: Ibid.

115 **"That was actually where**: Conrad L. Lohoefer, "Conrad L. Lohoefer Oral History," interview by Edward B. Williams, Library of Congress Veterans History Project, May 8, 2003, audio, https://digital.library .shsu.edu/digital/collection/p16042coll1/id/25.

115 **Lohoefer said the**: Ibid.

115 **His plane most likely**: W. F. Craven and J. L. Cate, eds., "The North Atlantic Route," in *The Army Air Forces in World War II: Volume VII Services Around the World*, University of Chicago Press, 1958, 92–100.

CHAPTER 20: Everyone Had a Role

120 **Over twenty million Victory**: Richard R. Lingeman, *Don't You Know There's a War On?* G. P. Putnam's Sons, 1970, 251.

120 **During WWII, the**: "Hollywood & the Home Front—75th Anniversary Special Presentation," Palm Springs Air Museum, February 15, 2020, https://palmspringsairmuseum.org/programs /hollywood-the-home-front-75th-anniversary-special-presentation/.

120 **One question Roosevelt and**: Clayton R. Koppes and Gregory D. Black, *Hollywood Goes to War: How Politics, Profits and Propaganda Shaped World War II Movies*, University of California Press, 1990, 66.

122 **The animated Disney film**: Walt Disney Studios, *Education for Death: The Making of the Nazi*, released January 15, 1943, by Walt Disney Productions, video, 10:43, https://www.c-span.org/video /?464005-2/education-death.

122 **The animated film starring**: Walt Disney Productions, *Der Fuehrer's Face*, released January 1, 1943.

123 **In 1940, Charlie Chaplin**: Charlie Chaplin, director, *The Great Dictator*, released October 15, 1940.

123 **"Soldiers! Don't fight for**: Ibid.

124 **"Against the fiercest assault**: Donald V. Coers, "Introduction," *The Moon Is Down* by John Steinbeck, Penguin Books, 1995, xxiv.

125 **As one nation, indivisible**: Historic Documents, *The Pledge of Allegiance,* https://www.ushistory.org/documents/pledge.htm.

PART V: THE EUROPEAN THEATER

CHAPTER 21: The Friendly Invasion

129 **"They are overpaid, overconfident**: Sir Hugh Saunders, "The Pleasure Is Ours," *The Rotarian,* April 1958, 26.

130 **An adage in one**: War and Navy Departments, *A Short Guide to Great Britain,* War and Navy Departments, 1943, 17.

130 **The publication date was**: Ibid., 28–29.

CHAPTER 22: East Anglia

131 **We won't do much:** Gerald Astor, *The Mighty Eighth*, Penguin Group, 1997, 3.

131 **In 1941, after the:** National Geographic, *Heroes of the Sky: The Real Mighty Eighth Air Force,* filmed by National Geographic, 2020.

131 **The Army assigned the:** Astor, *The Mighty Eighth*, 2.

131 **Brigadier General Ira Eaker:** Ibid., 3.

131 **When General Eaker arrived:** National Geographic, *Heroes of the Sky,* 2020.

131 **By August 1943, when**: Ibid.

131 **By mid-1944, the**: Ibid.

131 **Their first regular mission:** John F. Loosbrock, "A Lesson from History," *Air Force: The Magazine of Aerospace Power,* 45, no. 8 (August 1962):6.

132 **A year later, on:** "Regensburg/Schweinfurt, August 17, 1943," National Museum of the United States Air Force, https://www .nationalmuseum.af.mil/Visit/Museum-Exhibits/Fact-Sheets /Display/Article/1519655/regensburgschweinfurt-august-17-1943/.

132 **And on December 24, 1944:** Astor, *The Mighty Eighth*, 372–375.

132 **So, in just over:** "Eighth Air Force History," 8th Air Force/J-GSOC,

https://www.8af.af.mil/About-Us/Fact-Sheets/Display/Article
/333794/eighth-air-force-history/.

132 **In *One Last Look***: Philip Kaplan and Rex Alan Smith, *One Last Look: A Sentimental Journey to the Eighth Air Force Heavy Bomber Bases of World War II in England*, Abbeville Press, 1983, 35.

133 **A quote by one**: Ibid.

CHAPTER 23: Bassingbourn

135 **My father drew the**: Kaplan and Smith, *One Last Look*, 58.

135 **In October 1942, the**: Marion H. Havelaar, *The Ragged Irregulars of Bassingbourn: The 91st Bombardment Group in World War II*, Schiffer Publishing, 1995, 10.

135 **If an airfield met**: Roger A. Freeman, *Airfields of the Eighth Then and Now*, 6th ed., Battle of Britain Prints International, 1992, 8.

136 **Commander Wray took one**: Havelaar, *Ragged Irregulars*, 10.

CHAPTER 24: The Ragged Irregulars

139 **Because the leaders had:** The 91st Bomb Group Memorial Association, "The Ragged Irregulars," http://www.91stbombgroup.com/91st_info/raggedinfo.html.

139 **The 91st had four**: Havelaar, *Ragged Irregulars*, 9.

139 **Initially, the 91st aimed**: Documented in the 91st Bomb Group 1942 Dailies.

139 **By 1944, the bomb**: Ibid.

140 **The 91st Bomb Group's**: "91st Bomb Group The Ragged Irregulars," American Air Museum in Britain, last modified August 23, 2019, https://www.americanairmuseum.com/unit/544.

140 **They destroyed 420 enemy**: Ibid.

140 **They were the first**: Ibid.

140 **The 91st led the**: Ibid.

140 **The "Nine-O-Nine," another B-17**: Ibid.

140 **Last, the 91st was**: Ibid.

140 **When daylight strategic bombing was**: Havelaar, *Ragged Irregulars*, 263.

141 **He decided to create**: Ibid.

CHAPTER 25: A Plane Named "Bomb Boogie"

145 **On the website of**: "People," American Air Museum in Britain, last modified August 17, 2020, http://www.americanairmuseum.com /person/45135.

145 **Under this category, the**: "Aircraft," American Air Museum in Britain, https://www.americanairmuseum.com/aircraft/8299.

148 **He stated, "it was:** Ray Bowden, *Plane Names & Fancy Noses*, Design Oracle Partnership, 1993, 10.

148 **The names are highly personal**: John Steinbeck, *Once There Was a War*, Penguin Books, 2007, 30.

CHAPTER 26: Tempsford

151 **Edward Jablonski, in his**: Edward Jablonski, *Double Strike: The Epic Air Raids on Regensburg/Schweinfurt*, Doubleday, 1974, 126–127.

152 **When requesting permission for:** Kaplan and Smith, *One Last Look,* 36.

153 **Tempsford was home to**: John T. Correll, "The Moon Squadrons," *Air Force Magazine,* July 1, 2012, https://www.airforcemag.com /article/0712moon/.

153 **These specialized planes allowed**: Bill Gunston, *Classic World War II Aircraft Cutaways,* 3rd ed., Barnes & Noble Books, 1999, 22–23.

153 **Because there was no:** Ibid.

153 **The pilots would quickly**: Ibid.

153 **The agents, sometimes wearing:** Atlas Obscura, "Westland Lysander at the Shuttleworth Collection, Central Bedfordshire England," https://www.atlasobscura.com/places/westland-lysander-at-the -shuttleworth-collection.

153 **The pilots from Special**: Pathfinder Craig, "161 Squadron Operation Sorties Feb/Mar 1944," https://masterbombercraig.wordpress.com /bombing-operations/operations-no-161-squadron/.

154 **In an article in:** James Stuart, "R.A.F. Fly-by-Nights Beat Gestapo," *Evening Standard,* June 16, 1945, http://www.161squadron.org /historyoftempsford.htm.

154 **Today, in Tempsford, several**: "History," Tempsford Memorial Trust, http://www.tempsfordmemorial.co.uk/history.html.

CHAPTER 27: The Crew

157 An "**esprit de corps**" **and close**: Kaplan and Smith, *One Last Look*, 30.

CHAPTER 28: The Dailies

161 **An introduction to the**: "Dailies of the 401st Squadron," 91st Bomb Group Memorial Association,

162 **The author of the**: "Dailies of the 401st Squadron 1943," 91st Bomb Group Memorial Association, transcribed by Merle Choffel, October 6, 2005.

162 **As noted in *The***: Lord Moran, *The Anatomy of Courage: The Classic WWI Account of the Psychological Effects of War*, Carroll & Graf Publishers, 2007, xxii.

162 **What are the early**: Ibid., xxi.

163 **These country homes housed**: Keith Thomas, *Flak Houses Then and Now: The Story of American Rest Homes in England During WWII*, Battle of Britain International Limited, 2006, 7.

163 **The airmen were granted**: Ibid.

164 **The May 31, 1942**: "Dailies of the 401st Squadron 1942," 91st Bomb Group Memorial Association, transcribed by Merle Choffel, February 11, 2005.

164 **Life starts at Walla Walla**: Ibid.

164 **On August 23, 1942**: Ibid.

165 **The following note expressed**: Ibid.

165 **On October 14, 1942:** Ibid.

165 **On November 8, 1942:** Ibid.

166 **Captain Davison recounted the:** Ibid.

167 **Even the Dailies highlighted:** "Dailies of the 401st Squadron 1943," October 6, 2005.

168 **A beautiful, colorful drawing**: Larry Davis, *B-17 in Action*, Squadron/Signal Publications, 1984, 2.

CHAPTER 29: A Good Pilot

169 **The Dailies described the**: "Dailies of the 401st Squadron 1943," October 6, 2005.

170 **During my father's time**: Brian Todd Carey, "Operation Pointblank: Evolution of Allied Air Doctrine," *World War II*, November 1998.

171 **By the war's end**: "8th Air Force," Oakland Aviation Museum, https://www.oaklandaviationmuseum.org/8th-air-force.

CHAPTER 30: Little Friends

173 **Like Shepherd Dogs protecting**: Army Air Forces Aid Society, *Official Guide*, 88.

173 **During the last few**: National Geographic, *Heroes of the Sky*, 2020.

173 **On August 17, 1943**: Jablonski, *Double Strike*, 183.

173 **In a follow-up debriefing**: National Geographic, *Heroes of the Sky*, 2020.

173 **"The bomber will always**: Stanley Baldwin, "The Air Threat," Lord President of Council Remarks to House of Commons, *London Times*, November 10, 1932.

174 **He concluded that the**: Astor, *The Mighty Eighth*, 75.

174 **Evasive maneuvers close to**: Ibid.

174 **Le May often flew**: National Geographic, *Heroes of the Sky*, 2020.

174 **In November 1943, the**: Ibid.

174 **These fighter planes were**: Ibid.

175 **General Doolittle summed up**: Amy Pastan, *The Smithsonian Book of Air & Space Trivia*, Smithsonian Books, 2014, 160.

175 **Another reason that prompted**: National Geographic, *Heroes of the Sky*, 2020.

176 **In truth, Ira Eaker**: Ibid.

176 **He said, "We will**: Ibid.

176 **When Eaker adopted the**: Donald L. Miller, *Masters of the Air: America's Bomber Boys Who Fought the Air War Against Nazi Germany*, Simon & Schuster, 2006, 113.

176 **The Americans touted that**: Ibid., 6.

176 **"You flip on your**: Kaplan and Smith, *One Last Look*, 113.

177 **To create improved accuracy**: Ibid.

177 **The Air Force commanders picked**: Ibid.

177 **"The group lead crew**: Ibid.

CHAPTER 31: The Missions

181 In *A Tail Gunner's*: Gerald E. McDowell, *A Tail Gunner's Tale*, Vantage Press, 1991, 45.

183 **"Gentlemen, you are cleared**: National Geographic, *Heroes of the Sky*, 2020.

183 **He wrote, "On August**: Donald L. Hayes, *Synopsis of Schweinfurt-Regensburg Mission*, 1985.

183 **The Eighth Air Force lost**: Jablonski, *Double Strike*, 183.

183 **The 91st Bombardment Group**: Havelaar, *Ragged Irregulars*, 58.

183 **In his synopsis of**: Donald L. Hayes, *Synopsis of Schweinfurt-Regensburg Mission*, 1985.

184 **Jablonski summarized the**: Jablonski, *Double Strike*, 127.

CHAPTER 32: Captured by Krauts

185 **In his notes, he**: Donald L. Hayes, *A Tail Gunner in the 8th Air Force*, 1985.

186 **In the beautiful book**: Nora Krug, *Belonging: A German Reckons with History and Home*, Scribner, 2018, chapter 1. (Reprinted with permission of Scribner, a division of Simon & Schuster, Inc. from BELONGING by Nora Krug. Copyright © 2018 by Nora Krug. All Rights reserved).

187 **She described why it**: Ibid., chapter 2.

187 **She asked the same**: Ibid., chapter 1.

PART VI: PRISONER OF WAR

CHAPTER 33: Missing in Action

191 **We were merely young**: Elmer Bendiner, *The Fall of Fortresses*, G. P. Putnam's Sons, 1980, 238.

191 **If there was enough**: Elwood D. Arp, *American-British Military Intelligence Service Escape and Evasion Report No. 604*, April 27, 1944.

191 **After the Germans shot**: Ibid.

192 **It was thought that:** Ray Bowden, *Plane Names & Fancy Noses*, Design Oracle Partnership, 1993, 38.

192 **The crew began bailing:** In the paragraph from *Plane Names &
Fancy Noses,* the author states my father saw five parachutes open up.
Note: This is not a direct quote from my father and the number of
parachutes my father saw may differ from the five mentioned in this
paragraph.

192 **Most were quickly rounded:** Correction to quote in *Plane Names &
Fancy Noses,* 38. Six crewmen managed to initially evade capture and
four eventually made their way to Spain.

194 **In my father's MACR:** Army Air Force Station 121 MACR No.
514, September 6, 1943.

194 **First, the staff at:** Ibid.

194 **Second, military personnel presented:** Army Air Force Station 121
Missing Air Crew Report No. 514, September 19, 1944.

195 **The paragraph under the:** Ibid.

195 **"Pilot, co-pilot, top turret gunner:** Ibid.

196 **Not until the last:** Ibid.

198 **"I went out the:** Arp, *Escape and Evasion Report,* 1944.

198 **The copilot described his:** Howard Sherman, *American-British
Military Intelligence Service Escape and Evasion Report No. 608,*
April 29, 1944.

198 **And the bombardier's description:** Chauncey Hicks, *American-
British Intelligence Service Escape and Evasion Report No. 515,*
March 25, 1944.

199 **Pilot Arp describes his:** Arp, *Escape and Evasion Report,* 1944.

199 **After hitting down hard:** Hicks, *Escape and Evasion Report,* 1944.

199 **"There were 40 in:** Arp, *Escape and Evasion Report,* 1944.

199 **"The basket contained food:** Ibid.

200 **"During the crossing, I:** Ibid.

200 **The copilot, Howard Sherman:** Howard Sherman, *Escape and
Evasion Report,* 1944.

200 **As he marches to:** John Steinbeck, *The Moon Is Down,* 4th ed.,
Penguin Books, 1995, 111.

CHAPTER 34: Stories from Camp

203 **None of us would**: Ned Handy and Kemp Battle, *The Flame Keepers: The True Story of an American Soldier's Survival Inside Stalag 17*, St. Martin's Press, 2006, 227.

204 **In *A Tail Gunner's***: McDowell, *Tail Gunner's Tale*, 78–81.

204 **In 1943, the year**: "The Luftwaffe Interrogators at Dulag Luft-Oberursel," World War II—Prisoners of War—Stalag Luft I Online, http://www.merkki.com/new_page_2.htm.

204 **The Luftwaffe interrogators had**: Ibid.

204 **His name was Hanns**: Raymond F. Toliver, *The Interrogator*, Aero Publishers, 1978,190–191.

204 **One POW commented, "Hanns**: Ibid.

204 **On July 21, 1942**: US Army Air Forces, *Instructions for Officers and Men of the Eighth Air Force in the Event of Capture*, July 21, 1942, Stalag Luft I Online, http://www.merkki.com/documents.htm.

205 **"It is good to**: Ibid.

205 **And another reminder, "The**: Ibid.

206 **My father's new prison**: McDowell, *Tail Gunner's Tale*, 88.

208 **Ned Handy, in his**: Handy and Battle, *The Flame Keepers*, 48.

208 **There would be yells**: Ibid., 49.

208 **With answers back like**: Ibid.

209 **In *The Flame Keepers***: Ibid.

210 **Separated from the other**: McDowell, *Tail Gunner's Tale*, 88.

210 **The Germans built the**: Ibid.

210 **Due to the overcrowded**: Handy and Battle, *The Flame Keepers*, 53.

211 **"The winter here was**: Kay Sloan, ed., *Not without Honor: The Nazi POW Journal of Steve Carano*, University of Arkansas Press, 2008, 36.

213 **"We created a theater**: Senior Master Sgt. Minnie Jones, "The Real Hogan's Heroes visit 433d Airlift Wing," *433rd Airlift Wing Public Affairs*, May 13, 2011, https://www.433aw.afrc.af.mil/News/Article-Display/Article/179635/the-real-hogans-heroes-visit-433d-airlift-wing/.

214 **It turned out that**: Handy and Battle, *The Flame Keepers*, 5.

214 **He evaded capture for**: Ibid.

214 **I am not sure**: Lloyd R. Shoemaker, *The Escape Factory: The Story of MIS-X, America's Ultra-Secret Masterminds of World War II's Greatest Escapes*, St. Martin's Press, 1990, 161.

215 **Additionally, the POWs trained**: Ibid., 164–165.

215 **"Kurtenbach appointed Staff Sergeant**: Joseph R. Kurtenbach, "War behind the Wire: Life and Escape from Stalag 17B," *Air Force Historical Foundation: Air Power History* 58, no. 4 (Winter 2011), 4–13, https://www.jstor.org/stable/26276106?refreqid=excelsior %3Ae84e7553f12c2b85d02ba2617bf66528.

215 **"Matters were in such**: Ken J. Kurtenbach, "A Man of Confidence," *Hell's Angels Newsletter*, May 1988, 10, http://www.303rdbg.com /hanl/1988-05.pdf.

216 **"We needed the same**: Handy and Battle, *The Flame Keepers*, 227.

216 **"His sermons and stories**: Sloan, *Not without Honor*, 73.

217 **In the book, *No***: Doris Kearns Goodwin, *No Ordinary Time: Franklin and Eleanor Roosevelt: The Home Front in World War II*, Simon & Schuster, 1994, 467.

218 **And at times, letters**: Nichol and Rennell, *The Last Escape*, 100–101.

218 **For example, precious parcels**: McDowell, *Tail Gunner's Tale*, 99.

218 **After the war, the**: Ibid.

218 **Americans also believed their**: Ibid.

218 **After a devastating airstrike**: Nichol and Rennell, *The Last Escape*, 193.

218 **Rumors of the Nazis'**: Ibid., 355.

219 **In his journal, Steve**: Sloan, *Not without Honor*, 22.

CHAPTER 35: The Barbed-Wire Front

221 **In this war American**: Shoemaker, *The Escape Factory*, 16.

221 **Two intelligence organizations were**: Ibid., 17.

221 **MIS-Y was established:** Ibid., 4.

221 **In the book, *The***: Ibid., 5.

222 **The other covert unit**: Ibid., 4.

222 **So ultra-secret was this**: Ibid., 5–6.

222 **After the war ended:** Ibid., 1, 190–192.

222 **It was remarkable that:** Ibid., 20.

222 **When the Eighth Air Force:** Ibid., 7–12.

222 **Upon its inception, MIS-X:** Ibid., 12–13.

223 **In *The Escape Factory*:** Ibid., 20.

224 **Two fictitious organizations were:** Ibid., 28.

225 **In the end, MIS-X:** Ibid., 202.

CHAPTER 36: The March

227 **No one foresaw Hitler's:** Nichol and Rennell, *The Last Escape*, 189, 108–109.

227 **In mixed reports, the:** Ibid., 94.

228 **In *The Last Escape*:** Ibid., 357.

228 **Additional stories ludicrously declared:** Ibid., 94.

228 **In his book, *Kriegie*:** Kenneth W. Simmons, *Kriegie: Prisoner of War,* 2nd ed., 2019, 107.

228 **The Forced March for:** Eric Ethier, "A More Thorough Report," *America in WWII*, February 2006, http://www.americainwwii.com /articles/stalag-17-b/.

228 **Those prisoners too sick:** Ibid.

229 **In an article he:** Kurt Kurtenbach, "Kurt Kurtenbach's account of the last days of Stalag XVIIB," May 9, 2022, http://web.archive.org/web /sitemap/stalag17b.com.

229 **During the march, the:** Eric Ethier, "A More Thorough Report," 2006.

230 **The POW went on:** Nichol and Rennell, *The Last Escape,* 187.

230 **After eighteen days and:** "Krems, Austria–Stalag 17b: American Prisoners of War in Germany," prepared by Military Intelligence Service War Department, November 1, 1945, compiled and presented by Greg Hatton, 392nd Bomb Group, https://b24.net /powStalag17.htm.

230 **On May 3, 1945:** Ibid.

230 **Six days later, on:** Ibid.

CHAPTER 37: The Escape

233 **The POWs outnumbered the**: Richard H. Hoffman, *Stalag 17B*, 1988, 175.

233 **Being so close to**: Handy and Battle, *The Flame Keepers*, 288.

PART VII: HOMEWARD BOUND

CHAPTER 38: Demobilization

237 **The cigarette camps varied:** WW2 US Medical Research Centre, "RAMP: Administrative Repatriation Procedures & Evacuation and Disposition of Recovered Allied Military Personnel," https://www.med-dept.com/articles/r-a-m-p/.

238 **Many RAMPS suffered from:** Ibid.

238 **By the end of**: Kim Guise, "Camp Lucky Strike: RAMP Camp No.1," June 26, 2020, The National WWII Museum, https://www.nationalww2museum.org/war/articles/camp-lucky-strike.

239 **In the book, *A***: McDowell, *Tail Gunner's Tale*, 128.

CHAPTER 39: The Crossing

241 **Operation Magic Carpet:** Elly Farelly, "Bringing Home the 8 Million Boys after WWII; Operation Magic Carpet," *War History Online*, June 29, 2016, https://www.warhistoryonline.com/world-war-ii/brining-home-8-million-boys-wwii-operation-magic-carpet.html.

241 **In Europe alone, over**: Collin Makamson, "Home Alive By '45': Operation Magic Carpet," National WWII Museum, October 2, 2020, https://www.nationalww2museum.org/war/articles/operation-magic-carpet-1945.

241 **In the Pacific, the**: Ibid.

241 **In the ETO, the**: "Home Alive By '45': Operation Magic Carpet," National WWII Museum, October 2, 2020.

241 **Therefore, in the beginning:** Ibid.

241 **Luxury passenger ships such**: Elly Farelly, "Bringing Home the 8 Million Boys after WWII; Operation Magic Carpet," *War History Online*, June 29, 2016.

242 **The Military determined eligibility**: "Home Alive By '45': Operation Magic Carpet," National WWII Museum.

242 **You needed a score**: Ibid.

CHAPTER 40: Repatriation, Rejuvenation, and an Honorable Discharge

243 **In 1943, the Army**: W. F. Craven and J. L. Cate, eds., "Redeployment and Demobilization," in *The Army Air Forces in World War II: VI Men and Planes*, University of Chicago Press, 1955, 525.

243 **Later, in 1944, three:** Ibid.

244 **"Rest was stressed in**: Matthew M. Peek, "US Army Redistribution Stations in World War II: Asheville, North Carolina," *State Archives of North Carolina*, 2015, https://www.ncpedia.org/us-army -redistribution-stations-Asheville.

244 **In 1942, this thriving:** William H. Sokolic, "Atlantic City Was a Military Base in 1942 WWII," *Irish Brigade*, August 14, 2016, https://www.irishbrigade.com/blogs/http-www-irishbrigade-com -blogs/atlantic-city-military-base-in-1942-wwii.

244 **In 1943, Atlantic City**: Ibid.

244 **During World War II, when:** Juliana Deh Carvalho Machado and colleagues. "Refeeding Syndrome, an Undiagnosed and Forgotten Potentially Fatal Condition," *BMJ case reports*, vol. 2009 (2009).

CHAPTER 41: World War II Veteran

247 **The Honorable Service Lapel Badge**: The American War Library, *The Badge of Honorable Discharge: The United States Military Service Honorable Discharge Pin*," https://www.amervets.com/replacement /duck.htm.

247 **The young soldiers nicknamed:** Kirk Stotzer, "Ruptured Duck-Honorable Service Lapel Pin," Medals of America: Military Badges, December 21, 2011, https://www.medalsofamerica.com/blog /ruptured-duck-honorable-discharge-lapel-pin/.

PART VIII: LOOKING FORWARD

Bibliography

Army Air Forces Aid Society. *AAF The Official Guide to the Army Air Forces.* New York: Simon & Schuster, 1944.

Astor, Gerald. *The Mighty Eighth: The Air War in Europe as Told by the Men Who Fought It.* New York: Penguin Group, 1997.

Bendiner, Elmer. *The Fall of Fortresses.* New York: G. P. Putnam's Sons, 1980.

Bingley, Paul. *US Air Force Bases in the UK.* United Kingdom: Amberley Publishing, 2018.

Bowden, Ray. *Plane Names & Fancy Noses.* London: Design Oracle Partnership, 1993.

Bowers, Peter M. *Fortress in the Sky.* Granada Hills, California: Sentry Books, 1976.

Brickhill, Paul. *The Great Escape.* New York: Amereon House, 1950.

Brokaw, Tom. *The Greatest Generation.* 2nd ed. New York: Random House, 2004.

Chapin, William. *Milk Run.* Sausalito, California: WindGate Press, 1992.

Colby, John. *War from the Ground Up: The 90th Division in WWII.* Austin, Texas: Eakin Nortex Press, 1991.

Craven, W. F., and Cate, J. L., eds. *The Army Air Forces in World War II: Plans and Early Operations January 1938 to August 1942: Volume I.* Chicago: University of Chicago Press, 1948.

Craven, W. F., and Cate, J. L., eds. *The Army Air Forces in World War II: Men and Planes: Volume VI.* Chicago: University of Chicago Press, 1955.

Craven, W. F., and Cate, J. L., eds. *The Army Air Forces in World War II: Services Around the World: Volume VII.* Chicago: University of Chicago Press, 1958.

Davis, Larry. *B-17 in Action*. Carrollton, Texas: Squadron/Signal Publications, 1984.

Freeman, Roger A. *Airfields of the Eighth Then and Now*. 6th ed. London: Battle of Britain Prints International, 1992.

Freeman, Roger A. *The Mighty Eighth in Color*. Stillwater, Minnesota: Specialty Press, 1992.

Goodwin, Doris Kearns. *No Ordinary Time: Franklin and Eleanor Roosevelt: The Home Front in World War II*. New York: Simon & Schuster, 1994.

Gunston, Bill. *Classic World War II Aircraft Cutaways*. 4th ed. New York: Barnes & Noble Books, 1999.

Handy, Ned, and Battle, Kemp. *The Flame Keepers: The True Story of an American Soldier's Survival Inside Stalag 17*. New York: St. Martin's Press, 2006.

Havelaar, Marion H. *The Ragged Irregulars of Bassingbourn: The 91st Bombardment Group in World War II*. Atglen, Pennsylvania: Schiffer Publishing, 1995.

Hoffman, Richard H. *Stalag 17B: Prisoner of War*. Xlibris, 1988.

Jablonski, Edward. *Double Strike: The Epic Air Raids on Regensburg/Schweinfurt*. New York: Doubleday, 1974.

Jablonski, Edward. *Flying Fortress: The Illustrated Biography of the B-17s and the Men Who Flew Them*. New York: Doubleday, 1965.

Kaplan, Philip, and Smith, Rex Alan. *One Last Look: A Sentimental Journey to the Eighth Air Force Heavy Bomber Bases of World War II in England*. New York: Abbeville Press, 1983.

Kelley, Luther Erwin. *World War II From a Waist Gunner's View of Stalag 17*. Xlibris Corporation, 2008.

Koppes, Clayton R., and Black, Gregory D. *Hollywood Goes to War: How Politics, Profits and Propaganda Shaped World War II Movies*. Berkeley and Los Angeles: University of California Press, 1990.

Krug, Nora. *Belonging: A German Reckons with History and Home*. New York: Scribner, 2018.

Lingeman, Richard R. *Don't You Know There's a War On?* New York: G. P. Putnam's Sons, 1970.

MacDonald, Charles B. *The Battle of the Bulge*. London: Weidenfeld and Nicolson, 1984.

McDowell, Gerald E. *A Tail Gunner's Tale*. New York: Vantage Press, 1991.

Miller, Donald L. *Masters of the Air: America's Bomber Boys Who Fought the Air War Against Nazi Germany.* New York: Simon & Schuster, 2006.

Moran, Lord. *The Anatomy of Courage: The Classic WWI Account of the Psychological Effects of War.* New York: Carroll & Graf Publishers, 2007.

Nichol, John, and Rennell, Tony. *The Last Escape: The Untold Story of Allied Prisoners of War in Europe 1944–45.* New York: Viking Penguin, 2003.

Novey, Jack. *The Cold Blue Sky: A B-17 Gunner in World War Two.* Charlottesville, Virginia: Howell Press, 1997.

Pringle, Duncan John. *Life as a POW: What My Father Never Told Me,* 2016.

Rasmussen, Randall L. *Hell's Belle: From a B-17 to Stalag 17B.* Santa Fe, New Mexico: Sunstone Press, 2003.

Shirer, William L. *The Rise and Fall of the Third Reich: A History of Nazi Germany.* New York: Simon & Schuster, 1960.

Shoemaker, Lloyd R. *The Escape Factory: The Story of MIS-X, America's Ultra-Secret Masterminds of World War II's Greatest Escapes.* New York: St. Martin's Press, 1990.

Simmons, Kenneth W. *Kriegie: Prisoner of War.* 2nd ed., 2019.

Sloan, Kay, ed. *Not without Honor: The Nazi POW Journal of Steve Carano.* Fayetteville: University of Arkansas Press, 2008.

Steinbeck, John. *The Moon Is Down.* 4th ed. New York: Penguin Books, 1995. (First published in the United States in 1942.)

Steinbeck, John. *Once There Was a War.* New York: Penguin Books, 2007. (First copyright in 1943. First published in the United States by Viking Press in 1958.)

Stiles, Bert. *Serenade to the Big Bird.* Atglen, Pennsylvania: Schiffer Military History, 2001.

Thomas, Keith. *Flak Houses Then and Now: The Story of American Rest Homes in England During WWII.* Old Harlow, United Kingdom: Battle of Britain International Limited, 2006.

Thompson, Robert Smith, and Axelrod, Alan. *Nazi Germany History Examined.* New York: Penguin Random House, 2018.

Toliver, Raymond F. *The Interrogator.* Aero Publishers, 1978.

Verity, Hugh. *We Landed by Moonlight: The Secret RAF Landings in France 1940–1944.* 4th ed. Manchester, England: Crecy Publishing Limited, 2000.

Index

I

instructions in the event of capture, 198, 204-205

interrogation, 67, 203-206

J

Jablonski, Edward
Double Strike, 151, 184

Jewish Holocaust, 9, 25, 29, 47-48, 66, 218, 228-230, 262
United States Holocaust Memorial Museum, 66

K

Kaplan and Smith
One Last Look, 132, 157, 176-177

Katyn Massacre, 39-40, 72

Kimbolton, 135-136, 165

Krauts (German prison guards), 186

Krems, Austria, 76-78, 205, 229

Kriegsgefangener (Kriegie), 65-66, 208

Kurtenbach, Joseph R., 215

Kurtenbach, Kenneth "Kurt" J., 212, 214-216, 224-225, 229

L

Lamsdorf, Germany (now Lambinowice, Poland), 38, 40, 67, 72

lapel button, 92, 247-249

Las Vegas, Nevada, 105-111

The Last Escape (Nichol and Rennell), 65, 228, 230

Laval-en-Laonnois, France, 194-196

LeMay, Curtis, 174, 243

Lille, France, 146, 193-194, 197

Little Friends, 102, 173

Lohoefer, Conrad L., 114-115

long marches (also called forced marches), 9, 17, 20-21, 30-33, 61-62, 72, 75-76, 84, 227-230, 233-234, 262

Luftwaffe (German Air Force), 18-19, 38, 67, 70, 173-175, 183, 204
airmen POW camps, 38, 67, 71-72, 75-76, 78, 205
destruction of the, 140, 175

Lysanders, 153

M

MACR. *See* Missing Air Crew Report

Man of Confidence, 212, 224. *See* Kurtenbach, Kenneth "Kurt" J.

Map of Route Taken, 193-195

Marciano, Rocky, 93-94

Mauthausen (extermination camp), 218

McDowell, Gerald E.
A Tail Gunner's Tale, 181, 204, 239

MI9 (British Intelligence), 222-223, 225

Military Personnel File, 12, 57-58

Millward, Dean (waist gunner), 118, 142-143, 146, 158-159

Missing Air Crew Report (MACR), 84, 87, 146, 192-196

MIS-X (secret American intelligence agency), 215, 221-225

MIS-Y, 221

Mons-en-Pevele, France, 146, 193-195

The Moon is Down (Steinbeck), 124, 200

moon squadrons (RAF 138 and 161 Special Duty Squadrons), 153-154

Moosburg, 20-21, 76, 85

Moran, Lord
The Anatomy of Courage, 162

Moulsford Manor (country home), 162-163

Office of War Information, 120-
121, 217

Watkins, Claude, 71

Wehrmacht, 67, 76

Weilhart Forest, 229-231

Weltman, Nathan (navigator), 143,
146, 158-159

Wenninghoff, John B. (radio operator),
118, 142-143, 146-147, 158-159

World War II Prisoner of War Data
Files, 13, 17-18, 37, 77-80

World War II veterans, 6-7, 9, 48,
52-54, 63, 68-69, 80, 247-249, 253-
255, 262-263

Wray, Colonel Stanley T., 136, 139-
141, 165-166

Photo Credits

Photo 1. Stalag Luft III: The Long March. Source: 303rd Bomb Group website: http://www.303rdbg.com/pow-camps.html. Reprinted with permission.

Photo 2. Our Route through Germany and Poland. Source: Map created by the author.

Photo 3. American Red Cross Map of POW Camps. Source: 303rd Bomb Group, http://www.303rdbg.com/pow-camps.html. Reprinted with permission. Original source: The American National Red Cross.

Photo 4. My Father and Rocky Marciano. Source: Personal family photo.

Photo 5. My Father's Photo Shortly after Enlistment. Source: Personal family photo.

Photo 6. Get That Fighter. Source: "Prepared By Army Air Forces Operations Analysis Section And A.A.F. Training Aids Division In Collaboration With U.S. Navy And Central Flexible Gunnery Instructors School With The Assistance Of Time INC., November 1, 1943."

Photos 7a, 7b, and 7c. My Father with Wings. Source: Personal family photo. **US Army Air Forces Aircrew Badge** and **US Army Air Forces Aerial Gunner Badge** are from the author's personal collection.

Photo 8. The North Atlantic Air Ferry Routes. Source: Chapter 17: Establishment of the Eighth Air Force in the United Kingdom, in *Army Air Forces in World War II: Plans & Early Operations January 1938 to August 1942: Volume I,* Edited by W. F. Craven and J. L. Cate (University of Chicago Press, 1948), 643, https://www.ibiblio.org /hyperwar/AAF/I/maps/AAF-I-30.jpg. Public domain. Reprinted and credited in accordance with licensing agreement.

Photo 9. Crew Picture. Source: Personal family photo.

Photo 10. Eighth Air Force Installations: June 1944. Source: Steve Snyder. Reprinted with permission.

Photo 11. Bassingbourn Air Force Base. Source: United States Army Air Forces, 91st Bomb Group. Public domain. A copy of this photo is from the Imperial War Museum, Freeman collection (©IMW, FRE 3638). Used with permission. Original photo by Joseph Harlick, 91st Bomb Group photographer.

Photo 12. Control Tower at Bassingbourn. Source: United States National Archives and Records Administration. Public domain. Reprinted and credited in accordance with licensing agreement.

Photo 13. "Bomb Boogie" Crew Members with Redline—the Irish Setter Mascot of the 91st Bomb Group at Bassingbourn. Source: ©IMW, FRE 3526. Used with permission.

Photo 14. "Bomb Boogie" Crew and Mascot! Source: 91st Bomb Group Memorial Association. Reprinted with permission.

Photo 15. "Bomb Boogie" with Flight Crew Ready to Board. Source: Personal family photo.

Photo 16. "Bomb Boogie" with Flak. Source: ©IMW, FRE 0068. Used with permission. Original photo by Joseph Harlick.

Photo 17. My Father's Photo of Crew Members in Front of "Bomb Boogie." Source: Personal family photo.

Photo 18. "Bomb Boogie" With Her Bomb Doors Open. Source: National Archives and Records Administration. Photo from https://www.fold3.com/image/161312517. Public domain. Reprinted and credited in accordance with licensing agreement.

Photo 19. "Bomb Boogie" Dropping Her Bombs. Source: National Archives and Records Administration. Photo from https://www.fold3.com/image/37208568. Original photo by Joseph Harlick. Public domain. Reprinted and credited in accordance with licensing agreement.

Photo 20. The Bomber Raid on Stuttgart, Germany. https://historyshots.com/products/mission-91 Source: Courtesy of HistoryShots.com.

Photo 21. Map of Route Taken. Source: Missing Air Crew Report (MACR #514). Map references and interpretations of the MACR report are courtesy of Mick Hanou, President of the 91st Bomb Group Memorial Association.

Photo 22. One of the Foreboding Guard Towers at Stalag 17B. Source: Ben Phelper, *Kriegie Memories,* from www.b24.net. Reprinted with permission.

Photo 23. Stalag 17B Main Gate. Source: Ben Phelper, from *Kriegie Memories,* http://web.archive.org/web/sitemap/stalag17b.com. Reprinted with permission.

Photo 24. Stalag 17B Barracks Where the American Prisoners Were Detained. Source: Ben Phelper, from *Kriegie Memories,* http://web .archive.org/web/sitemap/stalag17b.com. Reprinted with permission.

Photo 25. Barrack 36A in the American Compound at Stalag 17B. Source: Ben Phelper, from *Kriegie Memories,* http://web.archive.org /web/sitemap/stalag17b.com. Reprinted with permission.

Photo 26. Roll Call—Appell. Source: Ben Phelper, from *Kriegie Memories,* http://web.archive.org/web/sitemap/stalag17b.com. Reprinted with permission.

Photo 27. Crew Photo of George N. Dillard (Toby) and Kurt Kurtenbach. Source: 303rd Bomb Group, http://www.303rdbg.com/. Reprinted with permission.

Photo 28. Stalag 17B Forced March. Source: Stalag 17b website, http://web.archive.org/web/sitemap/stalag17b.com. Reprinted with permission.

Photo 29. Building Shelter in the Weilhart Forest. Source: Stalag 17b website, http://web.archive.org/web/sitemap/stalag17b.com. Reprinted with permission.

Photos 30a and b. The Honorable Service Lapel Badge and Button. Source: Author's personal collection.

Photos 31a and b. American Prisoners of War Silver Dollar. Source: Presidential $1 Coin image from the United States Mint.

About the Author

Maureen Buick is a retired registered nurse and a World War II history buff. She is a member of the 91st Bomb Group Memorial Association and serves on the board as editor of the quarterly newsletter, *The Ragged Irregular*. She is also a member of the 8th Air Force Historical Society.

Maureen lives with her husband in San Francisco and spends most of her time traveling between Lake Tahoe and Sonoma County. She and her husband have two grown children and two grandsons, whom Maureen buys model airplanes for—mostly B-17s—every chance she gets. Maureen is currently writing a book about American Prisoners of War in World War II. She also writes a blog hosted on her author website titled "Finding Your Veteran," where she provides insight and resources for anyone searching to find out more about their veteran's World War II military service.

Author website: maureenbuick.com

Made in the USA
Las Vegas, NV
24 October 2023

79598959R10192